ADMINISTRATORS SOLVING THE PROBLEMS OF PRACTICE

ADMINISTRATORS SOLVING THE PROBLEMS OF PRACTICE

Decision-Making Concepts, Cases, and Consequences

WAYNE K. HOY

The Ohio State University

C. JOHN TARTER

University of Alabama

PEARSON

Boston ■ New York ■ San Francisco ■ Mexico City
Montreal ■ Toronto ■ London ■ Madrid ■ Munich ■ Paris
Hong Kong ■ Singapore ■ Tokyo ■ Cape Town ■ Sydney

Senior Series Editor: Arnis E. Burvikovs
Series Editorial Assistant: Erin Reilly
Marketing Manager: Erica DeLuca
Production Editor: Mary Beth Finch
Editorial Production Service: TexTech Inc.
Composition Buyer: Linda Cox
Manufacturing Buyer: Linda Morris
Electronic Composition: TexTech
Interior Design:
Photo Researcher:
Cover Administrator: Kristina Mose-Libon

For related titles and support materials, visit our online catalog at www.ablongman.com.

Between the time website information is gathered and then published, it is not unusual for some sites to have closed. Also, the transcription of URLs can result in typographical errors. The publisher would appreciate notification where these errors occur so that they may be corrected in subsequent editions.

ISBN 10:   0-205-50801-4
ISBN 13: 978-0-205-50801-3

Library of Congress Cataloging-in-Publication Data

Hoy, Wayne K.
     Administrators solving the problems of practice : decision-making concepts, cases, and consequences / Wayne K. Hoy, C. John Tarter.—3rd ed.
     p.   cm.
Includes bibliographical references and index.
     ISBN 978-0-205-50801-3
     1. Decision making—Case studies.   I. Tarter, Clemens John.   II. Title.
HD30.23.H69 2008
658.4'03—dc22   2007015476

Printed in the United States of America

5 6 7 8 9 10 V0CR 16 15 14 13 12

*Dedicated to our students
who taught us how to ground
our theories in practice*

*In memory of Elsie Kolter Hoy,
the heart of the family . . . and at her table,
all were family.*

ABOUT THE AUTHORS

Wayne K. Hoy received his BS from Lock Haven State College in 1959 and his EdD from The Pennsylvania State University in 1965. After teaching at Oklahoma State University for several years, he moved to Rutgers University in 1968, where he was a distinguished professor, department chair, and Associate Dean for Academic Affairs. In 1994, he was selected as the Novice G. Fawcett Chair in Educational Administration at The Ohio State University. His primary professional interests are theory and research in administration, the sociology of organizations, and the social psychology of administration.

In 1973, he received the Lindback Foundation Award for Distinguished Teaching from Rutgers University; in 1987, he received the Alumni Award for Professional Research from the Rutgers University Graduate School of Education; in 1991, he received the Excellence in Education Award from The Pennsylvania State University; in 1992, he received the Meritorious Research Award from the Eastern Educational Research Association; and in 1996 he became an Alumni Fellow of The Pennsylvania State University. He is past secretary-treasurer of the National Conference of Professors of Educational Administration (NCPEA) and is past president of the University Council for Educational Administration (UCEA). In November 2003 he was awarded the Roald Campbell Lifetime Achievement Award in Educational Administration.

Professor Hoy is coauthor with D. J. Willower and T. L. Eidell of *The School and Pupil Control Ideology* (1967); with Patrick Forsyth, *Effective Supervision: Theory into Practice* (1986); with C. J. Tarter and R. Kottkamp, *Open Schools—Healthy Schools: Measuring Organizational Climate* (1991); with C. J. Tarter, *Administrators Solving the Problems of Practice* (1995, 2004); with C. J. Tarter, *The Road to Open and Health Schools* (1997); with D. Sabo, *Quality Middle Schools* (1998); and with his wife, Anita Woolfolk Hoy, *Instructional Leadership: A Research-based Guide to Learning in Schools, 2nd edition* (2006); and with M. DiPaola, *Principals Improving Instruction* (in press). He is also on the editorial boards of the *Journal of Educational Administration* and *Leadership and Policy in Schools*.

C. John Tarter (EdD, Rutgers) is Professor of Educational Administration at the University of Alabama. He received a BA from the California State University, San Bernardino and an MA from the University of California, Riverside, after which he taught social studies and English at public schools in California as well as at the San Quentin Correctional Facility. He was an administrator and an adjunct professor of educational administration at Rutgers University. In 1987 he joined the faculty at St. John's University, New York City, where was a professor, program coordinator, and assistant chair of the division of administration and instructional leadership. He joined the College of Education at the University of Alabama in 2006.

Tarter's teaching and research interests are in organizational theory, decision making, and research methodology, and his work has been published in the *Journal of Educational Administration*, the *Educational Administration Quarterly*, the *Journal of Research and Development in Education, Planning and Changing*, and the *High School Journal*. He has been active in the University Council for Educational Administration in a variety of ways including leading the Organizational Theory SIG since its inception. He has served in various capacities in Division A of the American Educational Research Association. He was named an Outstanding Faculty Member at St. John's University. He received a special recognition award for reviews from the *Educational Administration Quarterly* and the Meritorious Research Award from the Eastern Educational Research Association.

CONTENTS

CHAPTER SIX
Shared Decision Making: A Comprehensive Model   121

CHAPTER SEVEN
Shared Decision Making: A Simplified Model   142

CHAPTER EIGHT

Decision Making: Final Cases   168

CHAPTER NINE

Putting It All Together   198

CHAPTER NINE

PREFACE

Decision making is the sine qua non of administration. *Administrators Solving the Problems of Practice* is a series of case studies designed to link current decision theory with solutions to contemporary problems. This book directly affects administrative practice by demonstrating the usefulness of theory and experience in guiding reflection. We believe in the good intentions of educational administrators, but intentions alone will not suffice.

Administrators can learn how to craft decisions skillfully, but they need practice. The case approach is our vehicle for teaching decision making in the context of schools. Case studies have a long tradition of bringing provocative problems from the field to analysis and solution in the classroom. The Harvard business and law schools pioneered the use of cases more than six decades ago, and, as programs in education take on a more practical tone, there is a refocusing on solving the problems of practice and, hence, the need for case studies.

As such national groups as the University Council for Educational Administration, the Council of Chief State School Officers, and the National Council of Professors of Educational Administration push the field toward a more practice-oriented preparation program, the benefits of theoretical knowledge must not be lost. The caliber of decision making is enhanced by combining actual problems from the field with pragmatic strategies from theory.

BOOK OVERVIEW

Eight decision-making models are explicated, and then their applications are illustrated with real contemporary cases. Educational administrators will recognize these situations from their daily work. In all forty-nine cases (**a dozen of which are new**), eight theoretical models, and an original contingency framework for decision making comprise the book. The cases were generated from the experiences of working administrators in different settings across the country. Ten cases were purged from this edition because they lacked relevance.

The chapters have a common structure. First, a theoretical model is explicated and critically analyzed. Then, the model is demonstrated through a case; that is, the reader is guided through the case as the model is applied. Thus, students not only study decision-making theories but are also presented with a hands-on demonstration of the model. The specificity and concreteness of the solutions make the theory accessible and meaningful. After this guided illustration, students are confronted with a new case to challenge their power of analysis in applying the model.

Chapter 1 introduces the use of case studies in solving problems. The issues of rationality, values, and ethics are integral features of decision making. Moreover, decision makers must learn to anticipate and manage the unexpected. Finally, the roles of theory and experience in reflective practice are discussed. Models of decision making can become ingrained habits of mind that shore up deficiencies in everyday problem solving, and the remainder of the book is a demonstration of this proposition.

In Chapter 2, two decision-making models are presented—the classical model of *optimizing* and the administrative model of *satisficing*. The classical model serves as an ideal comparison for the more practical administrative model. The strengths and weaknesses of each are discussed before the applications are demonstrated with solutions to a set of comprehensive practical cases. The chapter ends with another case to test mastery of the models.

In Chapter 3, two more decision-making models are examined—*muddling through* and *mixed scanning*. Again, each perspective is explained and contrasted before both are used to develop solution strategies for a new case. The advantages and disadvantages of the two frameworks are weighed and conclusions are drawn. Students are challenged to demonstrate proficiency with the models in still another case.

Chapter 4 considers irrationality, chance, and politics in administrative decision making. The *garbage-can* and *political* models are presented and illustrated. After each theory is explained, its utility is illustrated in aiding understanding of the apparent irrationality of behavior. This chapter concludes, as does each chapter, with a new case for solution. The pedagogical style of each chapter is similar—theory explication, guided illustration, and cases.

Chapter 5 begins with a synthesis of six models of decision making—optimizing, satisficing, muddling through, mixed scanning, garbage can, and the political model. Contrasts and comparisons are made, and a synthesis provides answers to the questions: Under what conditions is each model most appropriate and what is the best fit? A refined contingency model using information, time, and importance as criteria guides the student to match strategies with situations. In addition, the students are introduced to a SMART Case Brief to aid in their analysis of the cases. This chapter concludes with fifteen more actual administrative cases from public schools for further refinement of problem-solving skills.

In Chapter 6, we expand the notion of decision making to include leadership and shared participation in decision making. The leadership theory of managing participation in decision making by Vroom and Jago (1988) is explicated and summarized before several school cases are used to show its utility. Shared decision making has taken on added importance as reformers advocate teacher involvement in decision making; however, *always* involving teachers is as shortsighted as *never* involving them. Vroom and Jago offer a comprehensive model to guide leaders in involving teachers in decisions.

Chapter 7 presents our original simplified model of shared decision making, which is powerful yet user-friendly. The framework suggests under what conditions teachers should be involved in administrative decisions as well as the frequency, nature, purpose, and structure of teacher involvement. In addition, the model specifies different roles of the leader, depending on the situation. This is a simple though comprehensive perspective for guiding shared decision making. The structure of the chapter is the same as all the other chapters—explanation of the model, demonstration of its utility by solving actual cases, and then new cases for practice. In this chapter, however, the same cases used earlier in the comprehensive model of Vroom and Jago are reanalyzed using the simplified model, which enables a comparison of the strengths and weaknesses of each. Moreover, actual student solutions to contemporary problems using the simplified model are analyzed.

Chapter 8 compares the two shared decision-making models and develops strategies for using each. This synthesis suggests under which conditions each model is appropriate and concludes that, indeed, the perspectives complement each other and can be used either alone or together. The chapter ends with a set of twenty cases to master reflective leadership and shared decision making (including eight new cases from higher education).

Chapter 9, the last chapter, concludes with a comprehensive case study. *Redistricting* is by far the most complex problem of the text. We end with this case for three reasons: (1) students should now be ready to grapple with difficult social and organizational dilemmas; (2) the exercise encourages teamwork and group problem solving; (3) the scale of the questions requires knowledge of the internal dynamics of schools as well as the impact of the broad social context of the community.

COUNCIL OF CHIEF STATE SCHOOL OFFICERS INTERSTATE SCHOOL LEADERS LICENSURE CONSORTIUM (ISLLC) STANDARDS FOR SCHOOL LEADERS

The ISLLC standards, which appear inside the front cover of this text, expand in a series of concentric circles. The standards start with the vision of the school leader, and then move to the instructional program, the internal environment of the school managerially, and connections with the community. The fifth standard presents the ethical expectations of the school leader and the sixth, and final, standard expects the school administrator to respond to the social context of the school and education broadly. Within each standard are expectations of knowledge, the disposition or values to apply the knowledge, and behavioral performances that reflect the knowledge and values of the leader.

We present a matrix of cases and their matching standards (inside the back cover) for two reasons. First, the ISLLC standards provide a useful alternative entry in an analysis of the cases. One cannot predict what will become of the ISLLC standards politically, but it is hard to argue with the notion that administrative behavior reflects what principals know and hold dear. Moreover, the school leader should have a vision and that vision should guide efforts to improve instructional performance and the general operation of the school.

A second reason for our matching of case to standard is our understanding of the standards and cases. Clearly, though, there are overlaps. The case, "Controversial Speaker," for example, is considered to be a problem in the structure and culture of the school insofar as whether professional norms or bureaucratic necessity should take precedence (Standard 2). Still, a knowledgeable reader might well suggest that the case is a problem between the school and the community (Standard 4). We believe our analysis can serve as a foil to linking the cases with standards other than the ones we suggest.

Indeed, the cases may well serve a variety of pedagogical approaches. The case, "Controversial Speaker," illustrates this point. Hoy & Miskel (2001) use the case as a synthesis of open systems descriptions of schools. Readers are invited to employ bureaucratic, cultural, individual, or political perspectives in dealing with the case. They may also find applications from leadership, decision making, motivation, or communication theory. All that notwithstanding, the cases in *Administrators Solving the Problems of Practice* provide models for learning and applying different decision-making theories. Of course, the cases may be put to a number of uses, but we hope they will benefit readers in learning decision-making strategies. The matrix on the inside back cover will guide instructors and students as they select cases that illustrate each of the standards to analyze.

NEW TO THIS EDITION

- **Contemporary Cases** (12) with such current problems as community politics, cultural concerns, special education difficulties, dress codes, and internet problems.
- **A SMART Case Brief** to help students better analyze the cases.
- **New Studies**—more than two dozen decision-making studies to keep students apprised of the latest research and theory.
- **A Contingency Model** of decision making to help students chose the appropriate decision strategy depending on the situation.
- **Hidden Traps in Decision Making**—nine pitfalls and their escapes are provided to help students avoid making classic mistakes.

ACKNOWLEDGMENTS

First and foremost, we thank all of our students, who have supplied the reality in which these cases are grounded. We have used the case study approach for more than two decades; without exception, students are enthusiastic proponents of case methods. Two students deserve special mention: Cheryl Moretz and Fred Reiss.

It will be obvious that we have an intellectual debt to many scholars but especially to Edwin Bridges, Amitai Etzioni, Gerd Gigerenzer, Daniel Griffiths, Arthur Jago, Daniel Kahneman, Henry Mintzberg, Herbert Simon, Victor Vroom, Karl Weick, Donald J. Willower, and Phillip Yetton.

The following reviewers provided helpful suggestions: Dr. Ned B. Lovell, Mississippi State University, and Dr. Donald Leech, Valdosta State University. Finally, a number of administrators and professors read portions of the manuscript and made useful suggestions: James Bliss; Edwin Bridges; Steven Denig, C. M.; Patrick Forsyth; Harry Galinsky; Roger Goddard; Cecil Miskel; Robert Rimmer; Dennis Sabo; James Sinden; Frank Walter; and Anita Woolfolk Hoy.

Special thanks goes to Megan Tschannen-Moran of The College of William and Mary for her comprehensive review of the text and her thoughtful suggestions. We are also indebted to Michael DiPaola of The College of William and Mary, Thomas Reed and Nancy Nestor-Baker of The Ohio State University, and Sean Kearney and Page Smith of the University of Texas at San Antonio, Marilyn Quick of Ball State University, and Susan M. Kiernan of East Tennessee State University.

CHAPTER ONE

INTRODUCTION

*The real purpose of [the] scientific method is to make sure Nature hasn't
misled you into thinking you know something you actually don't know.*
— R. Pirsig, *Zen and the Art of Motorcycle Maintenance*

This book is about administrative decision making in schools. It is an attempt to
link decision theories to actions. It is a balance of analysis, description, and prescription. It is grounded in the problems of practice. Above all else, it is intended to
be useful to reflective administrators. We are of necessity selective in our discussion. Although there is a substantial and important body of literature on making
decisions, we consider only eight models. To be sure, there are other perspectives,
but we believe the theories describing the eight models provide a solid foundation
for solving the real problems that arise in the daily lives of administrators.

CASE METHOD: AN HISTORICAL PERSPECTIVE

Although the case study had its roots in Socratic technique, its formal use in the
United States was influenced by its introduction at the Harvard Law School in the
late 1800s. By the early 1900s, the case approach had proven itself as an efficient
means to teach the application of legal principles to specific cases. In fact, by about
1915 most well-known law schools were using cases in their teaching (Culbertson,
Jacobson, & Reller, 1960). Today, the case method has expanded and is used not
only in law schools but also in many medical training programs. Business schools,
as well, have widely adopted this method to apply principles of business organizations to specific companies. Again, it was Harvard, this time the School of Business, that pioneered the approach. By the mid-1940s, case studies were a common
part of the curriculum in many business and public administration programs. The
value of the method spread to such other fields as guidance, public health, social
work, and education (Masoner, 1988).

In 1955, Cyril Sargeant and Eugene Belisle developed one of the first collections
of cases in educational administration, published as *Educational Administration: Cases*

and Comments. Motivated by the success of the Harvard schools of law and business, the Harvard Graduate School of Education supported the development of Sargeant and Belisle's casebook. In their overview, the authors proclaim that "for those that are willing to look upon education as something of an adventure, cases offer this opportunity *par excellence*" (Sargeant & Belisle, 1955, p. 4). The thrust of their book was to get potential administrators to analyze and discuss the problems they would face in daily administration. Although there is an impressive bibliography, rich in conceptual capital, there is little systematic application of that capital. In fact, the orientation of the text is a freewheeling exploration of views generated by student discussion rather than a theoretical analysis of the issues or the development of theory-driven strategies for action.

Starting in the summer of 1952, a series of annual seminars was held at the University of Oregon. Over the next half-dozen years, university faculty wrote cases for "The Nature and Problems of Administration," as the sessions were titled. The classes dealt largely with decision making and human relations in schools as well as with communication and innovation. Culbertson and his colleagues published these cases as *Administrative Relations: A Case Book.* The text demonstrates how professors from different social sciences analyze administrative problems. For example, a case involving consolidation of schools is considered from four perspectives: education, political science, psychology, and sociology. The results illustrate how various social science constructs make sense of real situations. Different disciplines and experiences led to the contrasting constructions of reality.

Although Culbertson and his colleagues tried to encourage linking theory to practice, time has not been kind to their efforts. Perhaps they were ahead of their time. At any rate, the case study approach declined as an instructional tool in educational administration. It is true that new casebooks have appeared, but, by and large, they do not provide the theoretical focus of the earlier work. In brief, we now have more casebooks, but less theoretical rigor tied to analysis.

Educational administration is still faced with the problem of teaching both *about* and *how* to administer. Knowing what and knowing how are quite different. Here, then, is the vexing dilemma of relating theory to practice: Too much abstraction hides reality, too much prescription denies complexity. In fact, after three decades, the persistent charge abounds that courses in administration are either too theoretical or Mickey Mouse. Perhaps the real problem is that we have not yet found the appropriate methods for relating theory to practice.

The standards movement in educational administration (Council of Chief State School Officers, 1996) has led to a reemphasis on case analysis. States are beginning to test prospective school leaders by presenting them with vignettes drawn from problems in the field. Successful responses show applications of their knowledge to practice.

Are we in a loop? The fashion of the time calls for case studies. We need to advance beyond mere discussions that sensitize administrators to the problems of practice. Cases can be more than devices to stimulate discussions that simply allow the pooling of ignorance. It is time again to link good theory with sound practice. And a case approach grounded in theory provides the vehicle for this endeavor.

What seems clear is that the case method has an honorable past and a potentially bright future. If there is a weakness in the use of cases, it is a tendency toward drift. Our position is that theory provides purpose and gives direction. To be sure, one may argue that there is a valuable consciousness-raising simply in the analysis of important topics. We do not deny that, but our goal is not only to sensitize administrators but also to improve the quality of school decisions.

RATIONALITY AND DECISION MAKING

Decisions are rational if there is a reasonable connection between the means and ends, that is, if decision makers choose wisely the appropriate means for advancing their goals. Individuals are unable to maximize their decisions because of limited information and limited cognitive capacity to deal with complex problems. Because it is impossible to guarantee the best solution, people satisfice by looking for alternatives that meet minimal standards. Such limited rationality is "bounded"; decisions are made after only a moderate search for options (Simon, 1957). The impossibility of maximizing decisions is a theme to which we will return.

What is the natural state of rationality in individuals? Is it natural to be rational? Or is it more likely that decisions are based on feelings, values, and emotions? There is a wide-ranging debate between those who advocate increasing rationality in decisions and those who accept the fundamental, nonrational nature of decision makers (Etzioni, 1992; Herrnstein, 1990; March, 1994; Zey, 1992). We believe that nonrational choice is the natural state. Much, if not most, decision making is driven by normative and affective considerations. Not only are the ends selected based on feelings, but so too are the means. Rather than viewing people as rational or nonrational, it is more useful to examine the degree of rationality one brings to a decision (Etzioni, 1992). It is more useful to ask what conditions enhance or hinder rationality (Ashkanasy, Zerbe, & Hartal, 2002; Maitlis & Qzcelik, 2004).

Making decisions is both art and science. Our goal is to improve the scientific basis of the art of decision making. That position inherently pushes toward emphasizing logical and empirical considerations, which is not to say that normative, affective factors are unimportant. They *are* important. In fact, we have argued they are the natural bases for most personal decision making. To suggest that rational decision making should be both based on logic and open to science blends sound reasoning with evidence. It is a simple fact that something deep in most of us resists the essential position of rationality—that the world is explainable independently of the feelings of the observer (Brinton, 1990). The problem is that decision makers are constantly fighting against inherent, nonrational choice. That is, feelings, values, and biases are strong motivators.

Rational decision making in organizations can be crafted; the friction of affective considerations and biases can be controlled. Rationality is not free; its price is submerging natural tendencies. Administrators need to work steadfastly to recognize and understand the influence of their personal beliefs and biases. They must be responsible and responsive to the demands of the organization, to the needs of teachers, and to the care of children.

RATIONALITY AND VALUES

Values and feelings are an integral part of the decision-making process; they should be recognized and considered. It is not possible to be value free. Science itself has values. One of those values is rationality. However, the influence of other values on rationality is often subtle and difficult to measure. The influence of values, for example, shapes the definition of a problem or intrudes at different points in the problem's solution.

Values and moral choice are critical in what Dewey calls the *reflective method*. When administrators pursue actions that they believe will attain a valued outcome, they are making judgments of value between competing goods or the lesser of evils (Willower, 1991). Administrators, after all, are human beings who find some part of their own morality in their activity as practitioners. Administrators must learn to hold themselves to a rigorous standard of honesty in their work. Ideally, they must "humble part of their desiring self" (Brinton, 1990, p. 450).

Action requires more than good intention. For example, administrators often must weigh compassion for students against the judgments of teachers. Teachers may be threatened by students and react strongly to reestablish their authority. In the process, students may be punished for infractions that challenge teachers' positions. The welfare of both teachers and students is valued by most administrators, yet the administrator often must make decisions that favor one over the other. Judgments of value are inextricably tied to judgments of fact. The same kind of scanning and assessing used by decision makers to consider their options can abet moral choices (Willower, 1999).

Most school administrators (indeed, most educators) want to do a good job and are committed to their teachers and students. The challenge is knowing how to make difficult choices wisely and move things forward. Such action doesn't just happen but rather requires deliberate choice—using the best available theory and procedures to make sense out of the complexities of school life. Science and rationality are useful in this regard. Practical judgments will always be uncertain, but they can be considered hypotheses, open to testing and evidence. We believe that such procedures benefit from theory. This is not to say that social science concepts and theories should be separated from valuation. To the contrary, they are essential to intelligent moral action (Willower, 1992). The basic philosophic approach taken here is that science and rationality, and ethics and practice should not be sharply separated (Dewey, 1922, 1938; Evers & Lakomski, 1991; Willower, 1993). Ultimately, morals have to do with the common problems of living, and separating them from life in favor of some abstract creed creates rather than resolves problems (Dewey, 1922).

One goes through the same process to make an ethical judgment or a rational decision. Whether making ethical judgments or rational decisions, the reflective examination of alternative courses of action and their consequences is necessary. Hence, both moral choice and rational decisions require the formulation of hypotheses concerning probable consequences and outcomes. Our view of the practice of administration is that it is a continuing exercise in both rationality and valuation; it is both a rational and an ethical activity. To separate the activities is foolhardy and, indeed, impossible. Values and rationality are, in this view, symbiotic, not antithetical. The separation of ethics and the reflective methods of science promotes ritualism and mechanistic administration. If decision making is about moral choice, and thoughtful moral choice depends on informed explanation and inference, then philosophy and social science are both crucial to reflective administrative practice (Willower, 1993).

RATIONALITY AND THE ENVIRONMENT

The quotation from Pirsig at the beginning of this chapter should put one on guard against being misled by appearances. The obvious too often is wrong. The authors themselves have difficulty rejecting the "hot hand" phenomenon in basketball, that is, the tendency for success or failure to be self-sustaining. Who hasn't seen a basketball player "get hot"—sink six shots in a row—and thought, "keep shooting while you are hot." We want to believe that the player is in the groove and his shooting far exceeds his normal performance. Yet, using data and probability, Gilovich demonstrates that there is no hot hand phenomenon. There is just a chance grouping of sequential shots. Hard to believe? Yes. Gilovich captures this problem in his concisely titled work, *How We Know What Isn't So: The Fallibility of Human Reason in Everyday Life* (1991).

Representativeness, availability, and anchoring are three sources of error in decision making. The assumption that a few events in the environment indicate a general condition is the representativeness bias (Kahnehan & Tversky, 1996). One is tempted to accept as representative a few cases that confirm one's own bias. For example, successfully involving teachers in a management decision may tempt the administrator to conclude that teacher participation in *all* decisions is desirable. Perhaps, perhaps not: be careful that your information is truly representative before generalizing. Although representativeness is hard to define, the notion of a large sample is critical.

Availability is a bias that uses the strength of association (how well known something is) to predict the frequency of events (how often something will happen). In other words, availability is how easily something comes to mind. Consider the following question: Which is a more likely cause of death in the United States, being killed by falling airplane parts or a shark (Plous, 1993, p. 3)? The data describe death by falling airplane parts as thirty times more likely than death by a shark attack, yet most people indict the shark. Plous (1993) uses this case to illustrate the availability bias: people hear and read more about shark attacks than airplane-part fatalities, that is, the shark attacks are more available to them, and, therefore, they choose shark attack. In school decision making, the topical sometimes becomes a solution;

that is, if self-esteem has wide publicity, then self-esteem becomes available as an explanation of academic performance. Likewise, when phonics becomes a hot topic, legislators seize on that pedagogy to enact law mandating its use in schools. Decision makers need to be careful not to be taken in by what is immediately available. To do so is to risk error.

A third heuristic or bias that leads to decision mistakes is called anchoring and adjustment. People work from an initial estimate, the anchor, which may be incorrect, and then adjust their answers too conservatively; they stay too close to the anchor. Once an estimate is made, be it the appraised value of a house or the amount of time necessary to implement an educational innovation (Plous, 1993), people will often err as they adjust the estimate with additional information. The administrator who finds that the English department, for example, did not meet its timeline in the development of curricular innovation will likely not budget enough time even in light of the existing shortcoming. Decision makers must be cautious not to take what comes first as their anchor. We have selected three of the many heuristic traps that decision makers confront (Hammond, Keeney, & Raiffa, 2006). We extend our discussion of such traps in Chapter 2.

The biases described by representativeness, availability, and anchoring are the mechanisms by which the immediate environment distorts rational decision making. Three cautions for decision makers are in order:

- first, get sufficient data before generalizing (representativeness);
- second, don't seize on the obvious (availability);
- finally, push beyond initial thoughts and alternatives (anchoring).

RATIONALITY AND THE UNEXPECTED

It is rational to expect the unexpected. Social life has taught us many things, but one thing we can depend on is surprise. Rational decision makers try to anticipate the outcomes of the various alternatives, a process that we will discuss more fully in the next chapter. The point now is that anticipating consequences is a reflective activity of predicting the likely results of different actions. The effort to illuminate outcomes, *consequence analysis* (Willower & Licata, 1997), is an attempt to reduce unintended and unanticipated consequences whereas *mindfulness*, managing the unexpected (Weick & Sutcliffe, 2001), is a strategy for dealing with surprises once they have occurred.

Consequence Analysis

In consequence analysis decision makers grapple with options and consequences as they attempt to manage the unintended (Willower & Licata, 1997). First, using the social sciences as vehicles for general scanning, administrators should examine their alternatives in terms of psychological consequences for individuals, sociological outcomes for groups, political effects for the system, anthropological results for the culture, economic costs for the organization in terms of resource availability and allocation, and so on. This phase of outcome analysis underscores the importance of anticipating the likely results of different courses of action.

A second kind of scan is examining the possible outcomes of actions for various role players. What are the specific consequences for the key people and groups in the organization? For example, what will be the impact of the actions on teachers, students, parents, other administrators, taxpayers, associations, and any individual or group that is connected to the decision? A disciplined use of such scanning will reduce the likelihood of missing unanticipated results and increase one's ability to limit surprises. Further, although some participants may not be directly affected by the decision, it may be wise to communicate with them before the decision is implemented.

The procedures used to elaborate consequences are limited only by the ingenuity and creativity of those who use them. Brainstorming, scenario development, role playing, expert consultation, and "thinking outside the box" are only a few of the devices that can be used. Willower and Licata (1997) suggest an ongoing empirical side of consequence analysis. For example, as one scans for possible outcomes, it often becomes obvious that more data and information are needed; indeed, data collection can become a continuous process in decision making, especially where incremental approaches of deciding are used (see Chapter 3).

There is little doubt that consequence analysis can ground rational decisions and help one cope with unintended consequences, but there is a danger. Like any procedure, analysis has its shortcomings, and the one weakness that must be contained is the propensity to overanalyze. Although underanalysis may be more of a problem than overanalysis for decision makers, the latter can produce a kind of paralysis as administrators come to believe they don't have enough data, they have not considered enough consequences, there are other unintended effects that must be considered, and on and on. As John Dewey (1922) noted a lifetime ago, overanalysis is one of the vices of reflective thinking. Time and energy are scarce, valuable administrative commodities that should not be squandered in overanalysis.

In sum, consequence analysis and planning for rational action involve:

- drawing on relevant theory and research;
- using multiple perspectives and roles to predict consequences;
- thinking outside the box;
- scanning for unintended consequences;
- balancing analyses—avoiding both over- and underanalysis.

Mindfulness

Administrators can manage the unexpected by developing a state of *mindfulness* (Hoy, 2003; Hoy, Gage, & Tarter, 2006; Weick & Sutcliffe, 2001). To be mindful is to have a rich awareness of detail and advanced ability to scan for unintended consequences so that one can discover and correct errors before they escalate into major crises. Weick and Sutcliffe (2001, p. 10) argue that five processes promote such mindfulness in administrators: preoccupation with failure, reluctance to simplify interpretations, sensitivity to operations, commitment to resilience, and deference to expertise.

To be *preoccupied with failure* is to be continuously scanning for problems, large and small, but mostly small. Mindful decision makers avoid preoccupation with their successes. Instead, they search diligently for small mistakes and seek to eliminate them. For example, if data show high achievement levels for most students in their schools, then mindful administrators examine the data to find reasons for why the few failed. An old Vedic proverb captures mindfulness, "Advert the danger not yet arisen." To catch the early warning of trouble, one must be continuously open and alert to new information and subtle changes (Langer, 1989).

Mindful decision makers are also *reluctant to accept simplifications* because they feel the need to understand the subtleties of the situation. They simplify less and see more. Knowing that schools are complex and unpredictable, they position themselves to see as much as possible and try to reconcile different interpretations without destroying the nuances of diversity and complexity. For example, differences in the perceptions between African Americans and whites or between males and females toward shared decision making in the school need explanation and interpretation.

Sensitivity to operations signals a constant concern for the unexpected. Mindful decision makers know the "big picture." They detect problems, make continuous adjustments, and prevent further difficulty. They are unremitting in their scan for problems and never so removed from the day-to-day operations that they have difficulty understanding what is happening and why.

No system is perfect; mindful school administrators know this better than most because they develop a capacity to detect and bounce back from mistakes. They deal with the unexpected not only by anticipation but also by *resilience* (Wildavsky, 1991); that is, they learn to be sufficiently strong and flexible to cope with whatever negative outcomes emerge; they have a *commitment to resilience*.

Finally, mindful school administrators avoid the mistake of embracing rigid administrative structures. Instead they search for people with the specific knowledge to solve the problems. They encourage a fluid decision-making system by *deferring to expertise*, not to status or experience. In brief, anticipating the unexpected means developing a state of mindfulness in which scanning, anticipating, containing, removing, and rebounding from the unexpected are ever present.

In sum, the hallmarks of mindfulness are:

- preoccupation with mistakes and failure;
- reluctance to simplify events and interpretations;
- sensitivity to day-to-day operations;
- commitment to resilience as well as anticipation;
- deference to expertise rather than to status.

MINDFUL DECISION MAKING: REFLECTIVE, NOT MECHANICAL

Mindful decision making is not a mechanical skill. When models are depicted as diagrams or schemata, it is tempting to view them as lockstep procedures to be followed blindly. This is as wrong as seeing all decision making as so idiosyncratic as to deny patterns.

In the chapters that follow, eight models will be presented and discussed. These theories are no substitute for thought. Our intention is to provide a series of guides for grappling with the problems of administrative practice. We link systematic decision making with actual cases for three reasons: to demonstrate the utility of the models, to prompt reflection, and to encourage practitioners to link theory and reflection in the solution of problems.

The perspectives on decision making are strategies for action. Administrators are often overwhelmed and occasionally paralyzed by the sheer volume and complexity of their work. Using decision-making frameworks will not guarantee effective solutions, but they can provide reasonable tactics and strategies that improve the likelihood of success. A word of caution: conceptual tools are no substitute for reflective thought.

Decision-making theories, like all models in the social sciences, are probabilistic, not deterministic. One can make technically correct decisions and fail to achieve the predicted ends. Such is the nature of predicting human behavior. We may be able to improve the odds of success through thoughtful decision making, but we are never assured of the outcomes. Simply put, sometimes good decisions don't work out. This does not impugn systematic decision making; rather, it is a comment on the complexity of the task.

We ask ourselves as administrators, what can be done to improve everyday practice? One answer is to be reflective and systematic in our inquiry. This book is our attempt to illustrate the answer. Throughout this work is the injunction, sometimes implicit, that administrators should be more inclined to be guided by theories, as imperfect as they are, than by intuition, impulse, or the biases of dubious beliefs.

People will always be tempted to believe that everything that happens to them is controllable and explainable. Similarly, the tendency to impute rationality to random patterns is wired deeply into our cognitive machinery. These underlying causes of erroneous beliefs will probably never disappear, but we are convinced that they must be held in check by mental habits that promote sound reasoning (Gilovich, 1991). Models of rational decision making can become ingrained habits of mind that shore up deficiencies in everyday problem solving. In the end, decision making is simply a matter of making reasoned judgments informed by evidence (see Pfeffer & Sutton, 2006).

CHAPTER TWO

DECISION MAKING
Optimizing and Satisficing

Decision making is central to administration (Bazerman & Chugh, 2006; Buchannan & O'Connell, 2006). It is the sine qua non of administration—the process by which organizational problems are addressed, solved, and implemented. The good intentions of administrators do not guarantee good decisions. Rather, wise solutions require analysis and efficient action based on sound strategies. Schools are arenas in which administrators make decisions that ultimately affect the improvement of instruction. How do administrators make decisions? How should administrators make decisions? What are the tools for rational decision making? Is there a best way to make decisions? Do circumstances alter the choice of decision strategies? What are the effects of time, information, and bias on decisions? These are the questions that guide our inquiry.

THE CLASSICAL MODEL: AN OPTIMIZING STRATEGY

Classical decision theory assumes that decisions should be rational; decision makers seek the best alternatives to maximize the achievement of the goals and objectives of the organization. The manifest assumption of the model is that there is one best solution to problems that can be discovered and implemented. According to the classical model, the process is a series of sequential steps:

1. *Problem identification:* Problems are discrepancies between actual and desired outcomes. Administrators monitor school operations to identify problems, that is, to determine when performance falls short of expectations.
2. *Problem diagnosis:* Information that explains the nature and origin of the problem is collected and analyzed.
3. *Alternatives:* All the possible alternatives, options that are potential solutions, are developed.
4. *Consequences:* The probable effects of each alternative are considered.
5. *Evaluation:* All the alternatives are evaluated in terms of the goals and objectives.

6. *Selection:* The best alternative is selected, that is, the one that maximizes the goals and objectives.
7. *Implementation:* Finally, the decision is implemented and evaluated.

The classical model assumes an optimizing strategy of decision making. Such a maximizing approach is based on classical economic theory that assumes clear goals, complete information, and the cognitive capacity to analyze the problem. Is the optimizing strategy realistic? Probably not.

Decision makers are human beings who eat, sleep, and have families and a variety of interests; diversity and compromise are the stuff of their everyday life. While it is true that one objective may be favored over another, no one allows a single goal to dominate one's working life (Mintzberg, 1983). Moreover, the notion of clear and simple goals for organizations is similarly a gross simplification. Organizational goals are complex and often conflicting. Phillip Cusick (1983) describes, for example, the conflict in goals between an equalitarian ideal and an ideal of adapting to individual differences; there is goal conflict between what is best for an individual and what is best for the group.

The problem of uncertainty is intrinsic in organizational life. In fact, dealing with uncertainty is a problem that all organizations share (Thompson, 1967). In spite of that, there is no generally accepted criterion for dealing with uncertainty in decision making (Feldman & Kanter, 1965, p. 631). It is virtually impossible to know which of a number of actions to pursue when the consequences remain obscure. Therefore, the uncertainties of organizational life make maximizing an impossible choice.

There is yet another reason to question the optimizing strategy. The demands it makes on human cognition simply cannot be met. No person or organization is smart enough to maximize anything. There is no computer system large or fast enough yet to make the calculations necessary for a maximizing strategy (Feldman & Kanter, 1965; Simon, 1991). Even in a simplified game of chess, no extant computer can handle the quantity of information essential to select the best move (Mintzberg, 1983; Simon, 1991). In the much more complex world of organizational life, the limitations on human cognition preclude an optimizing strategy in decision making.

In summary, the prime objective of the classical model is to find the best solution. Unfortunately, that is easier said than done. Indeed, the model is unrealistic if not naive: decision makers virtually never have access to all the relevant information, nor can they generate all the possible alternatives and accurately anticipate all the consequences. The classical model is an ideal rather than a description of how decision makers function. Although the model is idealistic, it does suggest that a rational plan of action is preferable to arbitrary and biased responses.

THE ADMINISTRATIVE MODEL: A SATISFICING STRATEGY

As we have seen, the classical model has severe limitations for solving complex problems.[1] Decision makers often use a more realistic approach because the complexity of most organizational problems and the limited capacity of the human mind make it virtually impossible to use an optimizing strategy on all but the simplest problems. Herbert Simon introduced the strategy of *satisficing* in an attempt to provide a more accurate description of the way administrators do and should make decisions.

Skillful administration requires rational decision making. Decisions are rational if they are appropriate to the accomplishment of specific objectives. The rationality of administrative decisions is necessarily limited. Demands on human cognition are overwhelming; all the alternatives cannot be considered, simply because there are too many options that do not come to mind. Moreover, all the likely consequences for each alternative cannot be anticipated because future events are uncertain. Rationality is limited not only by the uncertainty of the situation and the extent of administrators' knowledge, but also by the administrators' unconscious biases and conceptions of purpose, which may deviate from organizational goals. Individuals are incapable of making completely rational decisions on complex matters; therefore, *they seek to satisfice because they do not have the knowledge, ability, or capacity to maximize.* Nevertheless, administrators continue to talk about finding the best solutions to problems. What is meant, of course, is the best of the satisfactory options.

Administrators look for satisfactory solutions, those that are "good enough." Their perceptions of the world are simplified models of the complex interacting forces of reality. Administrators oversimplify because they believe that most real-world facts are not important to the particular problem(s) they face and that most significant chains of causes and effects are short and simple. Consequently, they are content to ignore many aspects of reality that they consider irrelevant. Administrators make choices using a simplified picture of reality that accounts only for the factors they consider most important.

Rational organizational behavior consists of a means–ends chain (Simon, 1947, 1993). Given certain ends, appropriate means are selected, but once those ends are achieved, they in turn become means for further ends, and so on. After objectives are agreed upon (that is, the ends are defined by the organization), the subordinate's responsibility is primarily to determine the "best" means for attaining those ends. That pattern, along with procedural regulations, narrows the range of alternatives and establishes *bounded rationality.*

An individual's decision is rational if it is consistent with the values, alternatives, and information that were analyzed in reaching it. An organization's decision is rational if it is consistent with its goals, objectives, and information. The organization should be constructed so that a decision that is rational for the individual remains rational for the organization when reassessed from the organizational perspective.

School administrators are responsible for the following areas: curriculum and instruction; negotiations; physical facilities; finance and business; pupil personnel services; selection, supervision, and teacher evaluation; personnel and staff development; and public relations.

Decision making is essential not only in each of these school tasks but also in the broader functional areas of administration-policy, resources, and execution (Litchfield, 1956). A *policy* is a statement of objectives that guides organizational actions. The *resources* of administration include people, money, authority, and materials. *Execution* is the integration of resources and policy necessary to achieve purposeful organization.

The policy function is often termed *policy making* or *policy formulation*, but it is substantially more. Policies are not only formulated but also implemented and evaluated. Policy making is a special instance of decision making in which the goals and objectives of the organization are defined. Decision making is also the vehicle for dealing with resource allocation. In determining the need for personnel, supplies, physical facilities, and monies, the administrator is confronted with problems that require deliberate and reflective choice and action. Finally, in order to execute decisions, the administrator repeats the rational process of deciding.

Not only is decision making the same regardless of functional area, but each of the functions is a requisite of the total process. Furthermore, although policy helps shape the character of the resource and executive functions, resources have an equally important impact on policies, and execution brings policy to life in ways that achieve or impede organizational objectives. Hence, the three functional areas are interdependent.

Decision making—rational, deliberate, purposeful action, beginning with the development of a decision strategy and moving through implementation and appraisal of results—occurs in all types of organizations. The process is the same, for example, in military, industrial, educational, and service organizations. The pervasiveness of decision making calls attention to its uniformity regardless of the specific context in which decisions take place. Educational organizations are different, however, from industrial organizations in substantive ways. The technologies and products of each are quite different. Yet decision making in the areas of policy, resources, and execution is remarkably similar, indeed substantially the same. Consequently, we view educational administration as a general, abstract application of the decision-making process. Much can be learned about educational administration through comparative analyses of models of decision making in different contexts.

DECISION-MAKING PROCESS: A CYCLICAL PROCESS

Decision making is a dynamic process that solves some problems and creates others. Specific improvements that foster the achievement of the organization's purposes in one area often interfere with those in others. The process, however, usually results in incremental progress. As Peter M. Blau and W. Richard Scott (1962, pp. 250–251) explain:

> The experience in solving earlier problems is not lost but contributes to the search for solutions to later problems.... The process of organizational development is dialectical—problems appear, and while the process of solving them tends to give rise to new problems, learning has occurred which influences how the new challenges are met.

Consequently, it is quixotic to even hope that an effective decision-making structure is going to solve all problems. At best, thoughtful and skillful decision making leads to more rational decisions, but it typically will not result in final decisions. The inherent nature of decision making and organizations precludes that possibility.

In the process of decision making, those with the responsibility should go through five sequential steps:[2]

1. Recognize and define the problem.
2. Analyze the difficulties in the existing situation.
3. Establish criteria for a satisfactory solution.
4. Develop a strategy for action, including the specification of possible alternatives, the prediction of probable consequences, deliberation, and the selection of an action plan.
5. Initiate the plan of action.
   - Program
   - Communicate
   - Monitor
   - Evaluate

These steps will be developed, elaborated, and discussed. Although the process is conceived as a sequential pattern in which each step serves as a logical basis for the next, the process is also cyclical. Thus, decision making may be entered into at any stage. Moreover, the steps are taken again and again in the process of administering organizations. Decision making is a cycle of events; many decision-making cycles occur simultaneously. One elaborate cycle, regarding fundamental goals and objectives (strategic planning), may be proceeding at the level of the board of education, while smaller and related sequential cycles, regarding curriculum and instruction, pupil personnel services, finance and business management, and facilities planning, may be progressing at the district level. Litchfield (1956, p. 13) describes the complex interaction of events this way:

> There is . . . a series of wheels within wheels, tangent now at one point, now at another. The totality is administrative action, and the wheels are similar not in size but in the articulate and inarticulate uniformity of their components.

We now turn to a more detailed analysis of each step in the decision-making cycle.

Step 1. Recognize and Define the Problem

The recognition of a problem is the first step in the decision-making process. Effective administrators are sensitive to organizational actions and attitudes that are inconsistent with standard expectations. The administrative retort, "We don't have problems; we have answers," likely is a sign of an insensitive administrator who is headed for trouble. In such situations, it may be possible for the administrator to maintain equilibrium in the organization over the short run, but chaos over the long run seems inevitable.

The recognition and definition of a problem, important as they are, frequently do not receive sufficient attention. The way a problem is conceived is important to its subsequent analysis and solution. Not only is perceptual acuteness in the administrator necessary, but a thorough understanding of the formal and informal organizations is desirable to frame the problem. A quick and narrow definition of the problem unduly restricts options and frequently treats symptoms, not problems. For example, teachers requesting independence to select curricular materials can be seen as a challenge to administrative authority. The problem, so conceived, restricts the alternatives the principal considers. Such a teacher request, however, can expand the creative possibilities for long-range curriculum development. The example, coincidentally, underscores the importance of self-confidence because a secure administrator is unlikely to view such a request as a threat to his or her authority.

Complex situations often call for intricate solutions. Such circumstances are composed of many interrelated problems; thus, complexity typically requires reducing the general problem to manageable and specific issues, each of which is cycled through the decision-making process. Problems often require short- and long-term solutions. The difficulties of redistricting in a school system where many parents demand that their children go to Lincoln Elementary rather than Washington Elementary may be settled in the short run by a policy statement assigning children to schools solely based on residence. The long-run solution, however, will probably result in equalizing educational opportunities and improving the program of instruction.

Decision making is not merely reacting to problems. Effective administrators are alert to troublesome issues. They can limit conflict and promote organizational health and growth.

Step 2. Analyze the Difficulties

This stage of decision making is related to the first stage; in fact, some writers prefer to combine definition and analysis. However, analysis focuses attention on a different kind of problem. Is the problem unique? Or is it a new manifestation of a routine difficulty? What patterns of action have already been developed for similar problems? What do the rules have to say about this problem? Are the rules silent on the issue? A lack of guidance suggests that the problem is likely new and not merely a routine problem in need of attention.

Decisions come from above, from below, or from the initiative of the administrator. Chester I. Barnard (1938, pp. 190–191) identifies three kinds of decisions: intermediary, appellate, and creative. Intermediary decisions stem from formal communications from superiors that need implementation; appellate decisions emerge from the appeals of subordinates in such matters as job conflict and role ambiguity; and creative decisions originate in the initiative of the executive concerned. The latter decisions are those that no one but the executive himself or herself is in a position to raise, identify, and solve.

In contrast, Peter F. Drucker (1966) sees only two kinds of decisions—generic or unique. Generic decisions come from established principles, policies, or rules.

Recurring problems are routinely solved by formulaic rules and regulations. Most of the intermediary or appellate decisions that confront middle-level administrators are generic; that is, the organization has established mechanisms for these problems. Routine problems are not unimportant; they occur frequently, and the organization must deal with them. Generic decisions are needed when a principal implements board policy, monitors teacher absenteeism, mediates student–teacher conflicts, and enforces the disciplinary code. Administrators usually make generic decisions by applying the appropriate rule, principle, or policy.

Unique decisions are creative decisions that require going beyond established procedures for a solution. Unique problems are exceptions to the general principle or rule. Creative decisions to unique problems quite often change the thrust of an organization. In order to seek a creative solution, decision makers must be open to a wide range of ideas; they must break out of the standard organizational mind-set.

A unique decision might arise when the superintendent asks the principal and teachers to introduce a curriculum reform. Truly unique events are rare, but the distinction between routine and unique problems is important. Administrators make a mistake when they treat a routine situation as if it were a series of unique events or when they treat a new event as if it were just another old problem.

Once the problem has been classified as generic or unique, the analysis proceeds. How important is the problem? Can the problem be more carefully specified? What information is needed to clarify the problem? Problems are initially seen as global and general, but they take on sharper definition as more information is collected and analyzed; that is, the problems become more specific.

How much information is needed depends on such factors as the importance of the problem, time constraints, and existing procedures and structure for data collection. The more important the problem, the more information is required. Time, of course, is almost always a constraining factor. Finally, the existing data-collection procedures may facilitate or inhibit the search for relevant information.

Decision makers need relevant facts. Who is involved? Why is it involved? Where is it involved? When? To what extent? Answers to these questions are needed and information can be collected in formal, sophisticated ways, making use of operations research and computer facilities, or in informal ways, through personal contacts, by telephone, or in writing. Tedious analysis is often rewarded by the strength of the solution.

Step 3. Establish Criteria for a Satisfactory Solution

Before proceeding with the analysis, the criteria for an acceptable solution—the boundary conditions—should be established. The following questions are helpful:

- What must we have?
- What is good enough?
- What are the criteria for a satisfactory decision?

It is time to distinguish between what you desire as an ideal solution and what you will settle for in practice (Charan, 2006). At this point, ranking possible outcomes along a continuum from minimally to maximally satisfying is useful because compromise, adaptation, and concession cannot produce a completely satisfactory outcome. Such boundary conditions (what is acceptable) are needed and are the minimums that the decision maker must have if the solution is to be judged satisfactory. The limits (minimums) need to be specified *beforehand* so that the decision maker can evaluate the efficacy of the decision *after* it has been made.

Step 4. Develop a Plan or Strategy for Action

After recognizing the problem, collecting data, and specifying the problem and its boundary conditions, the decision maker must develop a systematic and reflective plan of action. The task involves at least four steps:

1. specifying alternatives
2. predicting consequences
3. considering options
4. selecting a plan of action

Let us review several limitations of this four-step process:

- First, administrators use simplified pictures of reality; they never have all the facts; hence, they select relevant and critical information, and draw general conclusions before selecting a plan of action.
- Second, administrators must not become paralyzed by the facts that "could be" indirectly related to the immediate problems: they cannot search endlessly for all the alternatives in fear of missing the "best" one.
- Third, administrators have limited information, time, and authority. The art of administrative decision making consists of four key practices (Barnard, 1938):
  1. not deciding questions that are not now pertinent;
  2. not deciding prematurely;
  3. not making decisions that cannot be effective;
  4. not making decisions that others should make.

Specifying Alternatives. The typical pursuit of alternatives is called "problemistic search." It is neither random curiosity nor a search for understanding per se. Rather, problemistic search is a straightforward inquiry limited to the areas of problem symptom(s) and current alternative(s). Only if the search is unsatisfactory is it expanded. It is also possible, however, to develop behavior-monitoring procedures to search the environment for opportunities that are not prompted by a problem. James Thompson (1967, p. 158) calls this process "opportunistic surveillance"; it is the organizational counterpart of curiosity in the individual.

Generating an Adequate Set of Options. Specifying alternatives is a listing of all possible options. In actuality, only some of the alternatives will be specified because, as we have indicated earlier, individuals have limited cognitive capacities. Nonetheless, in general, the greater the number of choices, the more likely that satisfactory alternatives will be discovered. Experts provide an exception to this general rule. For example, chess grand masters can generate quality options without generating a lengthy list of alternatives (Gladwell, 2005; Klein, 1997, 2003; Salas & Klein, 2001).

Creative decision makers are able to develop unique, viable, and simple alternatives. Creativity requires breaking routine habits of thinking, not an easy task. Unfortunately, too many administrators see the solution as a simple dichotomy—it is either this or that. Speed in decision making is often a symptom of sloppy thinking. The impact of a decision is more important than showy technique. Educational organizations need sound decisions, not clever techniques.

Developing alternatives requires time, but there are always constraints. One *must* force time for consideration, but there are some shortcuts and time strategies. Occasionally, for example, the alternative of "doing nothing" solves the problem; things work themselves out. Unfortunately, most problems do not solve themselves, but the decision not to decide should always be reflectively considered. Sometimes one can buy time by using temporary alternatives that provide opportunities for further deliberation. The key in preliminary and temporary alternatives is that, if successful, they "buy time" without creating hostility. There is always the risk that this tactic may be seen as stalling; hence, it should be used sparingly and adroitly.

Routine decisions often can be handled quickly and efficiently, but unique decisions demand more attention. Creative thinking is of particular value in non-routine decisions. It is enhanced by an organization that supports relativistic and less dogmatic distinctions, more willingness to consider and express irrational impulses, and trust—all necessary for effective brainstorming.

In brief, the development of effective alternatives typically requires:

- A willingness to make fewer black-and-white distinctions.
- The use of divergent and creative thinking patterns.
- Time to develop as comprehensive a set of alternatives as possible (Hoy & Miskel, 2008).

If time is short or the decision is not important, then a lengthy set of alternatives may be neither possible nor warranted. Under such circumstances, a *truncated satisficing* occurs; only a select few alternatives are considered before developing a strategy of action.

Traps in Generating Options.   In generating alternatives, administrators must beware of some common traps. In the first chapter, we foreshadowed a number of pitfalls caused by using representative, availability, and anchoring heuristics. Here we caution the decision maker on nine common traps that leaders often fall victim to as they grapple with deciding what to do. All of these traps are gleaned from the research literature (Hammond, Keeney, & Raiffa, 2006); they are common tendencies to make mistakes and to be seduced by bias, distortion, and carelessness.

Decision makers frequently give disproportional weight to initial information, that is, they fall into an *anchoring trap*. Subsequent analysis is determined by initial description. For example, if a teacher comes to your office with a discipline problem, the common tendency is to accept the teacher's version and make a decision.

Disproportionate weight is given to the initial information. You run the risk of making a premature and unwise decision without further investigation.

Similar to the anchoring trap is the tendency to place a higher value on the customary. The *recognition trap* entices individuals to seize upon the familiar rather than search for creative alternatives. Common student-discipline practices are not only the first ones that come to mind, they are often the only ones.

The familiar is comfortable; hence, there is also a natural tendency to accept uncritically alternatives that support the status quo. Options that maintain the existing situation are favored over those that cause change. Individuals don't want to rock the boat so they choose options that do not disturb equilibrium; they succumb to the *comfort trap*. In sum, first impressions, the familiar, and the comfortable yield a mindless generalizing in which significant information is ignored.

Often leaders are simply too confident. Success sows the seeds of its own failure because it produces an overreliance on one's ability—the *overconfidence trap*. Supporting overconfidence is the *memory trap*, a tendency to make decisions based upon a memory of past events, which is in turn colored by the immediacy and drama of those events. The vice principal for student discipline is likely to select options that have been successful in resolving recent problems, for example, the expulsion of students for fighting in the cafeteria. Reinforcing these tendencies is the conviction that a current problem is simply a version of a stereotyped incident of student misconduct, the so-called *representative trap*. In brief, overconfidence is supported by a memory that confirms stereotypic thinking.

Framing a problem has much to do with eventual action. Problems can be framed either too broadly or too narrowly—the *framing trap*. Poor framing may be a consequence of overoptimism, and overly optimistic beliefs can trigger the *sunk-cost trap* in which decision makers tenaciously cling to an option that should work but doesn't. They find themselves in a hole and just keep digging. Just as overconfidence is a trap so is hesitancy. Important decisions are often met with caution and conservative action. The tendency to be overcautious in high-stakes situations is a shortcoming known as the *prudence trap*.

In summary, seeing a teacher's question as a challenge to one's authority instead of a useful suggestion may be a matter of poor framing. And teacher criticism of a policy that has not worked well may be an antidote to the sunk-cost trap. The administrative response that seeks to reframe an issue and push the edges for a solution may overcome the reluctance to be a little adventurous in action, the prudence trap.

Mindful decision makers can avoid all of these traps. A few guidelines are in order:

- Be open-minded.
- Be skeptical.
- Embrace change.
- Seek disconfirming evidence.
- Search for counterexamples.
- Focus on novelty.
- Reframe and reframe again.

- Seek evidence.
- Push the edges.

Table 2.1 summarizes the traps hidden in decision making as well as means to escape them.

Predicting Consequences.   For each proposed alternative, probable consequences should be predicted. Although for analytic purposes, we have treated specifying alternatives and predicting consequences as separate operations, they often occur

TABLE 2.1 Traps Hidden in Decision Making and Escapes (Based on Hammond, Keeney, & Raiffa, 1998, 2006)

TRAP	COMMON ACTION	ESCAPE
Anchoring	Tendency to give disproportional weight to initial information.	• *Be open-minded and push for numerous options;* • *Be skeptical of information.*
Recognition	Tendency to place a higher value on the familiar.	• *Search for the unfamiliar; focus on novelty.*
Comfort	Tendency to a bias toward alternatives that support the status quo.	• *Always consider change and don't exaggerate its costs.*
Overconfidence	Tendency to be overconfident about one's ability to estimate and predict.	• *Always consider the extremes; check with experts;* • *Seek disconfirming evidence; be skeptical.*
Memory	Tendency to base predictions on memory of past events, which are overly influenced by both recent and dramatic events.	• *Assume data exist; find them; use statistics.* • *Avoid being guided by impressions.*
Representative	Tendency to see others as representative of the typical stereotype.	• *Search for counterexamples to the stereotype;* • *Be mindful.*
Framing	Tendency to frame the problem either too broadly or too narrowly; framing a problem impacts both options and consequences.	• *Consider the short- and long-term issues;* • *Reframe the problem several times;* • *Pose problem in neutral terms.*
Sunk-Cost	Tendency to make decisions that justify past decisions that didn't work well.	• *When you find yourself in a hole, quit digging.*
Prudence	Tendency to be overcautious when faced with high-stakes decisions.	• *Push the edges and adjust your actions;* • *Take some risks.*

simultaneously. The formulation of alternatives and consequences is a good place to involve others—pooling knowledge and experience to elaborate alternatives and improve prediction. Predicting consequences is difficult at best. One may be reasonably confident, for instance, in predicting financial costs but much less confident in anticipating the reactions of individuals or groups.

Predicting consequences accentuates the need for good management information systems. Schools that have built-in capacities to collect, codify, store, and retrieve information have a distinct advantage in the decision-making process. Consulting with knowledgeable individuals also improves predictive power. For each decision alternative, the consequences are determined in terms of probable outcomes. There are few certainties.

We have discussed the importance of scanning for the unexpected in the first chapter, but let's review a few suggestions:

1. Use multiple perspectives and roles in anticipating consequences.
2. Scan for unintended and negative consequences.
3. Focus on possible failures to prevent mistakes.
4. Resist the temptation to oversimplify; don't seize on the obvious.
5. Push beyond initial thoughts; think different and outside the box.
6. Involve others in analyzing consequences and defer to expertise not to status.

In brief, develop a state of *mindfulness* in which scanning, anticipating, containing, removing, and rebounding from the unexpected are ever present in your thoughts and actions.

Considering Options. The next phase of the process is a deliberate consideration of the alternatives and consequences. Sometimes it is helpful to list all the alternatives with their corresponding probable consequences (see Figure 2.1). The figure depicts a probability chain and is read as follows: Alternative A has three possible consequences (C1A, C2A, C3A), and the probability of each of these consequences

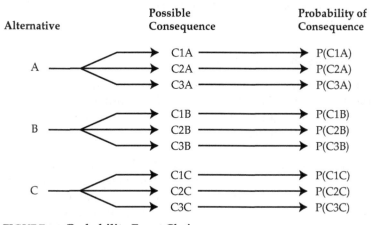

FIGURE 2.1 **Probability Event Chain**

occurring is designated P(C1A), P(C2A), P(C3A), respectively. Although such a formal procedure may not always be used, remember that every alternative has a number of probable consequences.

Selecting a Plan of Action.   Consequences of each alternative are considered using the criteria for a satisfactory solution. Decision makers then choose the best set of alternatives. They develop a solution strategy by selecting a series of alternatives that are linked together in sequential order—a plan of action. The more complex or problematic the issue, the more complicated the plan of action.

To illustrate the planning of action, let us simplify the procedure. It is possible to set up a strategy several moves in advance, just as a good chess player does. If the preferred alternative does not result in an acceptable solution, then the decision maker selects the next option and, if need be, yet another alternative, and so on, as long as the likely consequences are still satisfactory. Of course, unanticipated consequences may require a reevaluation of the plan.

If decision makers cannot find acceptable alternatives, then it may be necessary to reduce the aspiration level, that is, reestablish the criteria for a satisfactory solution (return to step 3). New objectives, different alternatives, and more feasible strategies need to be formulated. In searching for satisfactory alternatives, decision makers keep the activity manageable by using simplified decision rules called heuristics.[3] These simple rules of thumb guide the decision making. For example, rules about when to take a hit in blackjack or when to bet with the house or when to search for more information in decision making are heuristics. Some heuristics are valuable; others are misleading (Gigerenzer, 2000; Gigerenzer, Todd, and ABC Research Group, 1999). Refer to Table 2.1 for common mistakes and traps found in heuristics.

Many factors mediate the choice among preferred alternatives. The values of the administrator, the cultural context, perceptions of those involved, the significance of the situation, pressures on the school, and the importance of the goal—all these and other factors intervene in the selection of an alternative. Nonetheless, deliberate, rational, and reflective decisions generally result from following a systematic sequence of steps.

Step 5. Initiate the Plan of Action

Once the strategy and a plan of action have been formulated, the decision needs to be implemented—the final element in the decision-making cycle. The initiation of the plan of action requires at least four steps—programming, communicating, monitoring, and evaluating.

Programming.   Decisions must be translated into specific actions. For example, a plan to change the system of grading elementary school students contains a detailed set of operations that requires answers to a number of specific questions. Who has to have information about the plan? What actions need to be taken? By whom? What preparation is needed? The program must be realistic and capable of implementation.

What we call *programming*, others have called *program planning* or *strategic planning*—the activity designed to implement decisions. Program planning can be accomplished through a variety of techniques. The sophistication and capabilities of the school organization dictate the appropriate methods. Programming may include budgeting, setting behavioral objectives, mapping organizational charts, and using network-based management techniques, as well as other ways of allocating authority and resources.

Communicating. Once the plan has been programmed, it is essential that all involved are aware of their responsibilities. Existing as well as new opportunities for horizontal and vertical communication must be examined carefully. For a program to be successful, individuals need to know how their own roles and the roles of others relate to the total plan. Otherwise, efforts may be duplicated, counterproductive, or ineffective. Communication is crucial for initiating action and enhancing coordination.

Monitoring. Monitoring is overseeing the implementation of the action plan to be sure that it is proceeding as scheduled. Information monitoring and reporting should be built into decision making to identify discrepancies between expectations and actual events. Monitoring controls the implementation through systematic feedback loops. Standards of performance need to be enforced. Enforcement does not necessarily mean coercive action. Control devices include rewards and incentives, punishments, persuasion, and other means of inducing identification with the organization. The effectiveness of different modes of control depends upon the situation and the individuals involved. Continuous feedback is necessary in order to evaluate the progress of implementing the plan of action, changing communication procedures, or developing other monitoring techniques.

Evaluating. Once the decision has been programmed, communicated, and monitored, the outcomes still need to be appraised to determine the success of the decision. Has the action plan been satisfactory? Are there new problems? Even the most carefully planned and executed decisions can fail or become obsolete. Organizational decisions are made in a complex context—facts, values, and circumstances continually change. Therefore, a fully articulated decision—one that has been reflectively made, programmed, communicated, and monitored—in itself brings about sufficient change to merit further appraisal. Thus, evaluation is both an end and a new beginning. There are no ultimate solutions—only satisfactory ones, decisions, and solutions for the moment. The decision-making cycle is summarized pictorially in Figure 2.2.

You may find the preceding description of decision making too theoretical and, abstract, perhaps even boring. We know this can happen. Nonetheless the arduous tasks of reading and studying the model provide rewards in the real world of educational administration. No one ever said that administration or decision making would be easy. They are not. They are challenging and intellectual enterprises. At this point, you may not be convinced of this claim. We will illustrate the power and utility of the model with the analysis of an actual administrative case.

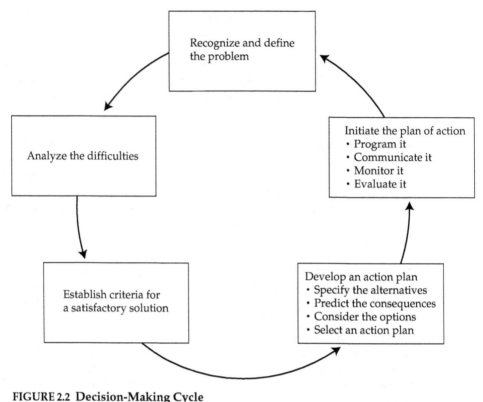

FIGURE 2.2 Decision-Making Cycle

CASE 2.1

The Teachers Council

Few would deny that Superintendent Beverly Edison had the best of intentions in setting up a teachers council elected by teacher-representatives of every public school faculty in this large industrial city.[4] Widely acknowledged to be an educator of the highest professional standing, Dr. Edison was a woman of impeccable integrity. She frequently assured large groups of her teachers that she wanted them to regard her as their "colleague with special responsibility." Her office was open to teachers who had problems of any kind. She routinely consulted teachers on proposed policies and rule changes before her recommendations were submitted to the board of education for adoption. It is true that teacher suggestions were not always adopted, but enough were accepted to give teachers both individually and collectively the feeling that their superintendent meant what she said in the matter of wanting a democratic school system.

After six years of service in Metro City, Superintendent Edison announced a plan for setting up a teachers council to give the superintendent a vehicle to meet and communicate with rank-and-file teachers. She wanted a direct connection with the teachers to assess their reaction to her and the policies and conditions in the schools. The teachers' union (AFT), having a membership of 8,000 and being the exclusive bargaining agent of the teachers, wrote to the superintendent, after due consideration and vote by the union's executive committee, that the proposed council would simply duplicate functions now performed by the union and other existing organizations. Dr. Edison responded that it was not her plan to have the teachers council vote or advise her on matters pertaining to teachers' benefits or welfare. She promised the union that she had no intention of having the council usurp the functions of the union. "All I want," she wrote, "is to have an opportunity to meet with teachers so that I can interpret our policies and to have the teachers advise me about educational issues in our schools. The council will not concern itself with issues of teacher welfare and benefits." Despite some protest from the union, Dr. Edison proceeded to set up the council.

Since its membership included approximately 80 percent of the teachers, the union adopted a more circumspect strategy to deal with the council threat. Union members would be elected to serve on the council to keep the deliberations under control. The union, working quietly through its membership and under the procedures instituted by Dr. Edison, was successful in electing union members to 90 percent of the council seats for an initial one-year term.

Trouble was not long in coming. Written minutes of the council's monthly meetings with the superintendent revealed detailed accounts of the deliberations. The union viewed with alarm the fact that questions of teacher welfare were raised and discussed at the meetings. Was the council already beginning to usurp the union's authority?

Vincent Riley, a long-time union leader, was outraged by the turn of events. He felt betrayed and undermined by Dr. Edison. After consulting with the executive board of the union, he officially notified Superintendent Edison that the union regarded the teachers council as inappropriate, counterproductive, and illegitimate; Riley wanted to abolish the council. He reminded the superintendent that the union was the exclusive bargaining agent of the teachers and that discussing questions of teacher welfare violated the contract.

Dr. Edison was surprised by this turn of events. She replied that the council's meetings were informal and that no votes or formal actions were taken. The council was merely an informal source of communication and advice. It enabled her to take the pulse of the teachers in this large district. Nevertheless, she yielded to the union. In light of the union's opposition, she would submit to the council the union proposal that the council be dissolved. The council promptly responded by voting unanimously to continue its existence. Union leaders were caught flat-footed by this show of independence by their members.

The union represented only 80 percent of the teachers. It had come into prominence at a time when Metro City teachers were not being paid very well and the state and local teacher associations were seen as inactive and controlled by the administration. Teacher pay and working conditions steadily deteriorated until Vincent Riley and a handful of union teachers waged a war to break the tyrannical hold the former superintendent and board of education had on the school system and its employees. The union swept into power first by winning the right to be the teachers' exclusive bargaining agent, and then by negotiating "the best contract teachers had had for a more than a decade." Many in the community, including most teachers, believed that the union had freed the school system from a despotic administration. Decisions were now made on the basis of merit rather than political influence, and the union was seen as an agent of responsible change. Unfortunately, the dishonesty and repression of the former administration left scars that had not healed. It was probably this history of distrust and manipulation that colored the union's reaction to Dr. Edison's proposal for the teachers council. Despite the fact that during her six-year tenure Dr. Edison had demonstrated a democratic and impartial leadership style, the union did not entirely trust any administrator.

Metro City is a blue-collar city. Trouble with one union could mean trouble with all the unions in the city. The school system could be paralyzed completely by a strike of its nonprofessional workers as well as its teachers. Union members across the city would observe picket lines around the schools. Unionized truck drivers would not make deliveries.

Many teachers, however, felt peculiar about being considered union members rather than professionals, and Dr. Edison sensed a need to go beyond simple labels. She had argued often with Vincent Riley over the union's assertion that it represented everybody. In point of fact, 2,000 teachers were not represented by the union. Many of these teachers had strong ties with the state educational association affiliated with the NEA. Dr. Edison contended that through the teachers council she could meet with the representatives of all the teachers.

The union, although well disposed toward Dr. Edison, was concerned that a future administration might resort to the old ways and use the council to destroy the union. Because the union represented most of the teachers, it did not share her concern for the minority that it did not represent; in fact, it viewed this group as freeloaders. Edison was concerned that the majority could completely disregard the wishes of the minority.

A superintendent faces many conflicting pressures. There is a constant push and pull of forces. No doubt, pressures were operating to get Dr. Edison to reduce its strength, if not eliminate the union. Representatives of large industrial and business establishments as well as taxpayer groups did not want labor-oriented groups to dominate the schools. However, because of the progress and good relationships during the past six years, union leaders did not believe that Dr. Edison would appease these groups by destroying the union. Dr. Edison was far too worthy a professional to succumb to such pressure. In fact, she was on record as describing the Metro City Teachers' Union as one of the most highly professional and responsible organizations that she had ever dealt with. She, in turn, was held in high regard. She welcomed the union's generous financial support of the Self-Help School Alliance, a federation of voluntary community associations providing opportunities for disadvantaged children in the school system. She approved of the union's lobbying of the legislature to increase state support for urban schools. In spite of her strong support of the union, she was unwilling to give in to its demand to abolish the teachers council. She believed that she had a right—no, an obligation—to consult with all the teachers, not merely union members.

In Edison's last meeting with Vincent Riley, Riley had said, "This most recent audit of our finances shows that out of a total of nearly 10,000 teachers, we have 7,953 paid memberships."

"You don't represent all the teachers," rejoined Dr. Edison. "I want to know how all my teachers feel about our programs and policies. I need information about educational issues, not union matters. It is curriculum and instructional matters that provide the salient topics for the teachers council. I need the professional advice of all the teachers if this district is to prosper and develop."

Riley paused momentarily, then responded, "Maybe you should spend less time in your office. I realize it's hard for a lady to go into some of these rougher schools. But I'm in the schools every day, and I can tell you that the professionals are union teachers. Furthermore, if you submit the question whether the teachers council should be continued to a vote of all teachers, I have no doubt that a majority would vote to abolish the council."

Dr. Edison could feel her face redden, and she fought back the urge to respond to his insensitive, if not sexist, comment. Finally, she said, "The council didn't vote that way, and many of your people are council members."

When Vincent Riley reported the result of this meeting to the union executive board, they agreed that Dr. Edison should be given a chance to explain her actions to the grievance committee before any formal grievance was initiated. It was hoped that the committee could convince Dr. Edison of the threat the council posed to good management–labor relations.

The executive committee conceded the good intentions of the superintendent, recognizing Dr. Edison's desire to democratize the school system. Despite good intentions, however, the union was worried about the turn of events. It saw itself as the guardian of the teachers' interests and of the integrity of the schools. It needed to act decisively.

Dr. Edison received a letter on Metro City Federation of Teachers stationery, over the signature of Donald Strickland, executive committee chairman (Strickland is a full-time employee of the union; he is not a teacher), requesting an appointment for the committee and Vincent Riley to discuss the advisability of continuing the teachers council.

ANALYZING THE CASE: USING THE SATISFICING MODEL

There is no one best way to solve a complex problem; rather, there are many satisfactory solutions, solutions that work. Let us go through the decision process using the satisficing model.

Recognize and Define the Problem

The critical first step in applying a satisficing model is identifying and framing the problem. What is the problem in this case? There are many ways to define the problem. The initial short-term issue here is to respond to the letter on Dr. Edison's desk. The long-term problem is to continue the good labor–management relations that the superintendent has developed over the past six years. Undoubtedly, there are other ways to frame the issue. The definition of the problem has a strong influence on the eventual solution. For example, one might also define the problem as how to improve communication with teachers. At any rate, framing the problem should be broad enough so as not to artificially constrain a solution, yet narrow enough to produce an action plan.

Analyze the Difficulties

In analyzing the problem, the second step in the process, Superintendent Edison must consider the kind of problem at hand. This is a problem that requires going beyond established procedures for a solution; it requires a creative decision. It is an important issue to Superintendent Edison; in fact, she sees the council as a necessary element in her open and democratic style of leadership. She feels the need to communicate with all the teachers, not merely the union teachers. The union leadership, in the person of Vincent Riley, on the other hand, responds to a perceived threat to the union's influence with teachers. Relationships between the administration and the union have dramatically improved in recent times. No one wants to go back to the bad old days. Edison needs to decide how badly she wants the teachers council. The problem has the potential for disaster—resurrecting old antagonisms, polarizing the faculty, labor–management hostility, boycotts, slowdowns, and strikes.

What are the critical facts of the case? Dr. Edison is a person of impeccable integrity who has improved administrative–union relationships. She is a democratic leader who wants to involve all teachers in decision making. In her desire to know the mind of the rank-and-file faculty, she instituted a teachers council. In spite of union opposition, she proceeded to set up the council by having teachers elected to represent each school in the district. Apparently unbeknownst to Dr. Edison, the union managed to have a disproportionate number of its members elected to the council. Whatever the intentions of the union, 90 percent of the council was union. Notwithstanding Dr. Edison's promise to abstain from discussion of welfare issues, written minutes of the council's meetings revealed that teachers did, indeed, raise and discuss teacher welfare issues.

This event triggered a disagreeable exchange between Edison and Riley. Riley, with the backing of the union's executive committee, demanded the council be abolished. Edison, in turn, submitted the issue to a vote of the council. Despite the fact that 90 percent of the council members belonged to the union, the council unanimously rejected the proposal to dissolve itself. This turn of events escalated the conflict between Riley and Edison. Riley saw the council as a threat to the authority of the union, and Edison viewed the council as an important forum for communicating with all the teachers. Riley suggested that Edison would have adequate information if she got out into the schools herself more often, rather than stay in her office. Edison pointed out that it was the council, not she, that decided to continue its existence. Before filing a formal grievance, the executive committee of the union decided to give the superintendent a chance to explain her actions.

Now, Superintendent Edison is confronted with a letter asking her to schedule an appointment with the executive board and explain her actions.

Establish Criteria for a Satisfactory Solution

What are the criteria for a satisfactory solution in this case? At this point, Dr. Edison must decide what is good enough, that is, distinguish between the ideal solution and what she will settle for in practice. What is the minimum that Edison must have for a satisfactory solution? Two factors are important: communication with the rank-and-file teachers and harmonious working relationships with the union. Ultimately, the effectiveness of the solution should be judged by these two criteria.

Develop a Plan of Action

How can Dr. Edison accomplish her objectives? She needs a strategy for action. To develop such a plan, she must examine the alternatives, predict their consequences, consider options, and select a course of action. What are the alternatives? The immediate problem is the disposition of the letter. Should a meeting be scheduled? Does she want to go to the meeting? Is there a way to avoid the meeting? Will the meeting be useful? Is the meeting a trap? What should be the topic? Where should the meeting be held? These are examples of only a few of the initial questions. It may be premature to raise these questions. Edison needs more information, but she has a letter on her desk. We begin our generation of alternatives and their consequences by examining Dr. Edison's options with the letter. Imagine yourself in Dr. Edison's position.

Alternatives	Likely Consequences
1. Don't respond to the letter.	1. Another communication and a likely hardening of the union's position.
2. Schedule a meeting at your office.	2. You will be asked to defend your actions.
3. Write a letter supporting the existence of the council.	3. Alienate the executive committee of the union and precipitate union action.
4. Write a letter agreeing to abolish the council.	4. Lose face with the teachers on the council and lose an open communication forum.
5. Write a tactful letter requesting more information about the meeting.	5. If the letter is tactful, it can produce more time without alienating the union.
6. Write a letter and invite the union executive committee to a meeting with the council.	6. The union will reject your proposal and harden its position.

This is just the beginning, but let us examine our options thus far. Of the six alternatives posed, option 5 has the distinct advantage of buying time to gather more information and develop a more elaborate strategy. The key to successfully implementing this alternative is to write a letter that is reasonable and will not alienate the union. For example, Dr. Edison might write the following letter:

November 27

Mr. Donald J. Strickland
Chairman, Executive Committee
255 Union Hall
Metro City

Dear Don:

Thank you for your letter of November the 25th. The problem you outline is an important one. I will be talking with Vincent Riley tomorrow or the next day about the teachers council. Vincent and I have a good working relationship, and I am sure that we will be able to work through the issue at hand in a mutually satisfactory way. I am surprised that the formation of the council has become an irritant, but, let me repeat, we will work it out.

After I have had a chance to talk with Vincent, I will be back in touch.

Best wishes.

Sincerely,

Beverly Edison
Superintendent of Schools

Selecting option 5 is merely a device to gain more time and information; it does not rule out the eventual selection of any of the other alternatives. Now, let us continue our generation of alternatives.

Alternatives	Likely Consequences
7. Meet with influential principals who are your confidants to assess saliency of council issue among teachers.	7. More information about teachers' concerns.
8. Touch base with the president of the board.	8. More information about the degree of community and board support for your position.
9. Talk informally with the council.	9. Elicit support and gain further insights.

10.	Talk informally with the PTA president.	10.	Elicit support and gain further insights.
11.	Write a press release publicizing the positive opportunities presented by the council.	11.	Elicit support from the community and harden the union position.
12.	Subject the disposition of the council to a vote by all teachers, as suggested by Riley.	12.	Close election, but divisive regardless of the outcome.
13.	Meet informally with Metro City Labor Council.	13.	Information on general union position.
14.	Have lunch with Don Strickland to feel out his position on council matter.	14.	Information.
15.	Telephone each member of the board.	15.	Information.
16.	Meet informally with Riley.	16.	Forge a compromise.

Before proceeding any further, it is obvious that the last alternative, meeting with Riley, requires another complete iteration of the decision-making process. The problem here is to develop a compromise that is satisfactory to both Edison and Riley. One way to proceed is to generate another set of alternatives to solve the compromise problem. These options should be developed and analyzed before the meeting with Riley; it is a matter of doing your homework. One useful strategy in this regard is to develop as many compromises as you can think of, then rank them in terms of desirability, and then draw the line—the point at which further compromise is unacceptable. Let us illustrate:

	Compromise		**Likely Consequences**
1.	Promise not to discuss teacher welfare issues at the council meetings.	1.	Union will reject as insufficient.
2.	Have the council reconsider the issue of abolishing itself.	2.	Union will reject as insufficient.
3.	Reduce the number of meetings held.	3.	Union will reject as insufficient.
4.	Unpublished minutes to be sent to Riley for review.	4.	Union will probably reject as insufficient, but it is a possible negotiating issue.
5.	Promise minutes will not be published.	5.	Union will reject as insufficient, but it is a possible compromise if linked to others.

Compromise	Likely Consequences
6. Adhere to preestablished agenda.	6. Possible compromise if linked to options 3 and 4.
7. Have council respond to only single issues of importance.	7. Union will reject as insufficient, but it is possible if linked to options 4 and 5.
8. Riley to approve agenda before each meeting.	8. Union will probably reject as insufficient, but it is possible if linked to options 3, 4, and 5.
9. Appoint Riley as an ex-officio member to monitor agenda.	9. Possible negotiating issue.
10. Appoint Riley secretary of the council.	10. If linked to other compromises, might be appealing.
11. Negotiate something the union wants for continuing the council (e.g., dues checkoff).	11. Might be appealing with options 6 and 7.
12. ~~Have a vote of all the teachers, in the district to determine the fate of the council.~~	12. ~~Probably will cause much divisiveness in the district.~~
13. ~~Have the union appoint members next year in proportion to membership (e.g., 80%).~~	13. ~~Might be appealing, but changes the nature of the council.~~
14. Propose a "graceful death." Only a few more meetings will be held this year and then no elections and no council next year. The council fades away.	14. Probably acceptable to Riley, but ends the usefulness of the council. Then the need for better communications with teachers remains.

The list of compromises is illustrative, not exhaustive. We have ranked them in order of the amount of authority given up by the superintendent. Reasonable people may well disagree on the order; however, each decision maker will have to establish not only the ranking but the point at which the compromises are no longer acceptable. The initial list should be as broad and creative as possible, even though some compromises are unacceptable and would be deleted upon further reflection. This is a good time to involve other key administrators in the process.

Compromise 12 would be deleted from the list because it is likely to cause divisiveness among the teachers. It is not clear what the result of an election would be. Riley is confident that he could control the election and get a no-council vote. We are less sanguine about the results. It is probable that many, if not most, teachers representing the various building faculties on the council are informal leaders in their respective schools. They are on record as favoring the council. In spite of the fact that most of the district teachers are union people, these informal leaders on the council could mobilize the teachers and win the election for the council. Thus, the superintendent could win a Pyrrhic victory whose cost would be polarized teachers. Here, winning is losing. The superintendent is not trying to break the union, but rather to improve relationships with the union while getting better communication.

Compromise 13 is also unacceptable to this superintendent. The cost of permitting the union to appoint 80 percent of the members would seriously limit free flow of communication. It would simply give the union another arm to control their members, and it would likely not yield the desired communication mechanism.

Compromise 14 is a drastic solution. The superintendent gives up the council in a face-saving manner, but she does not achieve one of her major objectives—a forum for general communication with all of the teachers. Thus option 14 is not a satisfactory solution (recall our criteria for a satisfactory solution), unless Edison can create another way to communicate with all the teachers. The line of compromise is drawn between compromises 11 and 12. Any solution up to and including compromise 11 will be acceptable to the superintendent. Compromises 12 and 13 should be excluded from the list of acceptable solutions. Alternative 14 is a possibility if another means of grassroots communication with teachers can be developed. This analysis might seem complicated, but it is simply a matter of systematic and reflective thinking.

A Strategy for Action

It is now time to link our options together in a plan. To do so, we must review each option and likely consequence in terms of our criteria for satisfaction. Let us eliminate some of the alternatives that are not consistent with the criteria because of likely negative consequences. Alternatives 1, 3, 6, 11, and 12 will surely alienate; therefore, they are eliminated. We have summarized the viable alternatives as well as the ones we have eliminated as follows:

A Summary of Possible Alternatives

Alternatives	Likely Consequences
1. ~~Don't respond to the letter.~~	1. ~~Another communication and a likely hardening of the union's position.~~
2. Schedule a meeting at your office.	2. You will be asked to defend your actions.
3. ~~Write a letter supporting the existence of the council.~~	3. ~~Alienate the executive committee and precipitate union action.~~
4. ~~Write a letter agreeing to abolish council.~~	4. ~~Lose face with teachers on the council and lose an open communication forum.~~
5. Write a tactful letter requesting more information about the meeting.	5. If the letter is tactful, it can produce more time without alienating the union.

Alternatives	Likely Consequences
6. ~~Write a letter and invite the union executive committee to a meeting with the council.~~	6. ~~The union will reject your proposal and harden its position.~~
7. Meet with influential principals who are your confidants to assess saliency of council issue among teachers.	7. More information about teacher concerns.
8. Touch base with the president of the board.	8. More information about the degree of community and board support for your position.
9. Talk informally with the council.	9. Elicit support and gain further insights.
10. ~~Talk informally with the PTA president.~~	10. ~~Elicit support and gain further insights.~~
11. ~~Write a press release publicizing the positive opportunities presented by the council.~~	11. ~~Elicit support from the community and harden the union position.~~
12. ~~Subject the disposition of the council to a vote by all teachers, as suggested by Riley.~~	12. ~~Close election, but divisive regardless of the outcome.~~
13. ~~Meet informally with Metro City Labor Council.~~	13. ~~Information on general union position.~~
14. Have lunch with Don Strickland to feel out his position on council matter.	14. Information.
15. Telephone each member of the board.	15. Information.
16. Meet informally with Riley.	16. Forge a compromise.

The first step is to implement option 5. This is a better option than abolishing the council outright (4). Writing the suggested letter will give the you time to do other important things. You need information, and options 7, 8, 9, 14, and 15 should help in this regard. The information should be collected quickly from key principals (7), the president of the board (8), the council members (9), Don Strickland (14), and board members (15). We would not talk informally with the PTA president (10) or the Metro City Labor Council (13) because such action might needlessly expand the problem. It is possible that there is resistance to the council in the community, among the teachers, within the board, and among the principals. If this is the case, you may want to replace the council with another structure to communicate with teachers. If, on other hand, there is support for the council among these groups, you need to work with Riley to seek a reasonable compromise and allay his fears about the council.

In either case, an informal meeting with Vincent Riley would seem advisable. The degree of support will determine the cutting point for the list of compromises. Strong support would argue a compromise between options 1 and 11. Weak support would argue for a graceful way to eliminate the council (14). If option 14 were chosen, it should not be selected until its negative consequences have been muted by agreeing on other mechanisms for communicating with teachers. For example, you might establish an electronic bulletin board for teachers to communicate directly, or you might make it a point to visit each school in the district to meet informally with the teachers over coffee.

We have a tentative strategy to address the issue of the teachers council. The plan is not set in stone; it can change as the situation changes. We have examined some of the contingencies but not all of them. As new information develops, we may have to develop new alternatives and a new strategy, which means engaging in another cycle of the decision-making process. Nonetheless, we do have a feasible plan, which we have presented graphically in Figure 2.3.

Initiate the Plan

The final step in the decision-making process is to initiate the plan. You can easily implement the tentative strategy (see Figure 2.3). The plan in this case rests primarily in your hands—you will coordinate a series of meetings to gather information prior to your meeting with Riley. The plan will be monitored carefully, and ultimately its effectiveness will be judged in terms of the criteria for resolution: Did the plan produce a good communications mechanism between you and all the teachers? Did the plan maintain or enhance harmonious labor–management relations?

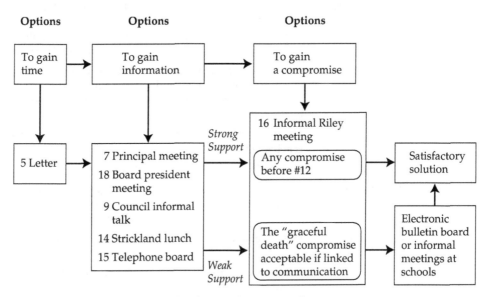

FIGURE 2.3 Solution Strategy for the Teachers Council

SUMMARY AND CONCLUSION

The two models of decision making are summarized in Table 2.2. The classical *model (optimizing)* is a normative ideal. It assumes complete information, total rationality, accurate prediction, and a best solution. Unfortunately, the organizational world is neither so neat nor so simple; hence, the optimizing strategy of the classical model is an ideal of limited use. The *administrative model* (satisficing) is better suited to day-to-day life in organizations because it substitutes a strategy of satisficing for optimizing. The goal is to find satisfactory decisions in complex matters. The model is anchored in rational analysis.

The argument developed in this chapter is that optimizing is inappropriate for most administrative decision making. Satisficing is more useful and realistic, but we suspect the satisficing model is not widely used. It is a normative model, which presents a set of guidelines and procedures to make complex decision making more rational and effective, but it has its costs. It takes time, it is difficult, it is complex, it offers no guarantees, and it is no better than the skill and creativity of the administrator. The model is a tool for reflective administrators, one that can be learned. As the strategy is systematically incorporated into administrative practice, its initial difficulty is overcome and its promise is realized. The keys to its effective use are discipline and practice. Thus we conclude with an actual case for practice with the model. See how well you can do.

TABLE 2.2 Comparison of the Classical and Administrative Models of Decision Making

	DECISION-MAKING MODEL	
CHARACTERISTIC	**CLASSICAL**	**ADMINISTRATIVE**
Setting objectives	Objectives are set prior to generating alternatives.	Objectives are usually set prior to generating alternatives.
Means–ends analysis	A means–ends analysis is always performed. First ends are determined; then means to attain them are sought.	Typically a means–ends analysis is performed; however, sometimes ends change as a result of analysis.
Test of a good decision	The best means to the ends is achieved.	A satisfactory end is achieved.
Decision process	Optimizing.	Satisficing.
Alternative search	Consider all the alternatives and consequences.	Engage in problemistic search to develop a list of satisfactory alternatives.
Underpinning	Heavy reliance on theory.	Reliance on both theory and experience.
Perspective	Normative ideal.	Descriptive and normative.

CASE 2.2

Controversial Speaker

"I can't stand those guys."

John Hill looked up from a note just handed to him by a student messenger. "What guys?" he asked.

"Gays, Mr. Hill. If one ever came up to me, I'd punch him out."

Before Hill could respond, the bell rang and the students quickly left the classroom to go to lunch.

"It was right at the end of class this morning," said Hill, speaking to Betty Hildebrand, another teacher in the social studies department. "One of the runners came by from the office to drop off an announcement. After he left, one of the kids told me he couldn't stand him because he was gay."

"What did you do?" asked Hildebrand.

"Nothing. I was saved by the bell."

"Do you deal with the topic of homosexual behavior in your Minority Studies class?" asked Hildebrand.

"No," replied Hill. "I deal mostly with racial minorities—you know, African Americans, Chicanos, and Native Americans. I have enough trouble getting students to deal rationally with race without getting into the problems of gays and lesbians."

Hill and Hildebrand continued their discussion over lunch. Hildebrand explained that she was dealing with a section on civil rights in her Problems of Democracy course and had touched on the problem of sexual discrimination against women, but she admitted that she had only briefly considered homosexual discrimination, and she, too, had noticed the evident hostility toward homosexuals. She chalked it up to the normal fears of suburban adolescents.

Over the course of that week, the two teachers talked about the problem again and decided to use homosexual discrimination as a topic in their respective classes, though only as a small two-or-three-day unit. Early in the next week, Hildebrand told Hill that she had contacted the public information office of the Society of Individual Rights (SIR), a national homosexual organization, and that SIR furnished speakers and would send, if requested, a speaker to the school.

"I don't know about the speaker," Hill ventured cautiously, "I certainly don't want some outrageous zealot in here. Really what I would like is someone to talk about the problems of discrimination in a legal sense; I absolutely don't want anyone giving 15 minutes on the joys of being gay."

"Don't worry," said Hildebrand. "I met the speaker who would be sent here. I had some reservations of my own about his being an ex-Marine who was in Iraq, but he said he would only speak on the legal problems faced by homosexuals. He seemed all right to me."

"Well, OK," said Hill. "Let's ask him to speak to both classes."

Hill and Hildebrand then talked with Tom Dannis, the department chairman. Satisfied that the speaker would aid in the class objectives and was thus justified, Dannis told the teachers to clear the speaker with the principal, Fred Beck.

Beck was proud of his high school. It was the smaller of the two high schools in Clearwoods, but he felt it was the better. Beck was hired as principal before the school was built and, consequently, had been in the enviable position of staffing the school as he chose and, with his staff, participating in the design of the buildings. Though the local townspeople were interested primarily in the athletic activities, the school district was the most pervasive institution in the town of 34,000. Most of the parents had attended the local school district.

Beck heard the teachers out and agreed with them that the speaker would fit the nature of their classes, but to satisfy his curiosity, he checked the SIR website to confirm the nature of the organization and their speakers. Satisfied, he gave permission to invite the speaker with two provisos: First, student attendance would be voluntary, and no one would be penalized for nonattendance at class the day of the SIR speaker. Second, Beck wanted teachers to apprise the parents of the class and receive parental permission slips from each youngster in the class. A student without a slip would not be allowed in class that day. It was true that parents had already given permission for their children to be in these two senior elective classes, but Beck felt that the alteration in the class justified a reaffirmation of parental consent.

While Beck was no stranger to controversy, he did not openly court it. He had in the past defended a teacher accused of teaching Marxism in his history class. Beck was quick to defend the teacher, though the fact that the class was one in Russian history made the defense easy. In general, the community was favorably disposed toward Beck and Clearwoods High. The school district had a good reputation; nearly 80 percent of the graduates went on to college, with a surprisingly high number accepted at schools of national reputation. Fred Beck saw no major problem in having a homosexual speaker in this setting.

"What are you trying to do, Fred? Do you want the parents to rise as one and descend on us with tar and feathers?" It was superintendent Jeff Ellis on the phone to Beck.

"What's the problem?" asked Beck.

"One of the school board members, John Sloan, told me that you were turning the school over to some gay activist group for the day."

"Well, I know what he's talking about. But that's not quite right. We have a couple of senior classes—Minority Studies and Problems of Democracy—and the teachers of these two classes are going to have a homosexual speaker talk to both classes about civil rights, legal problems, and that sort of thing. Both of the classes are senior electives, and we're covered by parental permission slips in both. According to Hill, one of the teachers, the guy seems pretty normal and we should be OK."

"Well, look, Fred, I'll get back to Sloan, and then I'll get back to you. Actually, I wish you had bounced the idea off me before going ahead with the speaker."

"Normally, I don't check with you about curriculum issues," rejoined Beck. "But, you know," he continued, "we probably should have some kind of policy for controversial speakers. In fact, that might be something for the next roundtable."

"It probably would be a good idea," Superintendent Ellis responded, "but you know, I try to keep a low profile on rules and regulations. I'm buried in paper as it is. Look, I'll get back to you, but in the meantime, don't get us in over our heads."

"No problem."

Superintendent Ellis had hoped the issue was restricted to a couple of crank calls. But his hope was not fulfilled. In the next two days, he had a dozen or so people call to complain about the proposed speaker, though none of the callers was a parent with a student in the affected classes. Later in the week, after two other members of the board called to protest a homosexual speaker at Clearwoods High, Ellis decided to call his principal.

"Fred, the phone lines are burning. I have three board members who are edgy. They keep asking what's happening with the homosexual speaker. The whole thing may be getting out of hand. Do you think this talk is really worth the trouble?"

After a slight pause, the principal responded, "I did tell my teachers they could have the speaker, and I don't like to renege. These are dedicated teachers whom I respect. Of course, I've had some calls, too. I just don't know if it's going to be a big issue or not."

"You know my policy, Fred. I don't interfere with my principals. And you're doing a great job there. But I see a potential catastrophe. We're still going to be in business after the speaker has come and gone. And if I can't bargain with the community here and there, I really can't do my job the way it should be done. Remember, it's you and I who have to live with these people, not the two teachers. I trust your judgment to do the right thing. Keep me posted."

"There really ought to be a policy about this," Beck thought to himself as he hung up the phone. "The speaker is coming tomorrow, and I may end up looking like George Wallace at the schoolhouse door. George Wallace! Gee, I'm getting old." With that thought, he left for the day.

As was his habit, Principal Beck got to school early the next day. He put a note in John Hill's box telling him to stop by in the morning during his break. When Hill came by, Beck told him only that there was a little trouble about the speaker and that he wanted the speaker to report to the principal's office before he went to the classes. Hill said he would get in touch with the speaker.

About half an hour before he was scheduled to speak, a well-dressed man in a pin-striped gray suit walked into the administration building and asked the principal's secretary where he could find Mr. Beck. "My name is Samuel Sheldon, and I'm going to give a talk for Mr. Hill and Mrs. Hildebrand today. John Hill asked me to stop in and see the principal for a minute before I went over to the social studies office."

"Have a seat, Mr. Sheldon. Mr. Beck will be with you in a minute."

Discussing the Case

- Assume the role of the principal in this case.
- Define the short-term and long-term problems.

- Use the satisficing model to develop a strategy of action.
- Is it too late to renege?
- What is the line between professional responsibility and community accountability?
- No matter what your eventual strategy, make sure it includes a plan to address the dysfunctional consequences of your actions.

ENDNOTES

1. This section draws heavily on Hoy and Miskel (2008).
2. Iterations of this process occur frequently in the organizational literature. For example, see Daft (2001).
3. A critical and intriguing examination of heuristics has been formulated by a group of cognitive psychologists called the *prospect school*. Their main thesis is that individuals cope with their limited abilities to solve complex problems by developing heuristic devices; however, although the heuristics help, they themselves sometimes introduce systematic biases that may subvert decision making. For an interesting debate on the utility of heuristics, see Kahneman & Tversky (1996) and Gigerenzer (1996).
4. The teachers council is a composite case based on the contemporary administrative issue of empowerment and unionism. It was inspired by the Advisory Council (Sargeant, C. G., & Belisle, E. L. [1955]. *Educational Administration: Cases and Concepts*. Boston: Houghton Mifflin).

CHAPTER THREE

DECISION MAKING
Muddling and Scanning

We have examined two models of rational decision making thus far. The optimizing strategy is an ideal model with severe practical weaknesses. The satisficing model, in contrast, is useful because it retains the rationality of the classical perspective while providing an approach that works well for practicing administrators. Both models rely on theory and are comprehensive strategies dedicated to means–ends analysis—establishing objectives and then determining logical means to attain them. Objectives, however, do not always precede action in the real world, nor is rationality obvious.

THE INCREMENTAL MODEL: A STRATEGY OF SUCCESSIVE LIMITED COMPARISONS

Sometimes administrative problems are so complex that even a satisficing strategy falls short. When alternatives are difficult if not impossible to discern or the consequences so complicated as to elude prediction, even satisficing does not work well. In such situations, decision makers are forced to make small incremental changes to avoid unanticipated negative consequences. They continually monitor the outcomes of each successive decision, carefully assessing the result of each small change. For example, to what new activities should a school administrator allocate more resources? This question can be answered by considering only those alternatives that differ slightly from existing conditions.

Charles Lindblom (1959) first described the incremental model of decision making as the "science of muddling through." He claimed that administrators actually muddle through much more than they engage in rational and comprehensive decision making. He suggested that successive limited comparisons may be the only feasible approach to systematic decision making when the issues are complex, uncertain, and conflict laden. What is striking about this model is that objectives, exhaustive analyses, and prior criteria for success are not necessary. In fact, means–ends analysis is inappropriate. Objectives and alternatives emerge simultaneously. Only a small range of options, closely resembling the current situation, are considered. The strategy proceeds by successively comparing the consequences of each incremental change until decision makers are comfortable with the course of action.

The incremental model has a number of features that set it apart from both the satisficing and optimizing models. Setting objectives and generating alternatives are not separate exercises. A priori objectives do not guide the analysis. Rather, a course of action emerges as alternatives and consequences are explored. The more complex the problem, the more likely it is that objectives will change as decisions evolve. The marginal differences in value among options, not established objectives, are the bases for decision making.

Few would admit they have no objective in making a decision. However, imagine a school administrator who finds day-to-day work far removed from educational theory. Faced with the task of allocating resources to new programs, for example, administrators often proceed slowly and incrementally. They dole out funds sparingly to assess the effects. Their decisions are frequently not driven by objectives but rather by nonspecified outcomes. Administrators recognize the daunting complexities of assessing the educational value of small programs, so the administrative team is inclined to say, "Let's fund this program and see what happens." If nothing bad happens, the decision is OK. Likewise, when they agree that the results are positive, a good decision has been made. No wonder administrators proceed slowly and carefully; they are unsure of their specific objectives. The criterion for a good decision comes after the decision is made rather than before. Decisions to continue the allocation of resources to new activities are based upon broad agreements among administrators about the outcomes. To use Lindblom's phrase, one "muddles through."

The incremental model greatly reduces the number of alternatives that administrators consider. Decision makers consider only those alternatives that are similar to the existing situation and only those differences between the current state and proposed outcomes. Options are ignored that are outside the decision maker's narrow problem focus; hence, the complexity of decision making is dramatically reduced and made manageable. Deciding what programs to fund does not mean examining all the possible alternatives; on the contrary, decision makers consider only a few options that are not far removed from the existing situation. The process is a slow evolution based on outcomes that administrators agree are acceptable.

Simplifying decision making by concentrating on alternatives that differ only slightly from the existing situation is not capricious. Limiting the focus to small variations from current situations makes good use of available knowledge. Decision makers who limit their search for solutions to a reasonable set of alternatives based on their experience confidently make predictions of consequences. By emphasizing only differences among alternatives, time and energy are conserved. Not straying too far from the existing situation can avoid the paralysis caused by attempts to analyze all the possible consequences of a specific course of action.

Successive comparison is often a pragmatic alternative to using theory. In both the classical and administrative models, theory is a useful guide to decision making. As problems become complicated, however, the inadequacies of our theories are evident. In complex situations, decision makers often make more progress by comparing a series of concrete, practical alternatives rather than by emphasizing abstract, theoretical analyses.

In sum, the incremental model has the following distinctive properties:

- Means–ends analysis is inappropriate because objectives and alternatives emerge simultaneously.
- Good solutions are those upon which decision makers agree regardless of objectives.
- Options and outcomes are dramatically reduced by considering only alternatives similar to the current state of affairs.
- Analysis is limited to differences between the existing situation and proposed alternatives.
- The incremental method eschews theory in favor of successive comparisons of concrete, practical alternatives.

When alternatives and consequences are exceedingly complex, administrators typically resort to an incremental strategy; they "muddle through." Small decisions are made in directions that do not steer far from the existing situation. These incremental actions are tentative and often remedial. Perhaps the best way to illustrate the incremental model is with an actual case. We turn to a case of conflict in a religious motif. As you read the case, consider the decision-making approach used by elementary school principal Thomas Evans. Successive comparison or muddling through, as it is more commonly referred to, can be effective or ineffective. How effective was the strategy in this case?

CASE 3.1

Conflict at Christmas

Background

Elementary Principal Thomas Evans passed the school auditorium while taking a routine stroll through his school.[1] The strains of "O Little Town of Bethlehem," filtering through the halls, underlined the religious nature of the season as the children practiced for tomorrow's Christmas program. But the background music failed to provoke the usual reaction on the part of Evans. Instead of stimulating thoughts of a religious nature or of the spirit of the season or even being a mundane reminder of the seven shopping days left until Christmas, the music prompted Dr. Evans to reflect on the old controversy stirred by a live nativity scene that had, at one time, been a part of the Christmas assembly.

Weeks before, as the holiday season approached, the customary plans were laid for the school Christmas assembly. Shortly after the implementation of some of these plans, however, Evans became aware that this holiday season might be different. What appeared as a routine decision became a controversy, the overtones of which were to be eventually heard throughout Central City. As Evans continued down the hall he reflected that tomorrow, on December 18, the Christmas assembly would be held in the wake of a controversy not yet fully resolved.

The Setting

Central City is a large midwestern city that is one of the biggest in its state. Steeped in conservatism and tradition, the city's general aura carries over to its public school system. The Central City schools are viewed by citizens as good, but the school administration is seen by some as following rules and channels rather than exercising dynamic educational leadership. A few of the vocal opponents of the schools point to the officialdom with which school administrators often become preoccupied and decry the apathy, as opposed to dynamism, displayed by many of the city's school administrators.

Lincoln Elementary is one of Central City's many elementary schools; it is not, however, the average Central City elementary school. The school's neighborhood is a traditional upper-middle-class section of the city. Although the area had been originally almost exclusively white and Protestant, an influx of Jewish people and still later of African American professionals had changed the demographic nature of the community, which retained its desirability as a place to live. The uniqueness of the neighborhood stemmed from the presence of a large private university. Local residents, committed themselves to education, placed a premium on involvement in the schools; it was not just something else to do for these parents. While the more aggressive parents are the well educated, they are not the majority. Because of the proximity of the private university, the attendance area is "loaded with college professors," according to Principal Evans. In fact, approximately 10 percent of adults in the area hold doctorates. The attendance area remains predominately (66 percent) white Protestant. The remaining population is split between Jewish and African American professionals.

One aspect of the school environment is especially relevant to the Christmas assembly conflict. Lincoln Elementary has traditionally had a strong and aggressive Parent–Teachers Organization (the PTO), a particularly vocal element for years. Often the PTO has been viewed by the administration as intrusive. Principal Evans was somewhat of an anomaly in that he liked the PTO and worked well with the parents. He had a settling influence on the parental turbulence at Lincoln.

Conflict Antecedents

At one time, the school Christmas program had included a live nativity scene with Lincoln pupils playing the various roles of the Christmas story. After some public protest and a short, though acrimonious, court fight, the nativity scene had been ended. The Community Relations Council (CRC) was instrumental in that success and continued to monitor the schools for practices that were offensive to Jews and other minorities. In fact, this year they sent a letter to all the members of the Central City Jewish community telling them that the CRC was ready to act on behalf of anyone who felt that the schools were favoring a particular religious interpretation of the holiday season. If advised of such practices, the CRC stood ready to take appropriate action on behalf of the parents.

Late in October, the mother of a Jewish child attending Lincoln called the CRC to complain that her child had been asked to take part in the singing of religious Christmas carols. The director of the CRC and a local rabbi decided to call Evans to talk informally about the Christmas program.

Evans was a bit concerned and decided to ask a teacher to sit in on the meeting to represent the interests of the school staff. A senior faculty member of the school, the CRC director, the rabbi, and Principal Evans got together to discuss the Christmas program. The CRC objected to the singing of religious carols and asked that they be eliminated from the program.

Requesting someone from another religion to participate against his beliefs was seen by the CRC as embarrassing and a violation of the rights of religious freedom. Principal Evans found that he was in some agreement with the CRC and said that he would consider the matter and get back to the CRC with a decision in the next few days. According to all concerned, rapport at this meeting was very good, although relationships were somewhat tense; further, all agreed that Principal Evans understood clearly just what the complaint was. Evans concluded the discussion by stating that he would take the matter under advisement and would consult with the Central City superintendent of schools.

Evans did speak with the superintendent of schools, who told him that whatever decision he reached would be acceptable as long as there was no repeat of the acrimony and upset caused by the last religious argument over Christmas. Evans assured him there would be no brouhaha.

A Decision Reached

Following their discussion with Evans, the CRC representatives were guardedly optimistic over the possibilities of achieving their goal, as was evident in the following letter from the CRC director to the local rabbi:

November 28

Rabbi David Rosenblatt
6001 E. 29th Boulevard
Central City, Lafayette

Dear David:

I would just like to summarize for both of us the Lincoln case. Several weeks ago, a parent called us in response to our community mailing on Christmas in the public schools. The parent objected to having a child forced to sing religious songs in the Christmas program. Consequently, on November 14th, we met with Dr. Thomas Evans, the Lincoln principal, and a teacher from Lincoln.

You will recall that we objected to the Christmas program because we thought it would be offensive to many Jewish parents and their children. We urged the removal of religious carols from the Christmas program. Dr. Evans promised to consult with the superintendent of the schools and the Lincoln faculty.

Our impression on leaving the meeting was that Evans and the teacher were sympathetic to our position. You will be pleased to learn that I received a telephone call from Dr. Evans on November 26th, during which he stated that there will NOT be singing of religious Christmas carols this year. I have asked several parents with children at Lincoln School to report to us what actually occurs.

Best regards.

Sincerely yours,

Dan Katz
Executive Director

As Principal Evans had said he would, he had taken the matter to both his superintendent and his teachers. The superintendent gave him free rein with the condition that things stay calm. He checked informally with his teachers and found them generally supportive.

He called the CRC to inform them that no religious carols would be sung at the holiday program. He then told Ms. Peters, the music teacher, that she should not include any religious carols in the program and explained the basis for the decision. She was not pleased. In fact, after a brief and bitter exchange, she stormed out of the office screaming, "We'll see about this!"

A Decision Reversed

One hour later, Evans received a phone call from the outraged president of the PTO. "What's the matter with you? We've had Christmas carols at Lincoln practically since there was Christmas, and now you just cancel them without so much as a by-your-leave. You can't do this; enough is enough. We have no nativity scene, and now you want to throw out Christmas carols. What kind of a Christmas is that? I understand that you have problems with the Jewish community, but why not sing some of their songs instead of getting rid of the spirit of Christmas? I've had five calls already from irate parents; things are getting out of control. They're insisting on an emergency meeting. This thing could get messy. By the way, what in the world did you say to Ms. Peters? She's threatening to resign as faculty sponsor of the Christmas program. You know she's a popular teacher with the parents."

Evans sat in his office and considered this new turn of events. Perhaps he had acted too quickly. Maybe he could have Christmas carols if he just didn't offend the Jewish community. He needed a few Hanukkah songs, and, maybe, everything would be alright. He decided to modify his decision canceling Christmas carols. His approach would be a multicultural program including songs and hymns representing not only Jewish and Christian communities but also some African American songs of the winter season and the solstice. "This decision is a good compromise," he thought. "Everyone should be happy."

The CRC was astounded when the parent who had originally complained about the Christmas program called to protest again. This time, they were asking her child to sing not only Christmas carols but also songs from other cultures celebrating, in some cases, pagan deities. They called Evans at once to lodge a complaint.

Another Decision?

The PTO was furious that Evans had so diluted the traditional Christmas program as to make it virtually unrecognizable and hardly a Christmas celebration at all. "This is a Christian county, you know," thundered the president of the PTO. "Aren't you forgetting us?" They requested an immediate meeting with Evans.

The teachers, hitherto uninvolved in the controversy, were divided over the question. Long-time teachers at Lincoln were fond of the Christmas program and saw no harm in it. Newer teachers were much more critical of the program. They made their discontent known to the principal.

The superintendent was dismayed at this turn of events. The old wounds were reopening. This is precisely what he had hoped to avoid. He picked up the phone and called Evans. Something had to be done and done quickly.

ANALYZING THE CASE: AN INCREMENTAL APPROACH

Principal Thomas Evans made an initial decision in direct response to an outside pressure. In the wake of controversy about the nativity scene, Evans was wary of provoking disharmony. He did not want his decision to upset the precarious equilibrium that had been reached. His strategy was to make small, incremental changes and gauge their effect on the status quo. Thus, when confronted by the director of the CRC and a local rabbi, he talked informally with them as he listened to their complaints. He established rapport with the CRC and the rabbi by his sympathetic ear.

Evans did not want to move too quickly and promised only that he would speak to the superintendent and avoid the acrimony caused by the last religious argument over Christmas. After consulting with the superintendent and a few teachers, he reassured the CRC that no religious songs would be sung at the holiday program. However, his music teacher was upset by the decision. Apparently, she immediately mobilized the PTO leadership, who supported the Christmas carol program.

Principal Evans, faced with a new turn of events decided to retreat from his ban on Christmas carols. He suggested the program include hymns and songs representing so many groups that no one, he reasoned, would be offended. He believed that the small change would satisfy everyone and not disturb the basic nature of the Christmas program.

Things are not always as simple as they seem. The CRC was surprised to learn that the parent who had complained about the program was upset again. Her child was being forced to sing not only Christmas carols but also "songs from other cultures celebrating, in some cases, pagan deities." Moreover, the PTO was angry because Evans had so diluted the original program that, they claimed, it was virtually unrecognizable as a Christmas celebration. Now the teachers were dividing and choosing sides. And the issue threatened further escalation of animosities.

What Evans engaged in is muddling through. He made small, incremental changes designed not to alter the program drastically but which seemed to have a reasonable chance of circumventing problems. In many cases, this is a successful strategy. In fact, many students of decision making (Lindblom, 1980) claim that muddling through, or decision making by successive incremental comparison, is the way most administrators make decisions. Indeed, often the strategy works quite well. In the current case, if the music teacher had been more sensitive to the dilemma and accommodating to the decision, the holiday program might have been changed without any serious disturbance.

When that did not happen, Evans was forced to make other changes. Note that in this case he took a small step back. Again he reasoned that a small change that would broaden the program would be acceptable to all parties. This might have worked had it not been for an adamant parent.

The Christmas problem demonstrates the differences between descriptive and normative models of decision making. This case simply describes what happened; it is likely typical of the responses of many administrators. What is lacking in the decisions of the principal is the anticipation of the possible negative consequences of his actions. But such an observation is a criticism drawn from a rational satisficing model. This case is a demonstration of the incremental model. Means and ends are not separated because the incremental model assumes that setting objectives and generating alternatives are too intertwined to consider as separate activities. The principal muddles through, trying to promote harmony. There is no means–ends analysis, only a series of small changes designed to maintain equilibrium. As it turns out, the case is not resolved by the incremental approach.

Perhaps a strategy of successive incremental approximation is inappropriate in this instance. After all, the problem is not so complex as to prevent the use of a more rational and comprehensive satisficing strategy. Alternatives are not so difficult to discern and the consequences are not so complicated as to elude prediction; a satisficing strategy could work well. What may be needed here is a strategy that draws the best from both the satisficing and incremental models. Thus we turn to an adaptive strategy of mixed scanning.

THE MIXED-SCANNING MODEL: AN ADAPTIVE STRATEGY

Although widely used, muddling through has its drawbacks—it is conservative and aimless. Yet most administrators are forced to make decisions under the press of time and with only partial information. Amitai Etzioni (1967, 1986, 1989) advances a model of decision making that is a pragmatic approach to its complexities and uncertainties. This adaptive strategy or mixed-scanning model is a synthesis of the administrative and incremental models (Langley, Mintzberg, Pitcher, Posada, & Saint-Macary, 1995; Thomas, 1984; Wiseman, 1979a, 1979b).

Mixed scanning is guided by two questions: (1) What is the basic mission of the organization? and (2) What incremental decisions will move the organization in that direction? In other words, the basic policy and mission of the organization guide even the smallest of decisions as the decision maker uses an adaptive strategy. Since all information is not known, the decision maker uses only partial information. This does not mean that the administrator proceeds blindly with little or no data; on the contrary, one proceeds deliberately without becoming paralyzed by a need to have all the facts before acting. It is "a mixture of shallow and deep examination of data—generalized consideration of a broad range of facts and choices followed by detailed examination of a focused subset of facts and choices" (Etzioni, 1989, p. 124). Incremental decisions are made within a framework of existing mission and policy. Mixed scanning is an adaptive strategy that unites the rationalism of the satisficing model with the flexibility of the incremental model. Unless decision makers assess incremental decisions in terms of some broad policy, drift is likely. The broad guidelines, however, are not incrementally determined; in fact, they have all the characteristics of grand, a priori decisions, which incrementalism seeks to avoid (Etzioni, 1989).

Mixed scanning has its roots in medicine. Effective physicians are guided by the general mission of patient health and make incremental decisions to achieve that end. Doctors know what they are trying to achieve. Moreover, they do not engage all their medical resources on the basis of an initial diagnosis, nor do they wait for every conceivable bit of scientific data and patient history before beginning treatment. They survey the symptoms, analyze the difficulties, initiate a tentative treatment, and, if it fails, try something else (Etzioni, 1989, p. 125). So too with adaptive organizational decision makers. Guided by policy and mission, they survey the problems, analyze the difficulties, initiate a tentative action, and, if it fails, try something new.

Etzioni (1989) advances seven rules or adaptive practices for a mixed scanning strategy:

1. *Use focused trial and error.* The procedure has two parts: searching for alternatives and continually checking the outcomes to adjust the course of action. Focused trial and error assumes that administrators must act despite the fact that important information is unavailable. Thus, decisions are made with partial information and then carefully monitored and modified in light of new information.
2. *Be tentative; go slowly.* Implied in this adaptive strategy is the principle of tentativeness, a commitment to modify when necessary. It is important that administrators see decisions as experimental, expecting to revise them as needed.
3. *If uncertain, procrastinate.* Waiting is not always bad; in fact, procrastination is another adaptive principle as the decision maker uses time to collect more information, process new data, and consider additional alternatives. Uncertainty and complexity frequently justify delay.

4. *Stagger your decisions.* Commit to a decision in stages, assessing the periodic outcomes of each phase and proceeding when the results are satisfactory.
5. *If uncertain, fractionalize decisions.* Staged decisions can be tested in parts. Do not use all resources in implementing a decision, but rather commit only in part until the consequences are satisfactory.
6. *Hedge your bets.* Implement several competing alternatives—provided that they seem to lead to satisfactory outcomes. Then adjust based on the results.
7. *Be prepared to reverse your decision.* Decisions that can be reversed without high cost are particularly useful in experimental and tentative decision making. Reversible decisions avoid overcommitment to a course of action when information is limited.[2]

Skillful educational administrators employ all seven of these adaptive practices. The techniques illustrate flexibility, caution, and the capacity to proceed carefully with partial knowledge. When time is limited or the decision is not that important, *truncated adaptive satisficing* may be sufficient, that is, both the range and number of facts and choices may be sharply reduced.

The mixed-scanning model has a number of distinctive characteristics. Organizational policy directs tentative incremental decisions. Good decisions are consistent with organizational policy, and good alternatives are experimental, reversible, limited, incremental, and typically not far from the problem. In spite of uncertainty and scarce information, action is necessary. A strategy of adaption can determine a course of action by mixing theory, experience, and successive comparisons. We return to our case to suggest how an adaptive strategy of mixed scanning might work.

ANALYZING THE CASE: AN ADAPTIVE STRATEGY

The central theme of a mixed-scanning model is that general policy guides the process as small, incremental decisions are made to adapt the outcomes to the policy. In the case at hand, there are three elements of a general policy that Evans could use: (1) holiday programs should have educational merit; (2) programs should benefit school–community relations; and (3) programs should not be controversial. Evans handled current problems simply by avoiding controversy.

When the CRC came to him, his response was a circumscribed decision to avoid trouble. Had he been guided by all the elements of the policy, he would have been forced to a comprehensive evaluation of his actions. He would have had to consider how his decision was related to the educational merit of the program as well as how the program might affect school-community relations.

The initial conference with the CRC and the rabbi should have prompted Evans to place the problem in the larger context of policy rather than in the narrower one of simply avoiding conflict. It is possible to make decisions using a focused trial-and-error approach and then carefully monitor and modify them in light of new information. Evans did not use this larger framework of decision making; consequently, his sequence of decisions never addressed the breadth of the problem. Evans neither searched for alternatives nor continually checked for consequences. Rather, he made small defensive decisions. His decisions were quick and not tentative. Each decision was seen as a solution, rather than as a trial test. For example, his decisions to cancel the Christmas carols and then to reinstate them as part of a multicultural festival were seen as solutions instead of tentative, experimental procedures.

Evans could have delayed his decisions or, at the very least, projected them as tentative possibilities to test the waters before fixing the actions. This is a case where procrastination encourages the collection of new information in order to gauge opposition to the final resolution of the problem. Evans did not wait for more information; he acted. And, some would argue, he acted precipitously.

When he did make a decision, as in the cases of cancelling and reinstituting the Christmas carols, he gave himself no leeway in dealing with potential negative consequences. In fact, it seems he did not even consider the possibilities. Between cancelling and reinstating Christmas carols there is a range of incremental decisions that might be made. Evans did not understand the uncertainties of his positions; hence, he jumped from one presumed solution to another. He did not hedge his bets, and he was unable to make strategic adjustments based on the responses to his decisions. Evans acted as if the adamant parent, the upset teacher, and the inflexible PTO would go along with his decision. He did not hedge against the possibility that they would not.

Evans was prepared to reverse his decisions. But, unfortunately, the costs were high because his initial decisions were not construed as either experimental or tentative. The consequence of Evans's reversal was to create a picture of vacillation, impulsiveness, and poor choice.

The situation might be resolved by using mixed scanning. Complexity and limited information suggest a strategy that is deliberate, tentative, fluid, cautious, open, and adaptive. Using a mixed-scanning strategy, Evans might have proceeded in the following way. First, he would have been guided by all aspects of the policy. That is, he would have considered the educational benefit of the program, community relations, and the limitation of conflict. Each small decision would be continuously evaluated in terms of how well it followed the policy. When the CRC first came to him, for example, Evans should have searched for alternatives beyond simply cancelling the carols. Such action was not wise because in reality it met none of the policy demands. A proposal to include Hanukkah songs would elicit reaction from the CRC, which would allow Evans to gauge the opposition to the program as well as to determine what the Jewish community would suggest in terms of education. It might well be possible to construe the problem as a multicultural issue in which parents and students learn to appreciate the diversity of other cultures. The focus of this process would then be on the educational benefit and the Jewish parents' reaction to it, thus developing sound community relations and avoiding controversy.

Similarly, Evans could frame the problem the same way with the music teacher. Again, the thrust of the holiday program would be defined differently. It would not be a program merely to celebrate Christmas, but rather a program to recognize the contributions of a diversity of cultures. Such a program might or might not have religious overtones. Perhaps the program could include activities that underscore the influences of Scandinavian traditions of the solstice; such ancient Middle Eastern religions as Mithraism and Zoroastrianism; activities that draw on the observance of the winter solstice in African, Asian, and European cultures; and the more traditional interpretations of the Christmas season. The program might include nonreligious songs of Christmas, Hanukkah, and African lore.

This is a complex problem, but one that has been reframed to broaden the possibilities for solution without falling prey to the religious controversy of the past nativity observance. Reframing the problem does not solve it; however, the decision maker can limit the effect of the emotion-laden religious issues and follow the general policy of educational benefit. There are no guarantees of success, but now there is potential for a positive outcome and general acceptance.

In sum, a reasonable decision strategy for Evans is to recast the problem in a broader frame that is consistent with guiding policy. He must search for alternatives, check the likely outcomes, and adjust the course of action as he deals with the protagonists—the CRC, the rabbi, the music teacher, parents, the PTO, and the superintendent. After deliberating with each of the protagonists, he makes small decisions that can be easily modified. The consequence of each decision is small enough in scale to leave room to revise it once more information becomes available. Waiting is not always bad; in fact, procrastination is an adaptive principle that can be used here to collect more information, process new data, and consider additional alternatives. Evans, for example, does not have to commit himself immediately to the CRC or the rabbi; he can hold them off until he has more information from the music teacher, the PTO, and the superintendent.

Having decided to refashion the Christmas program, Evans needs to move deliberately and cautiously so that the effects can be assessed as they are implemented. It would be helpful in this regard if the decisions were sequential or staggered so that changes in direction are possible without undue controversy. In this process, Evans needs to float a variety of competing options and hedge his bets. The options should be consistent with the general policy of educational benefit, community support, and harmony. A possible solution might readily be available. Consider the following scenario: The parent does not complain. The music teacher and Principal Evans work together with representatives of the CRC and the PTO. They change the Christmas program to a general celebration of the holiday season. They draw upon multicultural traditions and establish a program that becomes a model for its diversity and general appeal.

This happy ending may be overly optimistic, but never underestimate luck: It could work. Nonetheless, Evans should hedge against failure by being prepared to compromise. For example, the following possibilities might be advanced to various participants in the case:

1. Modify the program by substituting the performance of classical music of the season for the singing of Christmas carols.
2. Modify the program by presenting a series of student vignettes that dramatize the cultural roots of different celebrations of the winter solstice rather than singing Christmas carols.

3. Modify the program by replacing Christmas carols with an art festival that features holiday themes from different ethnic and cultural groups.
4. Modify the program by replacing the Christmas carols with a mix of these and other activities to celebrate the season.

The goal of mixed scanning is clear in this case. The policy of the school directs the decisions. What is desirable is a holiday program that promotes education, acceptance, and harmony in the context of diversity. There is always the possibility that the history of acrimony in this community will defeat such action. Evans still has a fallback position if he is unsuccessful in getting the groups to accept a reasonable modification of the program. He can cancel the program. This last step is only a short-term solution to this problem; it does not deal with the critical issues of education, tolerance, and harmony in a multicultural setting.

SUMMARY AND CONCLUSION

The two models of this chapter are summarized in Table 3.1. The *incremental model* is descriptive; it merely describes a common mode of decision making. It assumes that setting objectives and generating alternatives are intertwined. Decision makers

TABLE 3.1 Comparison of the Incremental and Mixed-Scanning Models of Decision Making

	DECISION-MAKING MODEL	
CHARACTERISTIC	INCREMENTAL	MIXED SCANNING
Setting objectives	Setting objectives and generating alternatives are intertwined.	Broad policy guidelines are set prior to generating alternatives.
Means–ends analysis	A means–ends analysis is inappropriate because means and ends are not separable.	Broad ends and tentative means focus the analysis.
Test of a good decision	Decision makers agree the decision is in the right direction.	Results in a satisfactory end, consistent with organizational policy.
Decision process	Successive comparing.	Adaptive satisficing.
Alternative search	Limit search to alternatives close to the problems.	Limit search to alternatives close to the problem, always evaluating in terms of policy and mission.
Underpinning	Comparison replaces theory.	Theory, comparison, and experience are used together.
Perspective	Descriptive.	Descriptive and normative.

limit their search for alternatives to those that are not dramatically different from the current state of affairs as they engage in a series of small incremental changes—always comparing the results with what is acceptable to them. The *mixed-scanning model* is a normative model of decision making that combines the best of the satisficing and incremental models. The goal is to find satisfactory decisions in complex matters where information is limited and anticipation of consequences is difficult. Mixed scanning is a pragmatic approach to complexity and uncertainty. Decisions are seen as tentative, fluid, open, and reversible.

The use of the incremental model has been criticized as muddling through without direction; its consequence is often organization drift. As Kenneth Boulding (1964, p. 931) pithily observed, the incrementalist's fate may be to stumble through history putting one drunken foot in front of the other. In contrast, mixed scanning is a coping strategy that capitalizes on incremental comparisons guided by organizational policy; it is directed incrementalism.

The argument developed in this chapter is that mixed scanning is usually a more appropriate strategy for administrative decision making than the incremental model. Although the incremental model may be more widely used than mixed scanning, mixed scanning can and should be used in those situations that call for an incremental approach. It avoids drift and guides the process. It forces the decision maker not only to consider reflectively the consequences of action but also to overlay organizational policy on the process. When time is crucial, information partial, prediction difficult, and complexity high, the mixed-scanning model is most appropriate. Mixed scanning is an adaptive tool for reflective administrators, one that can be learned. As the strategy is systematically incorporated into administrative practice, its promise is realized. Success in the use of the model requires practice; thus, we recommend that you practice using the model with actual cases. See how well you can do. We recommend that you develop a strategy for action based on the mixed-scanning model for the following case.

CASE 3.2

Crisis in Marshall Creek

Marshall Creek has long enjoyed a peaceful existence as a small rural town. This closed, close-knit community has traditional values, has been deeply committed to the education of its children, and has been suspicious of outsiders. Nonetheless, no town is an island, and Marshall Creek is no exception. New people, new ideas, and different values are creeping into the serenity of Marshall Creek. Cultural diversity has brought tension and conflict to a school system whose previous concerns about student deportment centered around tardiness, talking back to teachers, and an occasional smoke in the boys' lavatory. But now their problems are drugs, single parents, and even an AIDS case once in a while.

Such public meetings as the town council, the school board, the recreational authority, and, of all places, the hitherto sleepy meetings of the library board have been transformed from calm and deliberate meetings to arenas of rancorous and volatile conflict. Gone is the peace of the past. Diversity has brought opposing points of view, something that the old timers of Marshall Creek find uncomfortable, to say the least.

The argument at the library council is probably a case in point. The library had subscribed to a limited number of periodicals and popular magazines over the years, slowly cutting back as the costs of subscriptions grew. Newer residents in town expected to find magazines that catered to minority audiences and sometimes unpopular views. The older residents on the library board did not object to those views; they did object to the town library paying for them.

As the community has changed, new problems have emerged. The PTO, which has always supported the conservative norms of the community, has developed a militant faction of outsiders. These outsiders are families from urban communities who have migrated to Marshall Creek over the past five years. They have become vocal, assertive, and, some would say, antagonistic as they push for programs that are looked upon by the insiders as trendy, liberal, and decadent—who, after all, needs a program on modern living or whatever passes for sex education these days? These are personal problems that should remain in the family inner circle.

The board of education, however, has remained staunchly conservative. Seven of the nine members on the board are considered pillars of the community. But two recently elected board members hold to more contemporary views and present an enigma to the other board members. Without question, both have growing constituencies in the community. And one has become a gadfly on the board, calling into question the motives of many of the board's actions. He often describes the stodgy board as living in the past. The board does not care for this description. The other new member serves as the speaker for almost any group with an ax to grind at the board meeting.

The school has not gone unscathed in these conflicts. There has always been a powerful local clique that has been a leader in the activities of the informal organization of the school. However, a new and more progressive subgroup, composed mostly of younger teachers from outside the community, has challenged the status quo and made life in the school more interesting, if not more difficult.

Dr. Charles Frank, the superintendent of schools in Marshall Creek, is himself a product of the local schools. He grew up in the community, graduated from a local teachers college, started as a teacher in the system 25 years ago, and gradually worked his way up from teacher to high school principal to the superintendency, a post he has held for the past six years. Although Dr. Frank understands both the politics and the feelings of the community, he is also aware of aspirations and concerns of newcomers to Marshall Creek. He realizes that life in Marshall Creek is in the process of changing; nonetheless, he is gravely concerned about the infighting and polarization that are occurring in both the community and the schools. He considers himself an open and progressive educator who can deal with the realities of change. He has spent his life in Marshall Creek, but, except for a few outsiders, no one would call him provincial.

The most recent high school PTO meeting focused on sex education. The outsiders have been promoting a more systematic and comprehensive program that begins in first grade, develops gradually through successive grades, and includes such topics as contraception, safe sex, and abortion. The proposal to distribute condoms to sexually active students has polarized both the community and the teachers in the school, while making civil meetings almost impossible. Most people are violently opposed to a sex education program that goes beyond basic health and reproductive issues, taught in the high school. The growing and aggressive campaign of the newcomers, however, has spilled over into the student body. The students are choosing sides in this debate, and among high school students the notion of a condom clinic is popular.

Mr. Ross, the high school principal, telephoned Dr. Frank the morning after the latest PTO meeting to brief him on the discussion that had taken place. Dr. Frank understood the significance of the issues raised by the PTO in light of the increasing sexual activity of teenagers and the AIDS crisis. He realized that the matter of the sex education program, although controversial, needed to be confronted. But he thought he needed more time to prepare a sound analysis. He wanted to be able to respond in a rational rather than an emotional way. He decided to mobilize a study team comprised of parents, teachers, students, social workers, and medical authorities to prepare a report on which he could base his actions. Events overtook Dr. Frank, however, before he could act on his ideas. A seemingly inconsequential lunchroom fracas turned into a nightmare.

A fight between two boys in the high school cafeteria moved beyond the school when it was discovered that one of the boys had tested HIV positive. This hitherto confidential information came out as a result of rampant rumors among the students that one of the boys had AIDS. The news spread to surrounding towns and the television and print press soon descended on the school and the superintendent, demanding to know who had AIDS, what steps the school was taking to protect the rights of the infected students, and how the uninfected student body was being protected. The rush of publicity and public concern placed all the superintendent's deliberation in sharp relief. The press, parents, church and civic groups, administrators from neighboring schools—all were watching Frank to see what he would do. All these activities had occurred within the last twenty-four hours.

Dr. Frank quickly lost the initiative in the matter as a parents' group demanded immediate removal from the school of any student who tested positive for HIV and, moreover, the group was demanding that all teachers and all students be tested immediately. Until their demands were met, this group of parents, led by Mrs. Delgado, one of the board members, threatened to boycott the school.

The response to this threat was quick in coming. The state said that they would enforce the attendance laws and, thus, they would take notice of any failure to enforce the attendance codes. Dr. Frank sat back in his chair and reflected. It was only Wednesday afternoon at 3:00. His attempt to bring some sort of order to the problem could be seen in the formidable, perhaps intimidating, schedule of appointments he must make. He needed help to get ready. Whom should he involve? He had instructed his secretary not to interrupt him with any more phone calls. He had to develop his schedule of appointments for the next several days, and he was feeling besieged. He looked at the phone requests for meetings thus far today:

- Mrs. Delgado and three PTO parents
- Mr. Gerstein, lawyer for the ACLU
- Mr. and Mrs. Young, parents of the HIV-infected youngster
- Ray Jones, the prominent TV anchorperson for CBS
- Mr. and Mrs. Croy, parents of the youngster involved in the fight with Billy Young, accompanied by their lawyer
- Jack Mazza, president of the Marshall Creek Teachers' Association
- Robert Smathers, Assistant Commissioner, State Department of Education
- Fr. Louis Healy, pastor of Immaculate Conception parish
- Shirley Haggarty, Long Valley AIDS Awareness Federation
- Academic cabinet meeting (the six senior administrators in the district)
- Kate McLaughlin, president of the Marshall Creek High School student council
- Dr. Harvey Wheeler and Dr. Bernice Herriott, Frank's superintendent colleagues from the two adjoining districts

Superintendent Frank sighed, picked up his briefcase, and packed all the things he needed, including the requests for meetings. He had some difficult decisions to make. He needed to clear his head; he needed a plan. And this was not the place to create it.

Discussing the Case

- Where does one start?
- What is the appropriate decision-making model here?
- What are the priorities? What must be done immediately? What can wait? What must wait?
- Whom can Frank count on? Is he alone?
- What is the board's role?
- Is this a time to be careful? Is there time enough to be careful?

ENDNOTES

1. "Conflict at Christmas" is based on a case written by Glenn Immegart, "Conflict in Central City: The Christmas Assembly in P.S. 42." Used by permission of UCEA.
2. For an additional discussion of the principles of adaptive scanning, see Quade (1982), especially pages 217 ff. See also Katona (1975) who prefers the term *coping* to *adaptive*.

CHAPTER FOUR

DECISION MAKING
Garbage and Politics

In the previous two chapters, we have analyzed four models of decision making: *optimizing, satisficing, successive comparing*, and *mixed scanning*. Optimizing is impractical because decision makers do not have sufficient information, ability, or capacity to maximize the process. Satisficing—achieving satisfactory rather than optimal outcomes—is a realistic, rational strategy. Satisficing, however, is sometimes limited because of partial information and the complexity of the problem. Administrators faced with such problems often resort to muddling through, that is, making small, incremental changes and comparing the results. This successive comparing often produces organizational drift because decision making is guided only by the desire to avoid negative consequences. The danger here is aimlessness.

In Chapter 3, we offered mixed scanning as an adaptive strategy that combines the best elements of the administrative and incremental models; it unites the rationalism of satisficing with the flexibility of incremental decision making. Moreover, mixed scanning gives direction to the process of successive comparison and incremental change. In this chapter, we turn to two additional descriptive perspectives of decision making—the garbage-can model and the political model—to help explain the apparent irrationality and happenstance of actual decision making.

THE GARBAGE-CAN MODEL: IRRATIONAL DECISION MAKING

Creative people in organizations construct complicated theories to explain their actions. Sometimes they supplement a technology of reason with a technology of foolishness. Individuals and institutions need ways of doing things for which there are no good reasons. Not always, not usually, but sometimes people need to act before they think (March, 1982). This tendency has been analyzed using a garbage-can model of organizational decision making (Cohen, March, & Olsen, 1972).

The so-called garbage-can model of decision making is most likely to occur in organizations with extremely high uncertainty. Such organizations are typically characterized by problematic preferences, unclear technologies, and fluid participation. Problematic preferences are ambiguities that prevail in the decision process. Unclear technology simply means that cause and effect relationships within the organization are virtually impossible to determine: There is a lot of random activity. The notion of fluid participation underscores the rapid turnover in participants and the limited time available for any one decision.

Although no organization perfectly fits this organic and loosely coupled system, the model appears to be useful for understanding what otherwise would seem to be completely irrational behavior. The basic feature of the garbage-can model is that the decision process does not begin with a problem and end with a solution, but rather decisions are a product of independent streams of organizational events (Cohen & March, 1974; Cohen, March, & Olsen, 1972; Slater & Boyd, 1999).

Four streams of events are captured in problems, solutions, participants, and choice opportunities:

- *Problems* are points of dissatisfaction that need attention, but they are independent of solutions and choices. A problem may or may not lead to a solution, and problems may or may not be solved when a solution is accepted.

- *Solutions* are ideas proposed for adoption, but they can sometimes exist independently of problems. In fact, the attractiveness of an idea can stimulate a search for a problem to justify the idea. Cohen and his colleagues (1972) argue that, despite the dictum that you cannot find the answer before you know the question, in organizational problem solving sometimes you have the answer before you find the question.

- *Participants* are organizational members who come and go. Problems and their solutions can change quickly because personnel can change rapidly.

- *Choice opportunities* are occasions when organizations are expected to make decisions. Contracts must be signed, people hired and fired, money expended, and resources allocated.

The overall pattern of organizational decision making among these four streams of events often takes on a quality of randomness. Organizational decision makers do not perceive that something is occurring about which a decision is necessary *until a problem matches an existing solution that they find attractive* (Hall, 1987). When problems and solutions happen to match, a decision can occur. An administrator who has a good idea may suddenly find a problem to solve. When a problem, solution, and participant just happen to connect, a decision may be made and the problem may be solved. It will not be solved, however, if the solution does not fit the problem. Cohen and his colleagues (1972, p. 2) capture the essence of the process as "a collection of choices looking for problems, issues and feelings looking for decision situations in which they might be aired, solutions looking for issues to which they might be answers, and decision makers looking for work."

The garbage-can model explains why solutions are proposed to problems that do not exist, why choices are made that do not solve problems, why problems persist in spite of solutions, and why so few problems are solved. When events are complex and poorly defined, problems, solutions, participants, and choice opportunities may act as independent events; they may or may not connect. When they do mesh, some problems are solved; but in this chaotic decision process, many problems are not solved—they simply persist, waiting for the right solution (Daft, 2001). The research evidence (Heller, Drenth, Koopman, & Rus, 1988; Hickson, Butler, Cray, Mallory, & Wilson, 1986; Janis & Mann, 1977; Pinfield, 1986) suggests that while the garbage-can metaphor is an apt description of the ways some decisions are reached, it is not a general model of decision making, even in organizations of complexity, uncertainty, discontinuity, and chaos. It is a useful description that helps explain what seemingly is irrational decision making.

In brief, organizational objectives emerge spontaneously; they are not set prior to generating alternatives. Means and ends exist independently of each other; it is chance or happenstance that connects the two. A good decision occurs when organizational participants agree that a problem matches an existing solution. The process relies on chance rather than rationality. Administrators scan for matches among existing solutions, problems, and participants. The garbage-can metaphor is a description of how things sometimes happen; it is not a suggestion for action. We now turn to an example to illustrate its use.

CASE 4.1

Critical Friends Groups[1]

Wayne Miller, principal of Woodrow Wilson Middle School, sat in his office and mused over the unpredictable nature of school administration. He was continually amazed by how things happen in schools. It seemed to him that much of what happens was simply the working of chance. He thought back to a professor he had in graduate school who told him, "Never underestimate the power of chance, but then, too, never depend on it." Miller didn't think he depended on chance, but, at times, it was a good companion.

Six weeks ago, Miller had suggested to his faculty that they needed to find ways to deal with the individual needs of students. The school had grown dramatically and was bulging at the seams. Only five years ago, Miller had a friendly and supportive environment of 800 students in his middle school (grades 6–8). Teachers knew the kids and interacted with them informally, freely, and effectively. They knew when kids were in trouble and did something about it. The students, for their part, were compliant and fun to be around. There was mutual respect between students and teachers.

Could the school have changed that much in five years? The community had. A thriving computer industry had seen the relocation of two high-tech companies to Silicon Gap, bringing not only their share of middle managers but also a large core of blue-collar workers. The town grew as the computer industry prospered. Woodrow Wilson, the town's only middle school, swelled from 800 to 1,400 students. A new wing was added to the school building and the faculty increased by 30 percent. It was a new school. The student body was more diverse; the faculty less involved in the life of the school; the problems more complex—AIDS, drugs, vandalism, single-parent families, teen pregnancies.

The faculty had started to complain about their inability to control the students. It was evident that they were having difficulties. One of the assistant principals spent all her time on matters of student discipline. It had not been that long ago that a group of students had vandalized cars in the teachers' parking lot. Miller had resisted teachers' suggestions for in-school detention and a more punitive suspension and expulsion policy. He argued that what was needed was certainly not more punishment but rather more involvement of students in the life of the school. "These kids are crying out to us for help," he told the faculty. Their response was, "You're living in the past. The school has changed and so have the kids."

The more Miller thought about the difficulties in the school, the more convinced he was that structural changes were necessary to get students and teachers working together again. During the summer he had worked with his administrative staff to develop what he thought was an interesting and positive idea. It seemed possible that he could arrange the teachers into interdisciplinary groups and schedule students to teacher groups. This was not an especially new idea, and it was consistent with the middle school philosophy; it reminded him of the old notion of a school within a school. Before acting, however, he thought it would be a good idea to consult with the teachers to make sure that they were informed and influential in developing the details of the plan.

He was surprised at the resistance from the faculty. They argued that the plan would be too constraining on their work. Over the years, they had developed curriculum and teaching methods that accommodated to the size and sequence of classes. A new configuration of the school would require substantial revision of the program, and the faculty was not convinced that the changes would be worthwhile. They rejected out of hand his argument that it would have a positive impact on student–teacher relationships. They countered once again with what was becoming a familiar refrain: "We need more discipline, more support, and tougher sanctions." There was no question in the minds of the teachers that if the school cracked down on discipline, most of their problems would be solved, including academic performance. The more Miller pushed the school-within-a-school notion, the more vehement was the resistance of the teachers. Finally, after two acrimonious faculty meetings in which his plan was discussed and debated, the faculty voted almost unanimously to reject the plan. Miller was disheartened and a little angry, but he decided not to push the issue for now.

He turned his attention to the annual teacher in-service workshop that must be planned. (Two days of in-service each year was part of the teachers' contract.) He decided that if the faculty wanted to be autonomous, this might be a time to encourage it. Therefore, he charged the departmental chairs with the responsibility of organizing the day-long spring in-service. A little more than a month after his meeting with the chairs, two of them offered a proposal for the spring in-service. They outlined a program that included speakers who would present information and techniques on cooperative learning, behavior modification, classroom management, and Critical Friends Groups. Both the speakers and topics looked good, and the chairs and the assistant principals moved ahead with the arrangements.

In-service education rarely has dramatic effects on a school, and the in-service workshops at Woodrow Wilson were no exception. But the program on student responsibility was a success. Several teachers wanted a workshop devoted solely to cooperative learning. A few other teachers commented to Miller on the usefulness of some of the classroom management techniques, and several of the chairs were intrigued with the notion of Critical Friends. All in all, the in-service day was about as successful as an in-service day can be.

The principal's satisfaction and complacency were rudely interrupted by a weekend of vandalism. On Monday morning, he was appalled when his assistant principal informed him that someone had broken into the art department and smeared oil paints all over the walls and ceilings. It looked as though several fires were set in the girls' and boys' lavatories. There were empty beer cans and signs of marijuana smoking in the rest rooms. Obviously, somebody had a party. The teachers' room was thoroughly trashed and some not-so-complimentary graffiti were written on the walls. Rumors abounded, but it was clear that the damage to Woodrow Wilson had been done by students of the school. This was the last straw for the faculty. They wanted the perpetrators discovered and expelled.

Within a week, the students were found out. A wild flurry of activity and detective work by the assistant principal (and her informants) produced the names and confessions of eight students. Miller recommended a five-day suspension and fifty hours of school service for each student to clean and paint the school. Although the teachers were somewhat mollified, they remained sullen. They felt that the vandalism was symptomatic of poor control. They wanted a crackdown. In fact, at the next faculty meeting, little occurred except that teachers vented their anger and frustration. They recounted case after case of student misconduct: rudeness, cheating, fighting, lack of respect, class cutting, and vandalism. They were fed up.

Several of the department chairs approached Miller the day after the faculty meeting. They wanted to address the student behavior problem with more than rhetoric and anecdotes. These were the same chairs who were taken with the notion of Critical Friends Groups (CFGs). "Why couldn't student discipline be the focus of a CFG?" they asked. They explained that a Critical Friends Group would be a group of about six to eight teachers who would meet regularly to discuss and solve the problems of student discipline. Miller was intrigued by this suggestion. And as he discussed their idea, it became obvious that they were not talking about one CFG, but several. He encouraged each of the chairs to move ahead. The mathematics and the social studies chairs did just that. They formed volunteer groups of teachers, Critical Friends Groups for math and history, to deal with the problems of student discipline. Their initiative was the impetus for the other departments to develop their own CFGs.

As the CFGs began their deliberations, it became apparent that there were problems that cut across departments. In middle schools, the direction for cooperation has been interdisciplinary; thus, it was not surprising that there was a press for collaboration among groups. As the faculty developed ideas that required coordination across departments, they repeatedly turned to the administrative staff for help. As problems common to the interdepartmental groups emerged, it became important for the faculty to deal with the problems of interdepartmental cooperation. Accordingly, a meeting whose sole topic was coordination was scheduled.

The results of the meeting were as much a surprise to Principal Miller as to the faculty. In discussing the problems of coordinating departmental rules and procedures, several faculty members remarked on the difficulty of fitting students into their plans because the students were not members of departments; taking a math course did not make a student a member of that department. Thus, they were outside any one department's supervision most of the time. Someone suggested that each department be in charge of a certain number of students, a suggestion that provoked some laughter. However, the idea of altering student participation in the school led to other less humorous and more useful suggestions. At this point, one of the chairs suggested that the faculty consider dividing the student body into groups so that a member from each department would team with members of all other departments (interdisciplinary teams). Each team would form a CFG responsible for the discipline and instruction of their students. Miller could scarcely believe his ears: The school within a school was taking shape under a different name—interdisciplinary teams. So much for rational decision making. Things just work out, or do they?

ANALYZING THE CASE: GARBAGE-CAN MODEL

Is Wayne Miller right? Does luck govern outcomes in school organizations? Sometimes it does. The garbage can, as a descriptive model, suggests that there are times when solutions and problems connect by chance. While Miller's suggestion of a school within a school was rejected by the faculty, it remained an attractive solution to Miller. The metaphor of the garbage can is useful here because it describes a way in which a solution, in this case, the school-within-a-school idea, is kept alive, even though it solves no problems. Miller initially proposed his idea of smaller units of students and teachers to ameliorate the negative consequences of the school's large size. The idea was not attractive to his teachers. They saw only the difficulty of adapting their current teaching materials and strategies to a different learning arrangement. In short, it was more work, work they did not need.

Moreover, the teachers wanted to make their own decisions. Thus, when given a chance, they developed an in-service program that stressed cooperative learning, behavior modification, classroom management techniques, and Critical Friends Groups—topics that were consistent with their current practices and not threatening. Each of the topics appealed to a constituency of teachers. These topics joined the school within a school as good ideas to keep around; they stayed in the garbage can. Actually a hope-chest metaphor rather than the garbage-can metaphor may be more apt because these ideas are not garbage but rather good ideas that teachers and administrators hope will be implemented. Therefore, they are kept alive in the hope chest, not buried in the garbage can.

The school is also confronted by problems stemming from its rapid growth and changing demographics. Miller was initially concerned about the depersonalization of students, and he sought a way to address student needs that were academic, social, and emotional. The teachers were more concerned about specific problems of student misconduct as discipline deteriorated badly.

One idea that was intriguing to several of the departmental chairs was the idea of Critical Friends Groups. As the problem of student discipline became worse, the notion of CFGs became even more attractive to a select group of chairs. Circumstances seemed to connect these two relatively independent events—CFGs and the problem of student discipline. At the same time, Miller's notion of the school within a school fortuitously converged with the notion of Critical Friends, although each was originally developed in a different circumstance and not as a solution to the problem of student discipline. The opportunity for a school within a school occurred when the chairs chose to do something about student vandalism and the teachers struggled to coordinate the CFGs. In that struggle, they looked around for a good idea, and it was there in the garbage can.

The overall pattern of organizational decision making in this case takes on a quality of randomness. Neither Miller nor the departmental chairs perceived that something occurred about which a decision was necessary until a problem matched an existing solution that they found attractive. When the problem of school discipline, CFGs, interdepartmental coordination, and the idea of school within a school converged, a decision occurred. Miller had a good idea that may now be an acceptable solution. The problem, solution, and participants just happened to connect at a meeting and a decision to address the problem is now likely. The problem of student discipline will not be solved, however, if the solution does not fit the problem. The garbage-can model explains why original solutions to some problems are rejected but then reemerge as successful solutions to other problems.

Decision making here is a chaotic process. In fact, some might argue that the preceding example is itself too structured, and that the garbage can applies more appropriately to situations that are much messier. There is no question that fortuitous decisions often occur in ambiguous situations, that is, where logical connections within and between participants, events, choice opportunities, and problems are absent. Although the garbage-can metaphor is an apt description of the ways some decisions are reached, it may not be as common in most public elementary and secondary schools as in universities, colleges, and private schools. Nonetheless, the garbage can explains seemingly irrational decision making. For another actual case with less plot, see Kristian Kreiner's "Ideology and Management in a Garbage Can Situation," in March and Olsen (1979).

THE POLITICAL MODEL: PERSONAL RATIONALITY

The nature of organizational goals is an elusive but continuing subject of controversy. Do organizations have distinct goals? Or do only people have goals? These questions have occupied the theoretical literature for over a half century (Allison, 1971; Barnard, 1938; Georgiou, 1973; March & Simon, 1968; Mintzberg, 1983; Papandreou, 1952; Simon, 1964). Although there is still some disagreement, a consensus is emerging—organizations have goals.

Organizational goals are the intentions that lead to behaviors of organizations. Intended consistencies of behavior emerge from the ferment of activities and decision making in the organization. Strong ideologies that create shared beliefs, a dominant individual who imposes goals on everyone, or a group of powerholders who share personal goals or who rally around a set of goals produce such consistencies (Mintzberg, 1983).

In most organizations, there are conflicting goals that must be reconciled. In some cases, all goals are seen as constraints, and organizational decision makers simply try to develop reasonable solutions to the set of relevant constraints. In other organizations, one goal becomes a primary force. When the power within the organization is dominated by one individual or group, a single goal tends to absorb the discretion of the organization, and the energies of the organization are directed toward the primary goal. The primary goal is maximized in the sense that it can never be completely satisfied. There is perpetual pressure to achieve higher and higher levels of goal attainment. Other goals are seen as constraints. Once they are met, the organization is free to use more energy to attain the primary goal. Thus, the organization seeks to satisfy its constraints but always maximize its primary goal. Finally, there are situations in which there are multiple goals without a primary focus, a condition that frequently produces conflict. Organizations deal with the conflicts among multiple goals by addressing goals sequentially. Time ameliorates conflicts by enabling the organization to pay attention to one goal at a time. For example, at first a university is driven by the goal of research productivity, but as time passes and pressure mounts for excellence in teaching, the organization switches its emphasis. It is not surprising that organizations attend to multiple goals alternatively and in cycles as the pendulum swings back and forth (Mintzberg, 1983).

There are organizations, however, that do not have goals. As startling as that seems, a moment's reflection on the nature of the U.S. Congress or some school districts reveals institutions whose public purposes seem inextricably bound up to individuals' private concerns. These are organizations in which politics and power manipulations dominate the day-to-day activities. Personal preferences submerge organizational intention. Goals are merely public statements of official morality. Conflict, bargaining, game playing, and politics are intensive and pervasive. Chaos is the rule rather than the exception. It is in these organizations that administrative decision making is essentially manipulative, that is, pragmatic, personal, and, in a word, political.

Power is a fact of organizational life. All organizations must deal with political issues, which affect most, if not all, decisions. We are concerned here not with the routine of office politics nor with the political dimensions of decisions, but rather with *those situations in which control becomes the overriding force within the organization—that is, when politics replaces the legitimate procedures for decision making, and substitutes for goals.* It is naïve to suggest that most decisions do not have political elements; in fact, some see the organizational world as an arena of power politics moved by immediate self-interest, where morality is simply rhetoric for expedient action and self-interest (Alinsky, 1971; Klein, 1998). Our concern is not with legitimate decisions about the allocation of scarce resources. Individuals and legitimate interest groups will differ in their values, preferences, beliefs, and perceptions of reality, and, as a consequence, there is continuous bargaining, negotiation, and jockeying for resources (Bolman & Deal, 1997). These legitimate processes of negotiation are not what we are referring to as the political model. Rather our description of the political model is one in which personal politics has replaced legitimate organizational aims.

Are we saying that politics has no place in schools? Of course not. Are we saying schools would be better places if no one played politics? No. Are we saying that politics should not influence decisions? Certainly not. Politics has functional consequences; sometimes it is necessary to correct deficiencies in the formal structure; often, it is needed to promote organizational change that has been blocked by legitimate systems of control; on occasion, it is essential to ease the path for the execution of decisions; and, in a Darwinian sense, it assures that strong leaders and good ideas have a voice (Mintzberg, 1983). Although sometimes useful, politics in our view is generally illegitimate because it replaces legitimate organizational means of influence.[2]

The model of political decisions we describe is sharply circumscribed. Some may claim it is a personal model of decision making. We agree. It is a personal model in the context of organizations that have become politicized. Such organizations are arenas dominated by politics; individuals vie with each other to pursue their own personal goals. In fact, irrational behavior is a reflection of the fact that politics has immobilized functional decision making. At its best, a politicized organization simply satisfies as many constraints as it can. But at its worst, it becomes incapable of pursuing any collective goal at all as individuals act in their own interests: a circus of irrationality and chaos.

Decision making in politicized organizations is strikingly different from any of the proposed models because objectives are personal rather than organizational. Organizational goals play little or no role. Paradoxically, individuals may use incremental, mixed-scanning, or satisficing approaches in the process of developing strategies and agendas; however, organizational matters are merely fronts for political activity. Consequently, organizational trappings get in the way of understanding the dynamics in politicized organizations. Ultimately, the game is power—gaining as much influence and as many resources as possible. Decision making in these organizations can only be understood in terms of individual purposes, not as an organizational process. Organizational processes speak to operating goals of the organization, while political activities are rooted in the contest for power of organizational members and coalitions.

In sum, objectives in the political model are personal. Personal goals, not organizational goals, drive the process. A personal means–ends analysis substitutes for an organizational means–ends analysis. Personal ends are determined, and then organizational means are used to achieve them. The test of a good decision is whether the personal ends are met. Politics is a major force shaping the decisions. When a satisficing or adaptive satisficing strategy is used, it is employed on a personal level. The political model is a descriptive framework that relies on power to explain decision making.

Because politicized organizations are pervaded with conflict and chaos, it is difficult to understand decision making in these organizations. Much of the activity and decision making involves resolving conflict and enhancing power, processes that engender still more conflict. What seems to be at first blush irrational organizational behavior upon closer scrutiny is seen as the working out of personal rationality within the organization. Perhaps the best way to illustrate the political model is with another example.

CASE 4.2

Divided Loyalties

Suburban Center

Suburban Center was an old town on the outskirts of a large northeastern city. Its population, about 30,000, was a mix of different ethnic groups who had moved from the larger city to the suburbs, retaining much of their ethnic affiliation, and newer residents from skilled blue-collar and middle-class professional occupations. The town council was held firmly, however, in the grasp of an old guard who had moved from the city to the suburbs in search of a better life. The old guard influenced appointments on the city payroll, police and fire departments, and the schools. No superintendent had been appointed in the past twenty years without the explicit approval of the mayor. The mayor and his associates were very successful in getting their people elected to the school board. The old guard kept such city organizations as schools, police, and fire open enough so that they operated within acceptable guidelines, but not so open to new people that the guard lost its power to appoint some patronage employees. The schools, for example, were adequate but probably not as good as they could be.

Increasingly, however, the old guard was facing challenges from the young professionals who were moving into Suburban Center. For example, there was a constant battle for seats on the school board, with the balance of power shifting back and forth. But make no mistake about it, the old guard could still get out the votes to get their people elected when things became critical.

The Superintendent

It is in this context that the superintendent was hired four years ago. He was no stranger to Suburban Center, having himself been mayor fifteen years earlier. He had left the city to pursue his career as a school administrator. It was a successful career, beginning as a teacher in a nearby community. Then he became an assistant principal of a high school in another part of the state. While serving as an assistant principal, he completed his doctorate in educational administration and became principal of a high school in an exclusive adjoining community. A few years later, he became superintendent of schools in still another district, where he worked for six years before returning home as the head of the Suburban Center schools. His appointment was not without political machinations. He and the mayor had been political rivals but, as the new superintendent pointed out, he no longer had political ambitions; his aspirations were professional. An accommodation was reached—Patrick O'Shea was appointed superintendent.

The Board of Education

The most recent election for school board once again demonstrated the power of the old guard. They ran a slate of three people—a maintenance foreman at a local bottling plant, a local funeral director, and the owner operator of a large service station in town. All three were elected to the board, and the power shifted from the young professionals to the old guard. The new president of the board was the mayor's man, and the board was anxious to get back to business as usual. "Look," said the new president, "the public schools are owned by the people of the town, and it's only fair that they get some benefit from them. We need to hire our people to benefit the town and keep our loyalties at home." The reform movement of the past few years was over—at least until the next election.

The Principal

Edward "Ted" McGann had been principal at Suburban High for six years. McGann had been an undistinguished teacher in the school system for twenty years. Imagine the surprise of the young professionals when he became a finalist and subsequently was appointed principal over the strong challenge of two able and experienced candidates from outside the system. His uncle, the mayor, believed that loyalty was the greatest virtue and ought to be recognized. After a brief controversy, McGann took the helm of the school. The young professionals were successful in hiring two new assistant principals, who brought change and professionalism to the academic programs of the high school. In fact, McGann liked his two assistants and gave them relatively free rein to run the school. Even the young professionals admitted that there had been progress during McGann's administration of the school. Moreover, the faculty liked McGann. He was upbeat, gregarious, and left the teachers to their work. He did not interfere, and he was always good for a favor.

The Problem

The election of the new board was no sooner over than McGann was faced with a minor crisis. One of the assistant principals had been hired away by a neighboring district, and McGann needed a new assistant principal. He knew immediately that he was in for trouble. He liked the way things were, and they were about to change. In McGann's view, the most promising candidate for the job was Carl Forza, the social studies chairman at the middle school. Forza was also a favorite of the board president and the mayor because he had worked hard for their election.

Superintendent O'Shea did not, as a general policy, second-guess the decisions of his administrative staff, but he supported Darlene Baker for the assistant principalship. She had recently completed a doctorate in school supervision and had successfully worked as a chairman of the English department at the high school. O'Shea felt Baker was simply the stronger applicant for the job. In informal discussion, the superintendent was given to understand that the job was going to Forza. There was no question about Baker's qualifications, but this was not to be her day. O'Shea had a good sense of the political landscape of the situation and bowed to the inevitable; Forza got the job, but two months later, Baker was appointed curriculum coordinator of secondary schools.

Cooperation

Initially, Forza and Don Houser, the experienced assistant principal, worked well together. Houser knew the ropes at the high school and realized the political influence of Forza. "There's no sense fighting city hall," he thought. Forza, on his part, seemed genuinely grateful for Houser's help. Most of their work was routine, such as scheduling, discipline, coordination of the extracurricular program, and overseeing the maintenance staff. Six months had passed and cooperation between the two was high. The teachers were indifferent to their initiatives, but they were glad that they generally supported their professional activities without being intrusive. And some argued that there was beginning to be order in what many teachers had described alternately as "the jungle" and "the zoo."

Conflict

The beginning of the crisis emerged benignly enough. At the monthly meeting of the administrators council, Superintendent O'Shea had charged all the administrators in the district with the objective of improving the curriculum and instruction of Suburban Center. Forza and Houser returned to the high school determined to improve the school. It soon became apparent, however, that on educational matters there was a wide gulf between them. Forza believed in discipline, loyalty, obedience, and authority. Teachers should do as their superiors directed, and they would be rewarded. The role of the administrator is to direct the operation of the school. Houser, in contrast, argued for autonomy, initiative, cooperation, and professional responsibility. Teachers should act on their best professional judgments. The role of the administrator is to support the professional staff. Both were surprised at how heated their discussions were.

Their differences became manifest in their supervisory styles. Forza's supervisory style grew increasingly authoritarian over the next few months. Teachers described him as "popping up all over the place" especially in the classrooms of teachers whom he considered disloyal to the old guard. His supervision seemed to have little to do with the improvement of instruction; rather, it became the behavior of an enforcer. Houser was appalled, but found he simply couldn't talk to Forza. In fact, Forza questioned Houser's loyalty to the people who paid him and threatened to have him "taken care of." Houser reacted to the threat and Forza's authoritarian supervision by enlisting the help of Darlene Baker and Superintendent O'Shea. Houser felt that Forza was actually harming the existing program with his heavy-handed tactics.

A number of teachers, however, did not object to Forza's tactics. "He's the boss," they said, "and he has the right to do what it takes to improve the program." Privately, they also noted that Forza had risen in the school organization by doing what he was told. And they, too, were finding that the way to get ahead and stay out of trouble was to play ball. A substantial number of teachers objected to Forza's close, authoritarian supervision and found a sympathetic ear in the person of Houser. The faculty was dividing itself into three factions: the old guard—supporters of Forza; the young turks—supporters of Houser; and the indifferents—those who did not want to be involved.

Forza went to Principal McGann and complained, "Get this damn Houser off my back. He undermines everything I do. How can I work in this situation?" McGann was not happy at this division in his staff and called Houser in, hoping to smooth things over and get back to normal. Much to his surprise, the first words out of Houser's mouth were, "Ted, we have to do something about Forza. He's alienating half the teachers; he's making them choose sides; and he's turning the school into chaos. Can't you get him to back off?" McGann immediately responded that indeed things were out of hand when his two good assistants were at each other's throats. His assistant principals had always worked as a team in the past and that was what he wanted again.

The situation was bad and got worse. The phone rang, and it was an angry Mayor Valente who screamed, "Ted, get the boys under control. I don't want Forza complaining to the board or to me about his treatment in the school."

Houser had not sat idly by. He had informally spoken with some of the teachers who were disgusted with Forza's behavior. In particular, he had talked with John Pierson, one of the informal leaders among the teachers. Pierson was young, smart, charismatic, progressive, and active. Houser brought Pierson to a quiet lunch with Darlene Baker, the coordinator of secondary curriculum; the stated purpose was to brainstorm about curriculum improvement. Talk quickly changed to the current political climate in Suburban Center. The lunch ended with Darlene Baker assuring them that things would change after the next board election. She had contacts with the board, and the young professionals were mobilizing to elect a more progressive board. Baker also confided that Superintendent O'Shea was with them and had plans for Pierson.

Test Scores

Things were just beginning to settle down when state school test scores were released to the press. The evening paper carried the headline "Math and Reading Scores Fall: What Are We Doing Wrong?" The scores were down from last year. The expected increase had not materialized: In fact, the Suburban Center twelfth-grade scores were a hair below average for suburban schools in the state. (The state average was 489; Suburban Center had an average, this year, of 488, down from 512 last year.)

The test results were the catalyst for open hostility among the mayor, the superintendent, and the young professionals. Within the schools, the lines were clearly drawn among the old guard, the young turks, and the indifferents; between Forza and Houser; between superintendent O'Shea and the mayor; and between curriculum coordinator Baker and principal McGann.

Decision making in the district began to take on an aura of old-time horse trading. Each faction was leery of the other and unwilling to trust the other to work for the benefit of the district. Indeed, what was in the best interests of the district was the major point of contention. Forza argued that direct instruction supported by direct supervision would rectify the slip in scores. Houser maintained that close supervision had teachers meeting the letter of requirements rather than working creatively with students. Houser argued that the district would never pull out of the doldrums unless teachers were given the freedom to act as true professionals. Baker was for major curriculum reform and instructional improvement, while McGann argued for more authority on the part of the principal to deal with instructional matters. "Outsiders are screwing up my school," he proclaimed. And everyone knew that the outsider he was talking about was Darlene Baker. The superintendent and the mayor were feuding. O'Shea was becoming increasingly adamant in his attempts to keep the mayor and his cronies out of the school. And the mayor was incensed by O'Shea's lack of cooperation. The old guard teachers rallied around the mayor, Principal McGann, and Forza. The young turks supported O'Shea, Baker, and Houser. The board of education was split between the old guard and the young professionals. The president of the board was the mayor's man, but with the latest test results, the five–four majority the mayor and his people enjoyed was now in doubt as one of the board members became reluctant to take a position on virtually any issue at all. In the last election, some of the younger teachers worked against the candidacy of the old guard slate, a fact not lost on the mayor and the newly elected president of the board. The community and school were heating up.

McGann sat somewhat pensively in his chair. Things were getting out of control, he thought. Times had been worse, he reflected, and he always weathered the worst. Where should he start? he wondered. His reverie was interrupted by the phone. It was his secretary. Superintendent O'Shea was on the line.

"Ted," O'Shea began, "I have a solution to all our problems. Here is what we are going to do. Forza's a problem in a lot of ways. We need to get rid of him. He works well with the community leaders but not with teachers. I'm going to have the board create a new position for him. He'll be promoted to be our new district-level community liaison. John Pierson will take over as assistant principal, and he, Houser, and Baker will spearhead our reform team in the high school. I know I can count on your help in this matter. I'm sure there will be some flack about this from downtown, but I think if we stick together we can make this a better school district. After all, the schools are for the kids."

McGann hung up the phone, sighed, and wondered if they knew about this downtown. One thing was certain: They would soon.

ANALYZING THE CASE: THE POLITICAL MODEL

Not all solutions are driven by rational decision-making models. Such models require organizational goals. Do the Suburban Center schools have organizational goals? Public purposes seem inextricably bound to individual, private concerns in Suburban Center. Organizational decisions revolve around politics and power. Personal preferences seem to displace an articulated organizational mission. Goals in Suburban Center are merely public pronouncements of official morality. To understand how decisions are made in the Suburban Center schools, one must understand conflict, bargaining, game playing, and politics. Decision making here is essentially manipulative; it is pragmatic and personal.

At first blush, the motives of all the administrators in the Suburban Center district schools seem political. Even O'Shea, Baker, and Houser, whose decision making is oriented to professional issues rather than political ones, must engage in politicking and compromise if they are to survive and be successful. Their goals can never be wholly professional, that is, without political consideration. By the same token, those individuals motivated by purely political needs cannot escape some consideration of professional issues. The political game is played out in the context of legitimate problems: improving instruction, adequate supervision, public accountability, hiring procedures, community interests, administrative discretion, professional autonomy, and higher student achievement scores. But these are merely fronts for personal agendas and manipulation. The mayor would like the scores to rise, but not at the cost of losing control. In fact, the scores are important to the mayor because low scores pose a threat to his influence. O'Shea, for his part, would probably like to move Forza back to the middle school for the sake of organizational efficiency, but he cannot. Instead, he proposes a solution to the problems presented by Forza's behavior by suggesting that Forza be kicked upstairs to make room for Pierson, one of his own people. This suggestion is a political decision of accommodation. The issue is not what is best for the school but what is acceptable to the power players in the game. Why did O'Shea promote Forza in the first place? Was he the best person? Was he the most experienced? Were his views most consistent with O'Shea's? The answer in all three cases is no. His was a political appointment. O'Shea is a political player. He sets the tone by agreeing to the accommodation.

Virtually all of the important decisions in the Suburban Center schools are forced by politics. The games people play depend on their motives and where they are in the organization. Political games are not simple; they are intricate, subtle, simultaneous, overlapping, sometimes structured and other times unstructured. They do not proceed at random or at leisure (Allison, 1971). A political game is a specific mechanism in which people structure and regulate power relations (Crozier & Friedberg, 1977). Henry Mintzberg (1983) has made a taxonomy of political games that describes the purpose for which the game is played and the organizational level of the players. For example, the game "Rival Camps" is played to defeat rivals in the organization. O'Shea, Baker, Houser, and Pierson are a power alliance aligned against the mayor, the board president, McGann, and

Forza. The game has produced three groups: the old guard, the young turks, and the indifferents. There is a conflict among the personalities, values, and goals.

The mayor and the superintendent have a general disdain for each other. The mayor sees the superintendent as out of touch with the reality of life in the city and as a threat to his own power base. The superintendent views the mayor as an obstacle to the operation of the schools, one who is always ready to interject vested interests. Both agree on the value of loyalty, but they disagree on the focus of loyalty. The superintendent expects loyalty to the organization, while the mayor demands personal loyalty. The goal of the mayor is to increase his political base and use the school as an instrument to reward stalwarts. The goal of the superintendent is more circumscribed. Although not uninterested in political power, he is more constrained by educational issues and the success of the school.

Principal McGann is an extension of the mayor; he has been rewarded for his loyalty. Yet he wants to do a good job as principal. To this point, he has been skillful in working with two professional educators to maintain a reasonable instructional program. The appointment of Forza has upset the balance and produced conflict between the professional aspirations of Houser and the political loyalties of Forza. Events have overtaken McGann; he owes his loyalty to the mayor and, as such, he must do the mayor's bidding. That loyalty puts him into conflict with his own superintendent and Houser, his assistant principal.

We do not know much about Baker except that she is in the superintendent's camp and he wants to reward her with a job. It is not clear whether the reward is for her skill and knowledge or for her loyalty—probably both. Joining Baker are Houser and Pierson. Houser, who was appointed by the young professionals on the board, is loyal to them and to O'Shea. He is a professional who believes in the autonomy of his teachers; he believes they have the ability and the inclination to best serve students, if given sufficient latitude and a supportive working environment. He and Baker are committed to instructional and curricular reform, but, as does O'Shea, they spend a substantial amount of energy politicking. They have become political players in the rival-camps game to preserve as much professional autonomy as possible. More than that, they find themselves naturally opposed to the mayor's patronage and nepotism.

Pierson is sponsored by the O'Shea camp. He is being brought along in the organization because he is personally skillful, assertive, and sympathetic to the educational perspectives of the young professionals. He is being groomed by O'Shea for an administrative slot. He is also learning quickly about the political nature of decision making in Suburban Center. He has become part of the rival-camps game. No question, he is aligned with the young turks on the faculty and with O'Shea and Baker in the administration.

Additional support for progressive changes in curriculum and further development of the teachers' role comes from the young turks, a group of teachers whose intention is not simply to effect change but rather to counter the despotic authority of the mayor and his people. This means that they have become political; they are working in and through the community to influence the election of reform candidates to the board of education. The mayor in a different time would fire them all, but his hands are tied by tenure. The contest of the young turks is probably a tough game to play. An old guard of teachers, supported by the principal and Forza, resists them whenever possible. In fact, Forza has become a hit man aimed at the young turks. It is small wonder that a substantial number of teachers play it safe; they are indifferents on the sideline, struggling to remain a safe distance from the fray.

It is easy to lose sight of the superintendent's political ambitions because they are masked by an ostensibly professional orientation. His personal aim is power; he uses organizational means to attain that end. The mayor has the same end, that is, to increase personal power, but it is more difficult for him to mask the illegitimate quest for power. Clearly, the decision process in the Suburban Center schools is political. Objectives are personal but disguised by a professional cover.

We left Principal McGann about to call the mayor to discuss O'Shea's latest initiative. How will the mayor react? You can bet that he will see O'Shea's plan as a ploy to gain power, and he will react accordingly. Politics begets politics. Raising test scores is the context, not the purpose, of decision making. Decisions are an accommodation to power. The purpose is to extend influence and control.

The political model of decision making is not normative. It does not suggest how decisions should be made; rather the perspective describes the political and personal factors that guide a great many decisions in schools. These decisions are *not* made to achieve organizational objectives but rather to achieve personal ends.

SUMMARY AND CONCLUSION

The two models in this chapter are summarized in Table 4.1. Both are descriptive models. They describe common modes of decision making in school organizations. We do not advocate their use, but to understand the dynamics of school life, one must recognize that chance and politics are salient features of decision making.

The *garbage-can model* suggests that especially in organizations where uncertainty is high and coordination loose, fortuitous events often influence the way some decisions are made. When problems and solutions happen to match, decisions occur. Garbage-can decisions happen in schools, and they help explain seemingly irrational decisions. People often create complicated explanations for their actions. They sometimes act before they think; they get good ideas without problems; and occasionally, happenstance connects the good idea with the action and produces an unplanned decision. Organizational objectives are not developed beforehand, but rather they emerge spontaneously as the flow of problems and solutions connect by chance. Suddenly, people agree that a given solution is a good match for a problem, and a decision is made. The problems and solutions may float through the organization for some time before the fortuitous match.

The *political model* is another description of decision making. It is a framework for explaining what is, not what should be. Instead of chance, politics is a deliberate maneuver to influence organizational outcomes. The distribution of personal power is the critical issue in the political model. Objectives are personal, not organizational. The means–ends analysis is personal, not organizational.

TABLE 4.1 Comparison of the Garbage-Can and Political Models of Decision Making

CHARACTERISTIC	DECISION-MAKING MODEL	
	GARBAGE CAN	POLITICAL
Setting objectives	Objectives emerge spontaneously.	Objectives are personal.
Means–ends analysis	Means and ends are independent of each other. Chance connects means and ends.	Personal means–ends analysis performed. Personal ends, not organizational ones, are determined; then organizational means are used for personal ends.
Test of a good decision	Participants agree that the solution and problem match.	Personal ends are met.
Decision process	Chance.	Politics.
Alternative search	Scan for a match among solutions, problems, and participants.	Use adaptive satisficing on a personal level.
Underpinning	Heavy reliance on chance.	Reliance on politics.
Perspective	Descriptive.	Descriptive.

The test of a good decision is personal, not organizational. The strategy is personal, not organizational. The process is not wedded to theory but rather relies on power. Even when a rational model of decision making is used, it is usually adaptive satisficing on a personal level, not an organizational one.

Here is a case for you to practice on.

CASE 4.3

Politics at River Grove

River Grove is a K–12 district with 2,000 students and a professional staff of 175. The district, which has some of the highest test scores in the state, is organized into five schools: three K–6 elementary schools, a 7–8 middle school, and a 9–12 high school. The middle school and the high school share the same physical plant. An extensive building project will begin this summer. Two of the elementary schools, which are seventy-seven and ninety-two years old respectively, will be brought up to code, and the high school will be expanded to include twelve new classrooms. A separate gym and cafeteria will be provided for the middle school. Thus, the new 7–12 plant will have separate facilities for the middle school and the high school with the exception of the auditorium and the new media center. According to demographic projections, the plans should satisfy the physical needs of the district for the next decade.

The community has been termed "the community with character by the bend in the river," or so the current mayor claims. The district is a township district and is divided into three communities: two ethnic enclaves, one German and the other Italian, and a group of relatively affluent newcomers, whom the townspeople refer to as the "country clubbers." Each ethnic group is close-knit, homogeneous, and determined to preserve its roots. The families are second- and third-generation town residents; housing prices remain affordable; the parents have a preference for selling to their own sons and daughters. Both ethnic communities have strong and vocal senior citizen groups who consistently oppose the school budget. River Grove is a nice place to live if you are a local. It can be frustrating, however, if you are not. Each group has its own elementary school. The schools celebrate ethnic holidays and leaders. Most of the social events, though, revolve around high school athletics. It is the interesting case that each ethnic community works diligently to take care of their own and keep their kids separate until they come together after elementary school.

There is, however, an emerging third element of the township—the country clubbers, who live in a sprawling, largely undeveloped area on the other side of the highway that divides the town. As far as the locals are concerned, the country clubbers might as well be from another country. The housing in this area is considerably more expensive than that in town, and at the center of the area is the large country club and golf course that gives the residents their nickname. Unlike in the downtown, one sees many more BMWs than pickup trucks. Yet these people are outsiders. They vote in favor of the school budget, are generally supportive of education, and look upon the people in town with some condescension, a fact not lost on the locals. Although the country clubbers identify with the township, they interact mostly with each other and virtually not at all with the locals. They view themselves as cosmopolitans.

The nine-member board is generally split between the three country clubbers who support more money for the schools and the six members from the old groups who are fiscally tight. However, one would be mistaken to assume that the six members, three from each ethnic group, form a happy union. In point of fact, they disagree on virtually every program that would bring more resources to the other; the only thing they are in agreement about is their opposition to all programs that will raise taxes. This situation is best epitomized by a series of elementary science textbooks that are now twenty years old.

The country club contingent is appalled and works continuously to improve the antiquated programs of the school district. They are active on the PTA executive boards and the chamber of commerce, and they run for public office. They lobby hard and long for school improvement, but they are neither large enough nor strong enough to carry a school budget election. Their disputes and conflicts with the locals are numerous. For example, last year the board put out a referendum for a new high school based on enrollment projections. The existing high school would become a 5–8 middle school and each elementary school would become K–4. The old guard wanted the new school located on a tract of land already owned by the school board adjacent to the township recreational and office facility. It was in the middle of town, and neither the Germans nor the Italians felt that one was gaining an advantage over the other. The country clubbers, for their part, wanted the new school on their side of the highway where there was plenty of space and a modern, comprehensive state-of-the-art school could be built. They were successful in lobbying a major developer to donate forty acres of land for a new school. The attacks from the locals were vicious, and they won the battle; the new school was to be built in town. But ultimately, everyone lost the war: The country clubbers were disappointed in the location of the proposed school, and the two local communities were aghast at the projected tax increases. The result was an overwhelming failure of the referendum, with the community voting three to one against the proposal. The problem of inadequate physical facilities remained; the district failed the state monitoring for facilities and, under the threat of state sanctions, subsequently passed two referenda for renovation, hence the current building plan for the middle school and high school.

There has been superintendent turnover in the district, with one superintendent resigning after only a year to take a principal's position within the district and the last one leaving after only two years to accept a superintendency in a neighboring district. You have been appointed the new superintendent in the district. After being in the district as an elementary principal for two years, in a sudden move, you were appointed interim superintendent and then, two months later, superintendent. It is clear that the board has high regard for you and wants you to continue the directions provided by your predecessors. There were, however, whispers among the veteran teaching staff that you were simply a rubber stamp for the board because you were selected over the former superintendent, who was also an elementary principal, and the high school principal, a veteran of twenty-five years in the district.

The ethnic character of the town has been borne out in the selection of the two principals as well as your own selection. Mr. Mueller at the middle school and Mr. Rostelli at the high school have little regard for each other. The situation was worsened by the facts that their buildings were adjacent to each other and that they would be forced to share the auditorium and media center. As one might expect, Mueller was active in civic and social affairs in the German community of River Bend, while Rostelli was a stalwart of the Sons of Italy. Both saw their positions as, in large part, recognition of loyal service to their respective groups. Each felt responsible for addressing the educational needs of the children from his own part of the town. There was a constant competition for resources between the two principals. The hallmark of being an effective principal was the ability to get as large a piece of the pie as possible for one's own school. It would be an understatement to say that Mueller and Rostelli were rivals. They simply did not like each other and viewed the other's success as their own failure.

It became clear to you that your appointment to the superintendency was a result of an alliance between the Germans and the country clubbers. You wanted to be the superintendent of all the students in the system and make sound educational decisions to bring the communities together—perhaps a bit of idealism on your part. And you were enough of a realist to know that if you announced such a grand plan, you would be fired forthwith. This was an important opportunity for you, so you wanted to proceed carefully with any changes. You hoped to initiate change rather than simply react to politics.

Before you have had a chance to settle into your new position, "Black Tuesday" occurs. The state report card, published in the local newspaper, shows that River Bend's high school students have lower than expected verbal scores on the state proficiency tests. You act decisively, calling on the curricular and supervisory staff of the middle and secondary schools to discuss strategies that consider the problem. They agree that the low scores are probably a result of a lack of 6–12 articulation. They suggest that the animosity between the middle school and high school faculties contributes to the problem in virtually every subject area. There is more than a suggestion that Mr. Rostelli has fanned the flames of discontent. The high school stands aloof from a middle school that is indifferent to the high school.

To add to this problem, the high school faculty has recently presented you with a list of their complaints about the increasing discipline problem at the high school. The faculty are disappointed in the inability of the principal to maintain an orderly learning environment. Discipline is applied unevenly and, in the words of one of the teachers, "The school has no memory." There is also a small but vocal group of teachers who blame the disciplinary problems on the permissiveness of the middle school. "After all," they opine, "these kids are not taught responsibility at the middle school, so of course we have problems."

Mrs. Lavelli, president of the high school PTA, is a country clubber. She has asked to talk with you about the decline in scores. At a private meeting the next day, Mrs. Lavelli lists a litany of complaints about the high school principal's indifferent handling of discipline and his constant sniping at the middle school principal. She proclaims, "It's time for change. This is an opportunity to move the school forward. I want you to know that you have the support of my constituency for major change. We must make the high school better and more intellectual if we are to serve our children well."

You agree that the recent scores as well as persistent complaints reveal fundamental problems. You thank Mrs. Lavelli for her support and reassure her that her interests are yours. After all, you agree, the schools are for kids. Much to your surprise, you are caught off guard when Mrs. Lavelli suggests that Mr. Rostelli is nearing retirement and probably should be encouraged to turn over the reins of power to younger and more progressive educators like yourself. As she leaves, her parting words are, "I know we can count on you." She is gone before you can find out what it is that you are being counted on for.

You do not have to wait long. Henry Mintz, president of the board of education, calls to find out if you have begun to make personnel decisions. You don't know what he is talking about and ask him to explain. Mintz says that there are rumors that you have asked Rostelli to step down and open the way for someone younger and in better health. You are nonplussed, but assure Mintz that such is not the case. Nonetheless, Mintz is supportive and commends you on your work. "I realize this is a difficult situation," he says, "but you need to know you have our support. We hired you because you are the kind of leader who can bring people together and make decisions for the good of the group."

The next day you are thinking that perhaps Rostelli is the problem and he might be encouraged to retire. However, a call from Mr. Mazza, president of the Sons of Italy, points out to you that Mr. Rostelli is not without friends. "Look," says Mr. Mazza, "it may be that Frank Rostelli is not the most modern of principals, but that is not necessarily to the bad. He has been a friend of the community for more than twenty years. He cares about the kids and he is probably not as hard on them as the teachers would like, but he loves them. Such a man should not be cast out because he is no longer young."

It strikes you that the situation is becoming too political. The country club people are coming together with the Germans to try to unseat the high school principal. It might be good for the system to have a new and progressive principal, but surely the Italian community will see any attempt to replace Rostelli as an attack on their power. The system, however, does have a problem, as is amply demonstrated by the lower state proficiency test scores. It is sometimes difficult to separate political and educational issues.

You are not the only one thinking the situation is too political. Apparently, Mrs. Lavelli, Mr. Mueller, and some other people in town have been quietly saying that Mr. Rostelli intends to retire soon and that you might have had some influence on his decision. You are not quite sure where this rumor came from, but your secretary warned you that not all was calm in River Grove this morning. People in the community were talking, arguing, and choosing sides. The counterattack by Rostelli's forces was underway. Middle school and high school teachers were becoming openly antagonistic toward each other. Educational problems were taking a back seat to the power struggle at hand. Things were rapidly escalating out of control. Is this what the superintendency is all about? You need a plan of action that would defuse the politics, promote cooperation and understanding, and address educational issues in the district. It is time for leadership, and you are the appointed leader. While you are thinking this, the phone rings. Your secretary says that the high school principal, Mr. Rostelli, is on the line. You pick up the phone and Rostelli begins in a calm voice, "Bill, there are a lot of rumors floating around the community and my school, and we need to talk before things get out of control."

Discussing the Case

- Do you continue this conversation?
- Do you set up a meeting with Mr. Rostelli?
- If you do meet with Rostelli, what is your plan?
- Do you need to touch base with Mrs. Lavelli? The mayor? Mr. Mueller? The board president?
- Do you need to have a joint meeting with Rostelli and Mueller to clear the air?
- How can you limit personal goals and focus on school objectives?
- Which model of decision making is most useful in this case: political, garbage can, satisficing, incremental, or mixed scanning?

- Does this case call for a combination of approaches?
- Should you get help in making these decisions? From whom?

ENDNOTES

1. Information about Critical Friends Groups is at http://www.harmonyschool.org/nsrf/faq.html.
2. We use Mintzberg's (1983, p. 172) definition of *politics* to refer "to individual or group behavior that is informal, ostensibly parochial, typically divisive, and above all, in the technical sense illegitimate—sanctioned neither by formal authority, accepted ideology, nor certified expertise (though it may exploit any one of these)." In other words, legitimate systems of control and means of influence are those that are based on formal authority, accepted ideology, or certified expertise, not politics.

■ ■ ■ ■ ■

CHAPTER FIVE

USING THE BEST MODEL
Practice Cases

The previous chapters outlined and demonstrated six models of decision making that are used by school administrators—optimizing, satisficing, muddling, mixed scanning, and the garbage-can and political models. The optimizing model is a normative perspective, which in spite of its limited utility provides a rational ideal of decision making. It is this ideal of rationality that led Herbert Simon to develop his so-called satisficing model, a framework that refines and narrows the rationality of classical decision making to make it useful for administrators. Satisficing is more than a normative guide; it is an actual description of how some effective administrators make decisions.

The literature, however, suggests that most administrative decisions are made incrementally, that is, by moving through a series of small decisions, a process that has been termed *successive comparing* or *muddling through*. Muddling through is a description of how most decisions are probably made, but it is inherently conservative, guided by avoiding negative consequences, and is often without direction. If the situation is so complex as to require small incremental steps, then a strategy of mixed scanning avoids organizational drift by combining the rationalism of satisficing with the flexibility of incremental decision making. Mixed scanning is an adaptive strategy guided by the policies and mission of the organization.

Two other descriptive models were presented to explain the apparent irrationality of many administrative decisions. The garbage-can and political models examine decisions that lack an organizational plan. The garbage can shows how some problems are solved by fortuitous circumstances. Politics substitutes personal goals for organizational ones. Thus, what appears to be irrational organizational behavior is often the working out of happenstance or rational personal behavior, which is frequently dysfunctional for the organization.

DECISION-MAKING MODELS: A COMPARISON

How do the models of decision making proposed thus far compare with the rational ideal epitomized by the classical model? Recall that in the classical model, first objectives are set, then the best means are sought to attain the ends and the search is guided by appropriate theory, and finally the decision is evaluated by its success in maximizing the outcome. Accordingly, one may usefully compare all the models in terms of seven criteria drawn from the classic ideal: *setting objectives, means–ends analysis, the test of a good decision, the decision process, the search for alternatives, guiding principles,* and *normative perspective.* There is no simple continuum that captures the differences among these perspectives, but there are some consistent patterns.

For example, *setting objectives* varies from organizational to personal, with classical decision making occupying the organizational pole and with the political model resting at the personal extreme. Selecting the time to set organizational objectives distinguishes the models. Objectives are always set prior to generating alternatives in optimizing and usually in satisficing. Similarly, in the mixed-scanning model, general policy guidelines precede the development of alternatives. The setting of objectives and alternatives is intertwined in the incremental model, while in the garbage can they emerge spontaneously. In the political model, objectives are typically both spontaneous and personal. In brief, setting objectives ranges along the following continuum:

Classical	Organizational objectives are set prior to alternatives.
Administrative	Objectives usually are set prior to alternatives.
Mixed Scanning	Policy guidelines are set prior to alternatives.
Incremental	Objectives and alternatives are intertwined.
Garbage Can	Objectives emerge spontaneously.
Political	Objectives emerge spontaneously but are personal.

Means–ends analysis is another dimension along which the six models show some continuous variation. There is always means–ends analysis in the classical model, and it occurs frequently in the administrative model, but in the mixed scanning only broad ends and tentative means focus the analysis, while such analysis is inappropriate in the incremental model because means and ends are not separable. Furthermore, means and ends are independent of each other in the garbage-can model, and in the political model, personal ends, not organizational ones, guide decision making. In brief, means–ends analysis ranges along the following continuum:

Classical	Always begins with a means–ends analysis.
Administrative	Frequently begins with a means–ends analysis, but occasionally ends change.
Mixed Scanning	Broad ends and tentative means focus the analysis.
Incremental	No means–ends analysis. Means and ends are not separable.
Garbage Can	Means and ends are independent; chance connects them.
Political	Personal ends determine organizational means.

Next, we turn to what constitutes the test of a good decision in each model. A good decision in the classical model is the one that best accomplishes the ends, while the administrative and mixed-scanning models are concerned only with attaining satisfactory outcomes consistent with the overall mission of the organization. The incremental decision is good if the decision makers agree that the direction is right, but a good decision in the garbage can is one in which participants agree on the match of the solution and the problem. Finally, decisions in the political model are evaluated in terms of personal ends, not organizational ones; a good decision is one in which personal objectives are achieved. Thus, at one extreme—the classical— a good decision solves an organizational problem, and at the other extreme—the political—a good decision solves a personal problem. In brief, the test of a good decision ranges along the following continuum:

Classical	The best means to an organizational end.
Administrative	A satisfactory organizational outcome.
Mixed Scanning	A satisfactory organizational outcome.
Incremental	Decision makers agree that the decisions are in the right direction.
Garbage Can	Participants agree that solution and problem match.
Political	Personal objectives are accomplished.

The *decision-making process* can also be arrayed along a continuum from optimizing the organizational decision to using politics to achieve personal ends. Classical decision making always focuses on optimizing the best decision, while the administrative model has a more realistic goal of finding decisions that are satisfactory—that is, satisficing. It is often the complexity of the environment that produces a more tentative or adaptive satisficing in the mixed-scanning model, but the incremental model eschews satisficing in favor of successive comparisons. The garbage-can model depends on fortuitous circumstances to solve problems, while the political perspective is driven by politicking and personal preferences. In brief, the process ranges along the following continuum:

Classical	Optimizing organizational goals
Administrative	Satisficing
Mixed Scanning	Adaptive satisficing
Incremental	Successive comparing
Garbage Can	Connecting by chance
Political	Politicking to achieve personal ends

The *alternative search* also varies by model. At one extreme, the classical model is dedicated to searching for *all* organizational alternatives and their consequences, and, at the other extreme, the political model is a narrow search of alternatives and consequences that is driven by idiosyncratic personal needs. Again, the search moves from organizational to personal and from a comprehensive to an increasingly narrower examination of options. In brief, the alternative search ranges along the following continuum:

Classical	Find and consider all the alternatives.
Administrative	Search for a reasonable set of alternatives.

Mixed Scanning	Limit search to alternatives close to the problem.
Incremental	Limit search to alternatives close to the problem.
Garbage Can	Scan for a match among solutions, problems, and participants.
Political	Find satisfying personal alternatives.

These models are guided by a range of principles moving from a reliance on theory and experience to a reliance on chance and power. Classical formulation places heavy emphasis on theory, but the satisficing model acknowledges the importance of experience as well as theory. Mixed scanning adds successive comparison to experience and theory. In the incremental model, comparison replaces theory. The garbage can relies more on chance than anything else, and power drives the political process; theory is irrelevant in both cases. In brief, the guiding principles range along the following continuum:

Classical	Theory
Administrative	Theory and experience
Mixed Scanning	Theory, experience, and comparison
Incremental	Experience and comparison
Garbage Can	Chance
Political	Power

Finally, the decision-making perspectives that we have analyzed vary along a continuum from a normative ideal to descriptive explanations of the administrative world as it is. The classical model of optimizing is the normative ideal, while the political, incremental, and garbage-can models simply describe how many, if not most, organizational decisions are made. The administrative and mixed-scanning models are attempts to wed the reality of organizational life with the ideals of purpose and rationality. In brief, the decision perspectives range along the following continuum:

Classical	Normative ideal
Administrative	Descriptive and normative
Mixed Scanning	Descriptive and normative
Incremental	Descriptive
Garbage Can	Descriptive
Political	Descriptive

Our analysis has compared the models across seven standards. Table 5.1 summarizes the dominant characteristics of each model and provides both a vertical and a horizontal comparison.

TABLE 5.1 Comparison of Decision-Making Models

	CLASSICAL	ADMINISTRATIVE	MIXED SCANNING	INCREMENTAL	GARBAGE CAN	POLITICAL
Setting goals	Organizational objectives are set prior to alternatives	Objectives usually are set prior to alternatives	Policy guidelines are set prior to alternatives	Objectives and alternatives are intertwined	Objectives emerge spontaneously	Objectives emerge spontaneously but are personal
Means–ends analysis	Always begins with a means–ends analysis	Frequently begins with a means–ends analysis, but occasionally ends change	Broad ends and tentative means focus the analysis	No means–ends analysis; means and ends are not separable	Means and ends are independent; chance connects them	Personal ends determine organizational means
Test of a good decision	The best means to an organizational end	A satisfactory organizational outcome	A satisfactory organizational outcome	Decision makers agree that the decisions are in the right direction	Participants agree that solution and problem match	Personal objectives are accomplished
Decision process	Optimizing organizational goals	Satisficing	Adaptive satisficing	Successive comparing	Connecting by chance	Politicking to achieve personal ends
Alternative search	Find and consider all the alternatives	Search for a reasonable set of alternatives	Limit search to alternatives close to the problem	Limit search to alternatives close to the problem	Scan for a match among solutions, problems, and participants	Find personal satisfying alternatives
Underpinning	Theory	Theory and experience	Theory, experience, and comparison	Experience and comparison	Chance	Power
Perspective	Normative ideal	Descriptive and normative	Descriptive and normative	Descriptive	Descriptive	Descriptive

THE BEST MODEL: A CONTINGENCY APPROACH

What is the best way to decide? There is no best decision-making model, just as there is no best way to organize, to teach, to do research, or to do a myriad of other things. As in many complex events, the best approach is the one that best fits the circumstances. But what are the contingencies for selecting a decision strategy? (See Hoy & Miskel, 2001; Tarter & Hoy, 1998.) We turn to each model in an attempt to answer the question.

Under what conditions is the classical model of optimizing the best fit? There are few situations in schools in which optimizing is most appropriate. Only if the problem is narrow and concrete, and the decision maker can predict with certainty the consequences of all the alternatives, can optimizing be performed. Such circumstances are rare. Perhaps when purchasing a new fleet of buses, an administrator can obtain all the relevant cost-benefit data and maximize the decision. But even here, obtaining all the data is difficult. Buying the least expensive buses may not be the best decision unless they also have the best maintenance record. The point is that optimizing hinges on complete knowledge, but such knowledge is usually not available.

Under what conditions is the administrative model of satisficing the best fit? When complete knowledge is not available, satisficing rather than optimizing is appropriate. Complexity breeds uncertainty. That is, as the problem becomes more complicated, formulating and predicting consequences become problematic, cognitive limitations appear, and administrators must settle for a satisfactory decision rather than the best one. Thus, satisficing is the strategy of choice for most rational administrative decisions.

Under what conditions is the mixed-scanning model of adaptive satisficing the best fit? The line between satisficing and mixed scanning is not sharply delineated. As problems grow more complex, decision makers may be overwhelmed by the complexity. The problem of complexity is compounded by uncertainty. Outcomes can no longer be predicted with any reliability, yet time and circumstance press for action. One cannot get enough information to set the specific objectives of the decision; nonetheless, small, tentative decisions are made, which are guided by the policy and mission of the organization.

Under what conditions is the incremental model of muddling through the best fit? When the problem is complex, events are so uncertain that the decision maker cannot define satisfactory outcomes, and there is no guiding policy, the incremental model (muddling through) may be a sound short-term strategy. But it is, to be sure, only a *short-term* strategy until policy guidelines become clear.

Because a means–ends analysis is impossible in conditions of high uncertainty, limited information, and complexity, most administrators do nothing or muddle through. They make small, incremental decisions that symbolize action. These actions do not change much, but they reduce the pressure for action and, if there are no negative consequences, the decision maker continues further change in the same direction. The risk, however, is organizational drift, an aimless meandering that seeks to avoid negative reaction. Over the short run, such a strategy may be appropriate, but over the long run, it is dysfunctional.

Aimlessness in decision making can be avoided by always considering alternate actions in terms of their agreement with the mission and policy of the organization, that is, a strategy of mixed scanning that adapts the rationality of the satisficing model to the successive comparing of the incremental model. Therefore, when uncertainty and complexity are high, either the incremental or the mixed-scanning model may be appropriate.

Under what conditions is the garbage-can model the best fit? When decisions are complex and not constrained by time, and the organization can tolerate ambiguity and inaction, decisions sometimes occur by chance. Decisions just happen by fortuitous circumstances. This is not a model that lends itself to rational decision making. Rather, it is a description of how decisions sometimes happen in organizations like schools. We do not recommend this model for reflective decision making, but it is a useful explanatory framework for some decisions.

Under what conditions is the political model the best fit? Rarely, if ever. We define the political model as an illegitimate means of making organizational decisions because personal goals, rather than organizational objectives, guide the decision making. Nonetheless, when individuals in the organization pursue personal aims that are consistent with organizational interests, the organization can benefit; however, in most circumstances the political model is dysfunctional for the organization. The model is used to describe and explain decisions that are irrational from the perspective of the organization.

A summary guide for matching under which conditions each model is most appropriate is presented in Table 5.2.

TABLE 5.2 Summary of Matching the Decision-Making Model with the Appropriate Circumstance

MODEL	APPROPRIATE CIRCUMSTANCE
Optimizing	Narrow, specific problems; complete information.
Satisficing	Incomplete information; definable satisfactory outcomes.
Adaptive satisficing	Incomplete information; decisions complex; outcomes uncertain; guiding policy exists.
Incremental muddling	Incomplete information; decisions complex; outcomes uncertain; no guiding principles; short-term strategy until policy guidelines are established.
Garbage can	To understand fortuitous decisions.
Political	To understand irrational decisions.

A CONTINGENCY MODEL: MATCHING STRATEGY WITH SITUATION

Let's review the decision strategies and develop a model that matches strategy with situation. As we have seen, both the garbage-can and political models *explain* why some decision making seems nonrational or irrational, but neither model is a useful guide for making decisions. Moreover, the optimizing model is appropriate only when decisions are simple, information complete and certain, and a collective preference (no conflict) exists. Organizational problems are almost never simple, certain, and without conflict; hence, optimizing is not really a choice.

Thus, we have remaining three different decision strategies—satisficing, muddling through, and adaptive satisficing (mixed scanning). Which model is best? It depends; the appropriate model depends on matching the strategy with the situation. Three criteria are the basis for a simplified contingency model, each criterion defined by a simple question (Hoy & Miskel, 2008):

- *Information:* Do I have sufficient information to make a reasonable decision?
- *Time:* Do I have sufficient time to engage in a comprehensive search for alternatives?
- *Importance:* How important is this decision?

Do I have sufficient information to define a satisfactory outcome? If so, then satisficing is the model of choice. But depending on time and importance of the decision, the satisficing strategy may need to be truncated or adapted. Truncated satisficing means considering only a few of the possible options rather than seeking a comprehensive set of alternatives. If there is sufficient time to engage in a comprehensive search, but the decision is not that important, then truncated satisficing is the appropriate strategy. Don't spend time developing a host of options; it is not worth the effort.

If there is insufficient information, then adaptive satisficing may be the strategy of choice. However, depending on time and importance of the decision, adaptive satisficing may be truncated or moderated by muddling through. For example, if there is insufficient information and time, and the decision is not that important, then muddling may be an appropriate short-term decision strategy.

Thus, three questions guide the decision maker along eight possible paths depending on the situation—each path with a decision strategy that fits the situation. Satisficing, adaptive satisficing, and truncated versions of each, as well as muddling are appropriate depending on the situation. The situations are defined by information, time, and importance, and the decision tree in Table 5.3 summarizes the paths of our contingency approach to decision making.

DECISION MAKING: A PRACTICAL TIP

As you read the practice cases that follow and prepare to develop solution strategies, it may be helpful to highlight the major facts and organize them for deciding. One of our colleagues[1] has suggested a short **SMART** case brief as a way to prepare for class discussion and analysis. The brief is organized using the acronym—**SMART**.

S stands for stakeholder—who are the major players of this case?
M is the model or models used to analyze the case.
A is the application of the appropriate model(s).
R indicates the realistic chance of success.
T is the talk that a student prepares to defend her or his strategy.

Stakeholders are the important people in the case who will be affected by the outcomes of the decisions. A first step in elaborating a plan of action is to identify the key individuals of the case and those who will be affected by the decision. Focusing your analysis on these individuals limits negative unanticipated consequences. Knowing who will be materially affected can prevent unpleasant surprises—don't overlook someone who is likely to cause trouble.

Model selection is shaped by information, time, and importance. Do you have sufficient information and time, and how important is the problem? Table 5.3 will guide you in selecting the appropriate model.

TABLE 5.3 Contingency Model: Matching Strategies with Situations © Hoy, 2005

SUFFICIENT INFORMATION?	SUFFICIENT TIME?	IMPORTANT DECISION?	DECISION-MAKING STRATEGY

Apply the appropriate model to develop an effective solution strategy. What is your plan of action? What are the contingencies? Sketch and articulate your thinking as you come to a tentative path of action.

Realistic appraisal is an attempt to check your ideal against the real. Are you realistic? How confident are you that your plan has a reasonable chance of success? Decisions should be anchored in reality, not simply founded on hope.

Talk means crafting and defending your strategy. Be prepared to articulate, defend, and explain your plan. Prepare for negative consequences. Craft your position. What if your initial strategy is blocked or fails? Do you have a fallback position? What are the possible negative consequences? Are you ready for surprises? How? In spite of all your plans, surprises are likely. When anticipation fails, be resilient. Table 5.4 outlines the SMART strategy.

TABLE 5.4 The SMART Case Brief[1]

Stakeholders: Who are the important people in this case who will be affected by the decisions?

Model: What is the appropriate decision-making model to be applied and why?

Apply: Apply the model by selecting the appropriate decision-making strategy. Develop and express your resolution strategy for the case. What is your plan of action? What are the steps of your plan? What are the contingencies?

Realistic Appraisal: What are the realistic chances of the success of your strategy? How confident are you? Have you compared the real possibilities with the ideal vision?

Talk: Articulate, defend, and explain your strategy. How are you prepared for the possible negative consequences of your plan? How will you avoid them? How will you deal with them if they happen? Did you anticipate unexpected consequences? Do you have a fallback response?

APPLYING THE APPROPRIATE MODEL

The remainder of this chapter provides a series of actual cases in which you apply the models. You will find guiding questions at the end of each case that will help in the analysis. The contingency model just presented will also guide you in the selection of the appropriate strategy; use it.

CASE 5.1

Freak Dancing aka Dirty Dancing

The latest fad Principal Edward White had to confront as principal of Westmont High School was freak dancing. Freak dancing is a little hard to describe, but it's easy to recognize when you see it. The dancing involves bumping and grinding moves back to front in which a girl gyrates her hips against the pelvis of a guy standing behind her. A few years back, similar movements on the dance floor yielded a dirty dancing craze including a movie by the same name. The new wave of dirty dancing, freaking, includes crotch-to-crotch dancing, prone positions, grinding, and "sandwich dancing." The music is just as suggestive of sexual adventures as the dancing; consider the following popular titles: "The Thong Song" and "Back That Thang Up."

Principal White was still in shock. The band and drama teachers had just left his office after giving him a vivid description of Friday night's dance. He had spent the morning listening to parents on the phone complain vehemently about the sophomore dance in which the "kids went wild" on the dance floor doing what they called freak dancing. He had been appalled when the first thing this morning a parent rushed to his office with a video camera and showed an episode of the sophomore students doing the freak. White was not sure what the freak was before the showing, but he certainly knew now and was just as concerned as the parents. The visit from the band and drama teachers had really clinched the importance of the problem.

Mr. Leonard, the band director, and Ms. Rice, the drama teacher, had been adamant in their objections to chaperoning the dance. They flatly refused to be a party to any further "orgies," as they described the dancing. "Never again" was their exiting mantra. They complained that they actually had to work their way into a knot of gyrating students where they pulled girls off the dance floor half dressed. Unfortunately, someone had captured the whole affair on video and White had just seen it. He too was aghast and shaken. He knew this was just the beginning.

His immediate problem was to do some damage control with the teachers and parents. The chaperones had abruptly ended the dance a little after 11:00, just when, according to the students, things were getting started. The teachers were upset; parents were outraged; the students were divided, some defiant and others embarrassed. The superintendent had already called to vent her displeasure about the whole episode and to relay strong objections from members of the board of education.

The longer-term issue was what to do about school-sponsored dances in the future, especially the Spring Fling, which was just a few weeks away. Principal White decided to get a better sense of the problem by talking with some student leaders. He had good relations with the students in school and had had personal dealings with the president of the student council as well as the presidents of the freshman, sophomore, junior, and senior classes. He called in those student leaders who were already well aware of the outcry from teachers and parents in the community.

White had expected the students to be apologetic and cooperative about the uproar the freaking had caused. Instead, he got arguments supporting the dancing as a contemporary version of today's culture. In fact, one student claimed that freak dancing was to his generation what the twist was to the principal's generation. Another student said, "We just like to get a little wild and dance. We aren't doing any harm. We just like to dance close. It's a new world, Mr. White, and kids love the freedom of expression."

"Yes," added the student council president. "We are just expressing one of the freedoms guaranteed in the First Amendment of the Constitution. The First Amendment guarantees expression in all forms. No one is getting hurt, and we are not doing anything bad."

"Well," ventured the principal, "I have seen a videotape of some of the dancing and it looks like pornographic expression to me. Would you want your parents to see this dancing?"

The response was almost uncontrollable laughter from the students. "You've got to be kidding," Mr. White. But White was not kidding and he knew that he represented the dominant adult view of such dancing at school functions.

Principal White was in no mood for frivolous argument or an exchange of one-liners. He had heard enough and he threw down the gauntlet. There would be no Spring Fling this year unless the students could develop a set of rules and procedures, which would guarantee proper decorum on and off the dance floor.

The students' reaction was confrontational not conciliatory. They suggested that if the school did not provide a forum for free expression, students would have to find other venues. "You want to cancel the dance, Mr. White? Go ahead. We will just find somewhere else to go." The meeting ended on this less-than-cooperative note.

Principal White had less than three weeks to develop a plan of action. As he sat at his desk, he mulled over the issues and options.

Discussing the Case

- Opinion may be divided among students, but there is a substantial number of students who believe that freak dancing is neither sexually charged nor offensive.
- Teachers are upset and for the most part unwilling to be sponsors or chaperones for such dances.
- Likewise, parents are generally appalled and opposed to such dancing.

- The superintendent and board of education are united in demanding that you get control of this situation.
- What immediate actions should you take to mollify parents and teachers about the freaking that took place at the Friday's sophomore dance?
- What kind of policy should be developed about school-sponsored dances?
- What are the appropriate roles of students, teachers, parents, and administrators in developing such policy?
- The Spring Fling is scheduled to be held in three weeks. What needs to be done in preparation for this annual dance? Should it be postponed or cancelled?
- Perhaps a better question would be, "Under what conditions should the Spring Fling be held?"
- Assume the role of Principal White and develop a strategy and plan for dealing with the set of events that has just occurred.

CASE 5.2

Sexual Harassment

Kelly Croy, a new teacher in her tenure year at Elm Road Elementary School, was not unaccustomed to fending off unwanted attention. She was a recent graduate of the state university and had not only been a diligent student but also had had a full social life. She had been active in her sorority and won the most-popular-student award during her senior year. She was a likable young woman. Although she was only beginning her third year of teaching, her vivacious personality and her professional skill combined to make her one of the most popular teachers among parents and teachers at Elm Road.

Brent Rader had been the principal of Elm Road Elementary for three years, coming directly to the principalship after serving only four years as a sixth-grade teacher at Elm Road and then a year as acting principal. Brent was thirty years old, married, with two children, and had already established himself as competent, reliable, and well liked. He was close to finishing his doctorate in educational administration at the state university. His future as an educational leader in the state was promising.

Kelly Croy was nonplussed the first time it happened. What she had taken to be innocent conversation with the principal had developed into sly innuendo. Conversation led to touches that were questionable. She had not minded his occasional hugs, chalking them up to the warm friendship they had, but the first time he actually grabbed her, she was shocked. She searched her actions to see if she had encouraged his advances, but she could not find anything to justify his obvious sexual interest. She was sorry she had not protested more strongly and sooner, but she just could not believe it. She liked Brent, and they were good friends, but he was happily married (so she thought), and she was not interested in developing anything more than a professional relationship. Things were more complicated, though. After all, she was in her tenure year, he was her superior, and she loved Elm Road. He would be the one to recommend her for reappointment with tenure. If someone had told her that she would be having this kind of problem at work, she would have laughed. But now the situation was not amusing.

Just before Valentine's Day, she had occasion to stay late at school to prepare for a Valentine party in her class. She was working alone, and Brent saw her light and decided to offer assistance. Looking back, she realized that she had made a mistake in accepting his help. As she stood on a chair attaching a paper heart to the ceiling, Brent's hands encircled her waist and lingered there. She nearly fell, but he caught her. She broke loose and demanded that he leave. He ignored her demands and asked, "What's wrong? Should I have let you fall?"

"You know what's wrong," she said harshly. "This is not fun, and I don't like it."

"Oh, c'mon," cajoled Brent, "we're both adults. Don't be a prude. We like each other and what's the harm?"

"You're married and I'm not interested," she rejoined.

"OK. OK. I apologize, and I'm sorry."

Kelly felt relieved that she had made herself abundantly clear that she did not share Brent's romantic interests. She was sure that he had gotten the message. And, indeed, for the next month, they acted like good friends and their relationship was warm, though correct. Kelly was proud of herself for the way she had handled a difficult situation. She had protected herself and Brent by not blowing the incident out of proportion and by keeping it to herself.

She was dismayed to find that her next evaluation suggested her teaching had deteriorated. Her two previous evaluations had been glowing, but now she saw in the evaluation the picture of a teacher who was marginal at best. She was worried. On the one hand, she had a reputation as a good teacher and a series of good evaluations since her employment at Elm Road. On the other hand, she was worried about her recent evaluation and the forthcoming tenure decision. She realized that she had better tell someone about this situation. She decided to go directly to the superintendent. She did not know Dr. Ortiz, but he had a reputation as a fair administrator and she was sure that he had heard of her good work at Elm Road. She picked up the phone and called for an appointment.

Ed Ortiz was puzzled by Kelly's request to meet with him without an explanation. He had not had time to check with Brent Rader about the teacher, but since she only wanted a few moments of his time and he knew by reputation that she was a good teacher, he was looking forward to her visit. The intercom buzzed, and the secretary announced that Kelly Croy was in the outer office.

He got out of his chair and walked to the outer office to greet her and escort her in. They exchanged pleasantries, and he was impressed by her poise and pleasant demeanor. Imagine his surprise when Kelly recounted the entire story. Kelly was not vindictive and, indeed, broke down and cried when she described the events that led up to visiting his office. She exclaimed, "I don't want to cause trouble for anyone, but I don't want to be harassed by Brent or anyone else. I don't want this to be a formal complaint, but I do want you to know about it. I don't want to risk a job I really love, but I don't want to work in such circumstances. Please help me."

Superintendent Ortiz reassured her that all decisions in the district would be made on a professional basis and there was no place for any hint of sexual harassment in his school district. This last point he made emphatically and told her she had done the right thing in coming to see him.

After Kelly Croy left, Ortiz sat back in his chair, clearly troubled by the turn of events. He liked Brent Rader; he was a good principal and a strong supporter of Ortiz's. "Could the story be true?" he wondered.

Discussing the Case

- What decision-making model would you use in this case?
- What should have been the superintendent's first step? Could he ignore this complaint?
- He needed to talk to Rader, but what should his approach have been?
- Was this a formal complaint of sexual harassment, in spite of Kelly Croy's insistence that it was not?
- What were his legal responsibilities in this matter?
- What should his role have been in this case?
- How could he protect the best interests of all concerned?
- What were the policy implications for the district?
- What decision model was most appropriate? Could he afford to muddle through? Or could he do otherwise?
- Develop a strategic plan of action to deal with Kelly Croy's complaint.

CASE 5.3

Late Again: What to Do?

Decatur is a small town close to a northeastern population center. In some ways it is more of a bedroom community than a traditional small town. Most of the faculty live in adjacent communities, and many of the parents commute to work. With its carefully planned small town atmosphere Decatur has become a favorite choice for young professionals to live and raise their families. The community expects high academic standards, but they also are proud of their strong athletic program, which in large part is a reflection of a conscientious coaching staff.

Decatur High School is a small 7–12 school with about 700 students. The largest minority is an Asian contingent of about 10 percent. The school clearly has an academic orientation: a substantial number of students, about 75 percent, go to college. Mark Rodriguez, the longtime and popular principal, has just hired a new assistant principal, Mike DeLisi. DeLisi was a young mathematics teacher who had taught for seven years during which he attended the state university and earned his master's degree in educational administration and a license to be a principal. This was DeLisi's first administrative position—the vice-principal at Decatur High School—and he was eager to do well.

"Well, Mike, here is a small project for you. Some students who caught detention for coming in late complained about unfair treatment. They were late and punished, but they claimed that Coach Thorne often comes in just as late and they are upset at uneven treatment: 'If teachers can be late, why not students?' Talk to Bill Thorne and see what you can do to fix this. If you have any questions, let me know," finished Mark.

"OK," said Mike. "I will look into this and let you know how it goes."

True to his word, Mike found a break in the day to talk with the department chair and to Coach Thorne and found that, indeed, the coach was routinely late. Thorne lived about twenty minutes away and there didn't seem to be any reason why the coach would be late. Thorne pointed out the long hours he spent after school and on weekends, but he did apologize for being tardy and said it would not happen again.

It did happen again, and not just once. Coach Thorne was about five minutes late twice in the past week, and VP DeLisi found out that, as a matter of courtesy, other faculty members would cover for Thorne. Thorne was a likeable teacher and colleague, so other teachers did not feel put out by covering his homeroom for five or ten minutes.

The problem persisted. During the next two weeks, vice-principal Mike DeLisi monitored the situation and determined that in the last ten days Coach Thorne had been tardy nine times, never more than ten minutes late but always at least five minutes tardy. VP DeLisi could see why students would be upset because Thorne was not merely a coach but also a social studies teacher and should behave as a professional. Much to his dismay, DeLisi decided that he must have another talk with Bill Thorne and he would stress the importance of starting the school day on time to model the behavior the school expected of students and to be sure student attendance was recorded properly during his homeroom.

The second meeting went well. Thorne apologized for being late and agreed with DeLisi about the importance of punctuality. Thorne explained that he worked long hours as a coach, arrived home late every night, stayed up to prepare for the next day's classes, and was often so tired that he slept right through the alarm. Actually, DeLisi empathized with Thorne and suggested that since he himself was an early riser, he would call every morning to make sure that Thorne was up and on time. Thorne seemed genuinely grateful at his concern and help.

As it turned out, this new procedure worked well for about three weeks, but then the old pattern returned. Even with the calls, Thorne was late routinely. When the vice-principal asked, Thorne was always apologetic and rationalized his behavior because he was working so late with his student athletes. Nonetheless, DeLisi persisted, "You need to get here on time, Bill."

When the vice-principal recounted his actions and Thorne's responses to the principal, the principal just shook his head and said, "It's not worth the effort; forget it. It is what it is. We're not going to be able to change Thorne's behavior and his colleagues seem to understand and accept his tardiness."

DeLisi retorted, "It just isn't right. We have to get Thorne to be responsible; for Pete's sake, we can't have a faculty member coming in late all the time."

Principal Smith rejoined, "Do what you need to do, but I don't think he'll change."

DeLisi was not one to let this lie. At the next evaluation, he confronted Thorne and reviewed all he had done to help, Thorne's promises, and the persistence of Thorne's tardiness in spite of all efforts to help him overcome it. The vice-principal included the description in Thorne's written evaluation report. What was Thorne's reaction? He was sullen, annoyed, unsympathetic, and uncooperative. Moreover, at the end of the year, notwithstanding all of DeLisi's efforts, Coach Thorne continued his wayward ways; he was late almost every day. If Thorne were not a good teacher and a fine coach, the resolution would be easier, but, in point of fact, Thorne was pretty good in the classroom, respected by colleagues and students, and to top it off, Thorne was a very good coach and the school was happy to have him. DeLisi's principal had as much as said to let this problem go, but DeLisi's professional sense of decorum was offended.

Discussing the Case

- Take the role of the vice-principal.
- Is there a problem here? If so, how serious?
- Would you make amends to Coach Thorne?
- Would you just forget it?
- Do you have a cause for action here? If so, why? And, if so, what strategy could you devise to resolve the issue?
- Would you consider withholding the annual salary increment, if possible?
- Options seem limited with a tenured teacher. What can you do?

CASE 5.4

Excessive Force?

Superintendent Monica Jones sat back in her chair and reflected on recent events in Addington Unified School District. Addington enrolled about 3,500 students in the school system. Her high school currently was the home of 1,800 students, and the high school was much like the entire system—typical of small-town Midwest. On the state report card, Addington scored toward the middle with about 75% of the students passing the high school proficiency tests.

Superintendent Jones was perplexed and a little disturbed at the recent turn of events at the high school. She was holding in her hand a petition signed by nearly 500 high school students asking her to stop police from using Tasers in the school after a police officer stunned a ninth-grade student with the a Taser in breaking up a fight.

The story she got from the principal was the following. Two students had been fighting at the school and the assistant principal ordered them to stop. When they did not, he tried to separate the boys with no success. While he was engaged with the boys, two police officers showed up. The police warned the boys to stop, and when they did not, they used a Taser on one of the youths to end the confrontation.

This was the second time this year that a police officer had used a Taser in response to violence. Earlier in the year, a seventeen-year-old boy was stunned by police in school after he had allegedly attempted to assault an officer. Superintendent Jones recalled the chief of police's statement in a recent newspaper article, "The officers involved were 100 percent justified in using such force." He claimed the officers were simply following established department policy.

The high school students at Addington disagreed as was evident from the petition that Superintendent Jones was holding in her hand. The students were really up in arms and their petition was causing waves in the community as reports of the use of the Tasers became an item in the local paper and as the chief of police tried to justify their use on students.

One high school student, Samantha Kincaid, observed, "Does this make sense? The school has a policy of not paddling students, but then they call in the police to shoot them with Tasers. Two ninth-grade boys, neither of whom weighed more than 140 pounds, should be able to be controlled by the school officials without calling in the police and permitting them to use excessive force."

Her friend added, "It seems to me that the school administration should be able to handle their own routine discipline problems without calling the police. Schools aren't prisons—at least they shouldn't be—they are institutions of learning."

The superintendent was also taken aback by the alleged quote from the high school principal, Brett Mulhane, that "the two police officers who regularly patrol the high school carried the same protective gear and equipment as street officers, and they react as they see fit."

Superintendent Jones was deeply troubled by the use of what she considered to be excessive force. Moreover, she agreed with the students and with a number of parents who had called that the school system was abdicating its responsibility in permitting the police to control the schools. After all, schools are places of learning, and self-control is a learning goal. Jones pondered the situation.

Discussing the Case

- Was her administrative team at the high school too quick to rely on the police?
- Was the high school really out of control such that external force was necessary? If so, why?
- Did the school, including the administration, have a responsibility to guarantee the safety of all students?

- Is there a reason now to talk with the chief of police? Why, or why not?
- Should you ask the principal and her staff to justify using the police?
- How much latitude should individual school leaders have in discipline?
- Is the high school abdicating its responsibility in using the police in such situations?
- Should the high school administration be called on the carpet?
- Could a plan be devised and a policy established so that police were called into a school only on rare occasions and for crime-related activities?
- If you were the superintendent of this district, how would you work with the junior and senior high schools to establish a policy on school violence that protected students while they were in school and used the police only in those cases where the life and safety of students were at risk?

CASE 5.5

Discord and Disharmony[2]

As you leave the Kiwanis meeting, a community business leader asks to have a few words with you. In a tone more of concern than anger, he says that "people are really fed up with the band, especially after last Friday night. You are the superintendent; you should be able to do something."

"What do you mean?"

"I mean the dumb music. You call that band music? It was my kid who told me they were playing Bono's music. I didn't know if that was the name of the band or the song, or if my kid was just putting me on. What I do know is that a marching band ought to play marches, rouse the crowd, play the school song, and make people come alive. Do you think most people want to hear a concert at a football game?"

With an inward sigh, you listened as he aired his feelings. His concerns were not news to you. For the past several years, disgruntled residents have complained about the band's performance and participation during Friday night football games. The complaining members of the community want a traditional football band, with plenty of team spirit and some rousing marching during half-time. As superintendent you are not unsympathetic to such complaints. You like team spirit and Sousa marches, too.

The band parents, on the other hand, don't think that the band exists to serve the football team. The band and its boosters are active participants in a band competition program that emphasizes concert performance and avant-garde formations. To hone their competition skills, the band repeatedly performs its single competition piece at half-time, to the puzzlement of the fans who want some show tunes and a good march rather than the discordant (though very difficult) postmodernist music.

Recognizing the unhappiness of community members, and bowing to the wishes of the high school principal, the band director had agreed to rev up the half-time offerings and to play the school song more often during the game. But the compromise was not a success. Tempos were slow, movement was virtually nonexistent, and the school song was lost. Even worse, your principal seemed to have little ability to influence the director's choices and behavior.

You are troubled by the discord between the community and the band. Being a big fan of the state university marching band, known fondly as the best darn band in the land (TBDBITL), you know how much a strong, traditional marching band can add to the enjoyment of the game. And you certainly want to keep your community members happy; you have an operating levy on the ballot and need all the support you can get. But you also understand the band parents' point of view.

As a registered nonprofit organization, the Band Boosters are a stand-alone group, with few legal ties to the school system. The band parents raise thousands of dollars to subsidize the district funding of the band program. The boosters hire assistant directors, choreographers, and drum line coaches; they pay travel expenses for competitions; they raise money for new uniforms and for vehicles to haul instruments. They firmly believe that their investment of time and money entitles them to choose the type of extracurricular programming done by the band. For the last decade, their belief has not been challenged.

You've tried to smooth things over for the past few years, but discord is growing. You have decided that the school system must get more control over the situation. However, events are complex and changing rapidly: the band director has resigned in a huff, angry with what he perceived as lack of support from the administration. Not only are the boosters demanding to participate in the selection of a new band director, they have also made clear their desire to choose a band director that agrees with the current type of programming. The booster president called last week to inform you that the booster parents are tired of the administration's lack of respect for the band's efforts, and that they "will not sit idly by while educrats pick the next director."

What to do? How can this mess be resolved without infuriating the boosters or alienating the community? Must you let the boosters participate in choosing the new band director? Will you insist on a different performance format? These questions and many others run through your mind as you listen to your fellow Kiwanians. Thanking him for his concern you get in your car and drive back to the office. You resolve to get a handle on this whole situation—and quickly. But how?

Discussing the Case

- What decision-making model would you use for this case?
- What is the basic problem here?
- What are your options?
- What is the minimum you must have to resolve this situation?
- What is the role of the principal in this case?
- How much delegation of the decision should you make to the principal?
- What are the constraints on the principal?
- Should you maintain final authority over the decision?
- How will you organize for this decision?

CASE 5.6

Superintendent's Hiring Dilemma

Superintendent of schools Mary Beth Kerner once again looked through the pile of résumés on the desk before her. She was under pressure from the board of education to hire a new high school principal who could replace Jimmy Johnson, who had been the venerated principal of Kingston High School for twenty-eight years. Kingston, a college community, is located in a large northeastern state and is the home of a prestigious private university. The board places a heavy demand on the school system in its insistence that the school offer what is essentially a college preparatory program. There is, however, a substantial minority population that has become increasingly vocal in its demands for a more comprehensive curriculum. The list of grievances is long and growing: lack of concern for the non-college-bound student; lack of minority teachers serving as role models, no African American administrators in the district, an unofficial tracking program that gives resources to the college prep curriculum and deprives the other programs, not enough concern for poor performance of minority students, and a snobbery among the students that offends the less advantaged.

The school board is also undergoing change. The past board had been pleased with the number of students accepted at good colleges, the consistently high SAT scores of students, their numerous winners of the Westinghouse awards for science, and a recent article citing the school as the best in the state. The board was comprised of four men and five women, eight whites and an Asian. The president of the board was a professor of sociology at the local university. Two of the five women were spouses of successful professional leaders in the community and were committed to serving the school and community; the other three were a college professor at the state university, an owner of a local business, and a realtor. The additional three men were a successful attorney, a mathematics professor at the university, and a community college professor. This was a professional board of education; it was the board that had hired Dr. Kerner six years ago. They had given her early tenure in her position and the accolades and the salary that go with success.

But things were changing at Kingston. The African American community was increasingly disillusioned with a school system that paid little attention to their needs. They did, after all, represent 25 percent of the population. The parents had mobilized, formed an African-American Alliance for Progress, and elected two of their own to represent their interests on the board. One, who replaced the attorney, was the minister of the local Baptist congregation. The other was an outspoken woman, a parent of three school-age children. She replaced the wife of a socially prominent banker. The new board was sensitive to the demands of a hitherto unheard minority. At the first board meeting, the newly elected members demanded change; they wanted an African American high school principal, more minority teachers, and a curriculum that realistically addressed the needs of their children. Their top priority was clear: the principalship. The board in general was not opposed to hiring a minority principal; in fact, most agreed it was a good idea. However, they were adamant in their desire to get an educator of the highest standing with impeccable credentials; quality was the ultimate criterion.

William Levine had been the popular vice-principal for six years. Dr. Levine had had numerous opportunities to move on, but he was always reminded by his principal that his future was in Kingston. "Bill, don't move. I'll be retiring in a few years, and the job is yours." He had heard that refrain at least three times in the past six years. At last the opportunity was here, but now there were complications.

Levine was something of a scholar in his own right. He graduated from Harvard with a major in history, received a master's in political science from the University of Chicago, and went back to Harvard for his doctorate in educational administration. His academic career had been interrupted with teaching stints at Phillips Andover as well as in the public schools of Highland Park, Illinois. He was a successful teacher and administrator. Students liked him, faculty liked and respected him, and his fellow administrators seemed at times in awe of his abilities. He was a skillful and dynamic leader. Clearly, he was ready to assume the principalship at Kingston. In fact, it was a foregone conclusion that William Levine would be the next principal. The sudden death of the former principal in an auto accident had saddened the district and the school and propelled Levine into the role of acting principal, the job that everyone assumed was his permanently. That was before the board election. Now what?

Dr. Kerner, herself, at times had implied to William Levine that he would be the next principal at Kingston High School. He had every right to expect to be appointed the next principal, she thought, as she pondered her next steps. Things were not so simple. She concluded that an open search for the new principal was not only desirable but necessary.

The board balked at hiring professional consultants to carry out a national search for the principal. The two new members of the board wanted to be involved directly in the search and selection of the new principal. Consequently, a five-member search committee was appointed; it included the two new board members. Its charge was to find the best possible principal for Kingston. After a long and exhaustive search, which involved screening hundreds of applications, conducting several scores of interviews, and holding repeat interviews with five finalists, two people remained in consideration: William Levine and Roger Washington.

Levine's work at Kingston had reinforced its academic prominence. He had been successful in involving the local university with a variety of advanced placement courses, and some of the Kingston students moved easily between the classrooms at Kingston and well-equipped laboratories of a highly competitive university. Levine was aware of the limitations of the curriculum for some of the students, but he felt that the hard work and the excellence of college-bound Kingston students should be rewarded.

Roger Washington had been a principal for three years in a middle school in a large northeastern city. He had built a reputation as a no-nonsense administrator respected by both students and faculty. Parents marveled at his ability to handle kids. During his tenure as principal, he had reorganized the curriculum, increased the school averages on standardized tests, and reduced the student absentee rate by 40 percent. He was an articulate young man, committed to the problems of minorities. He saw in Kingston an opportunity to help a group of children who were not being served.

As was Levine, so too was Washington an anomaly in school circles. He had been a scholarship student at the University of California, Berkeley, where he had graduated with honors in a double major of mathematics and physics. In the course of graduate education at the University of Michigan, he had worked with local schools and found, he felt, a calling. He became a high school science teacher and gradually rose through positions of increasing responsibility.

Either Levine or Washington would be a good choice for the school, but the decision as to who was the better probably hinged on their respective interviews. Levine held that the school should continue to focus on the excellent job it was doing with high-achieving students and devote resources to the middle- and lower-range students as a secondary focus. It was not the case that Levine was indifferent to these lower-performing students, rather it was a conviction that the school's emphasis on academic quality had paid off for hard-working high-achieving students.

Washington also considered the school's success with the high achievers important; however, he felt that the school's emphasis should be placed on those students who really needed a more intensive education than they were now receiving. Washington advocated shifting some of the school's resources away from the faster tracks to the other sectors of the school. Not to do this, he argued, would deprive the slower students. Washington believed strongly in education for the gifted, but not to the degree he found at Kingston. He thought the school had an obligation in justice to shift its focus.

The board recognized the problem presented by the views of Levine and Washington. They seemed unable to come to a decision on which to hire; they were deadlocked—four for Washington, four for Levine, and one who abstained, saying that either was a good choice. Finally, after long debate, they called in Dr. Kerner. "Mary Beth," said the president of the board, "whoever is hired will have to work with you. What we need now is a strong recommendation and rationale. We all agree that you are critical in this decision and we trust your judgment. What is your recommendation in this case?"

Discussing the Case

- What decision-making model would you use for this case?
- Is there another way out, or does the buck stop with Kerner?
- How important is her decision here?
- Is this a win–win situation? Or perhaps a lose–lose one?
- To what extent is this a political decision?
- Anticipate the negative consequences of Kerner's decision and make plans to mute them.

CASE 5.7

Electives

Samuel Peterson, the English department chair at Central High School, was making the best case he could with Principal Jack Morris.

"As we increase the number of electives we offer, we reduce the coherence of our program. We don't concentrate our efforts on what the kids really need—grammar, composition, and mainstream literature. Dispersing our resources does no one any good. We can't afford to give any more teachers electives that distract from the basic thrust of our program."

Morris responded, "Let me think on this for a few days and get back to you. I'm sure we can work this out to both the department's and Emily's satisfaction. You'll hear from me before there is any decision. But I will have to talk with Emily again."

Emily Dotson, a five-year veteran of Central, had inadvertently become the center of a controversy for exercising a tacit understanding at Central. If you had been a good teacher, and you had put in about five years of service at Central, you could offer an elective in your department. Most teachers saw this as a kind of reward for good service and continued academic interest in their field. Not all teachers availed themselves of this opportunity; in fact, relatively few of them did, but the ones who did were considered the better teachers by their peers.

Emily Dotson wanted to teach a Latin American literature course as an elective in the English department. She was well qualified to do so. She had double majored in English and Spanish, had taken graduate work in Latin American literature, and recently received a Master's degree in comparative literature.

Sam Peterson had no doubts about Dotson's ability; rather, he was concerned about the effects of more electives on the program. Peterson had served as chair of the department for more than a dozen years, and he was not about to see his program, nurtured so assiduously for so long, decline. In his time as chair, he had watched good teachers develop electives in areas of their particular interest. The department now had courses in science fiction, mysteries, Russian novels, and American novels. These were academically demanding courses, but Peterson felt that further electives would move students away from developing a general competency in language and literature.

Peterson had been instrumental in hiring Emily Dotson. He had not been disappointed in his decision. Dotson was a fine teacher—knowledgeable, skillful, conscientious, and interested in kids. She was becoming one of the more popular teachers. She was willing to do her share and a little more of the department's work, and the other teachers in the department saw her as a good colleague. As Peterson saw it, in spite of the fact that he had exchanged harsh words with Dotson, the problem was not with Dotson; the problem was with the electives.

When they spoke informally about the elective, Peterson had argued, "The electives water down the overall program. I'm not disputing your skill as a teacher. I think you do a great job, and I'm pleased to have you in the department. But I'm afraid that you may be pursuing an intellectual hobby, rather than developing the students as much as we might."

"Well, that could be," responded Dotson judiciously. "Let's see if the students who take the electives are the better or worse ones. My guess, based on informally watching the department, is that the better students take the electives and they profit from them."

"I'm not convinced," rejoined Peterson. "Maybe we can talk about it more later."

Emily Dotson was not about to give up. She made a formal appointment with Principal Morris to present her case. "This is a kind of fringe benefit that helps everyone," she told Morris. "It keeps teachers like me intellectually alive, and it encourages kids to broaden their academic horizons. There aren't many electives that are offered, but those that make it are pretty good. They're taught by the good teachers, and the kids like them. I'm not saying the school has to offer Latin American literature as a requirement. I'm just asking to be allowed to take my chances on putting together a course that is both academically challenging and popular enough to draw students. After all, the chance to offer an elective has always been given to other teachers once they have proved themselves. My teaching evaluations have always been good, and you know I wouldn't offer a course that traded a grade for popularity. You're the principal. All I'm asking is that you put the course on the schedule and see if it makes it."

Morris responded, "I can't unilaterally put your course on the schedule."

"Of course you can," interrupted Dotson. "You're the principal."

"Of course I have the power to do it, but that's not the point. I don't schedule courses without the recommendation of the faculty."

Dotson continued the conversation aggressively, "If we go to the faculty on this issue, we're just going to have a lot of trouble. I've been reluctant to say it, but I think Sam is discriminating against me. And he may have something against Latinos. You know, we have a substantial number of Hispanic students who would like to study the literature of their native culture."

"I have known Sam Peterson a long time," said Morris stiffly, "and no one has ever accused him of discrimination or favoritism."

"Well," Dotson said hotly, "everybody else has gotten his elective, but when I come along and ask, suddenly there's a problem." With that, she stalked out of his office.

Discussing the Case

- What decision-making model would you use for this case?
- Is this a personal or a professional problem? Does it make a difference?
- Which model seems most appropriate here? Satisficing? Mixed scanning? Incremental?
- What obligations does the principal have to the chair? To the teacher?
- Is this case about sexism? Racism? How can the principal find out?
- Use the appropriate decision-making model(s) and develop a strategy for action.

CASE 5.8

Sour Notes[3]

The phone rings again. When you pick it up, you hear the voice of a school-board member on the other end.

"Hey, what's going on with the choir schedule? We've had an all boys choir and an all girls choir at your middle school for four years, but I'm getting calls from some irate parents telling me that you've changed all that. They say that the choir director said you are forcing her to do this against her will, and that a mixed-sex choir will hurt their children's vocal and social development. They're demanding that you restore the format we've had for the past few years. What's up?"

It is early Monday morning in this district of 10,000 students, and you've already had six phone calls and eleven E-mail messages from parents about the choir. With this call, you know that the board is now involved. You take a breath and gather your thoughts as you prepare to explain the situation to the board member.

The choir program in the middle school where you serve as principal has an excellent reputation. When the present choir director was hired four years ago, she said she felt mixed-sex choirs at middle school were detrimental to student vocal development and willingness to participate, particularly in regard to boys. You acceded to her wish to have same-sex choirs, and scheduled accordingly. Choir enrollment soared, and now approximately one-third of the school's 750 students are involved. Same-sex scheduling may or may not have contributed to that growth, but surely the choir director did.

Gender-specific classes were not new in your building. Physical education classes had been gender specific for forty years before you joined the district, and, because the parents were generally happy with that, you had continued the practice during your twelve years as principal. But, as this school year began, one of the central office administrators told you that your gender-segregated physical education classes seem to be in violation of Title IX. It was clear that central office expected changes to be made. After scrutinizing the schedules, you determined that the least disruptive way to mix boys and girls in phys ed was by changing the choir schedule. You spoke with the principals of the other two middle schools in the district to confirm that their choirs were mixed gender. Because school had been underway only a few days, you felt the changes could be made painlessly for the students. You met with the physical education teachers and the choir director to inform them of the coming change and the reason for it. The phys ed teachers were unconcerned and left your office quickly. The choir director, on the other hand, was incensed.

"How can you do this to my program? Haven't you seen all the good that has come from these same-sex choirs? Everybody knows that same-sex education is better for adolescents. Don't you care that you are hurting these children?"

Insisting that she would fight this change, she stormed from your office. Nonetheless, you proceeded to make the changes in student schedules.

That was last Wednesday. On Thursday, the choir director met with the teachers' union representative. The union rep counseled the teacher to accept the changes gracefully and work with the newly mixed choirs. Thursday night was Open House for parents. The choir director gathered her students' parents together and told them that the administration was forcing her to mix the choirs, even though all the latest research showed that their children's development would be irrevocably damaged. She went on to say that Title IX was supposed to be the reason for the change, even though, in her opinion, Title IX had nothing whatsoever to do with her choirs. She ended her comments by exhorting them to go to both the board and to the principal and get this horrendous decision reversed. By the weekend, the parents were mobilized.

You have asked the choir director to report to your office during her planning period. As yet, you have not determined a course of action, but feel strongly that you must address this situation with her as well as with the parents.

As you look at your watch, you realize that you have an hour to prepare for your meeting with the choir director. You resolve to plan a strategy that will ameliorate this difficulty.

Discussing the Case

- What decision-making model would you use for this case?
- Is this simply an insubordinate teacher?
- How can you convince this teacher to acquiesce to the wishes of the board?
- How much room is there for compromise?
- Should others be involved in this decision? The music department?
- Are you open-minded enough to be convinced that your decision is wrong?
- Should you get another legal opinion on Title IX?
- Should you get the irate parents involved? How? Why?
- Develop a strategy and set of talking points for your meeting with the choir director.

CASE 5.9

Zero Tolerance Policy: The Eagle Scout[4]

You are the principal of Martin Luther King High School (MLKHS), a high school in a northeastern urban city. You have come up the ranks beginning as a middle school teacher and then moving to the senior high where you were a teacher and vice-principal for six years before you were promoted just three years ago. You got the job in large part because of your ability to get along with students, parents, and teachers, and your reputation as a hard-charging but fair administrator who was dedicated to the improvement of instruction.

Your first three years as principal have not been easy ones. Your curriculum and instructional initiatives were not without some battles with parents and teachers, but in the end most were satisfied with the changes. You are happy with your progress, yet there remains the myriad problems associated with most urban high schools—absenteeism, drugs, violence, racial tension, single-parent families, and on and on. Your superintendent and board have been very supportive of you and the high school; in fact, you are gaining a solid reputation as a reflective principal who cares about students.

Notwithstanding its confidence in you, the board has developed a "Zero Tolerance Policy" on a number of issues including drugs and violence. Most recently the board passed a policy that stated: "Students found in the possession of weapons of any type, cell phones, and any other articles that pose a potential threat to the safety of the school face automatic suspension and an expulsion hearing." The get-tough policy gave you the leverage you needed to deal with even the roughest and most recalcitrant students. As you sit in your office, you are feeling good about your school, its progress, and your relations with students, teachers, and parents. Your reverie is interrupted by the phone and the secretary who tells you that she has just received an anonymous tip that an automobile in the school parking lot contains a weapon. Your secretary continues with a description of the car, but adds that she thinks the whole thing is simply a student prank.

As you consider the situation, you decide that there is no sense taking any chances. Ever since Columbine, you and your staff have been hypervigilant. You resolve that this is no time to let down your guard. Classes have already begun and you ask the vice-principal and security guard to check the student parking lot for the car in question. A half hour later they return, having identified two cars matching the description—one is a faculty member's car. After checking the license plate number, the other car is identified as the automobile of Brian Agnew.

You know Brian. He is the kind of young man that most parents would like to have. He's a member of the National Honor Society, plays the trumpet in the school band, and is president of a group called Warriors for Christ. Indeed, his father is a leader of the African American community and pastor of the local Baptist Church. Brian is an Eagle Scout, the highest rank in scouting, in the troop sponsored by his father's church. To be an Eagle Scout an individual must prove himself as a leader, show unquestionable commitment to service, and be of high moral character. Eagle Scouts who enter the military service automatically get extra recognition of their achievements and skills.

You scoff at the idea that Brian has dangerous weapons in the trunk of his car and are ready to forget the whole affair, but your vice-principal is adamant that you need to check it out. Brian is called to the office, and you and the vice-principal accompany Brian to his car and ask him to open the trunk, which he does without hesitation, although he is curious about what is going on. You inform him that someone is probably pulling a prank that needs to be checked out.

Imagine your surprise and chagrin when Brain unlocks the trunk and you find his Boy Scout equipment: a cell phone for emergencies, an axe that he used the night before to teach about Scout safety, and his scouting pocketknife. Possession of any one of the three items could be construed as an automatic suspension from school according to school policy.

Discussing the Case

- What decision-making model would you use for this case?
- What do you do? Should you check out the teacher's car also?
- What is "Zero Tolerance" Policy? Is this really a zero tolerance situation?
- Is zero tolerance policy too rigid?
- What is your short-term strategy?
- What is your long-term strategy?

CASE 5.10

The Slap

Martha Hildebrand was a seventeen-year veteran home economics teacher, who honed her teaching skills to an enviable level; not surprisingly she was highly regarded by her colleagues and students at Monroe High School. Marshall Johnson was that professional school administrator who found harmony in the operations of the school and yet developed open and friendly relationships with the faculty and staff.

Johnson was sitting at his desk one Wednesday during the last period of the school day with his door shut working on a district report due at the end of the week, when his door burst open and Martha Hildebrand rushed in—"I need to talk!" she exclaimed without her customary aplomb. "I need help," she gasped.

"Sit down. Calm down," said Johnson. "What's going on?"

"I was in the lab working with my students when Jesse Slocum, the class clown, started to act up. I asked him three or four times to turn around and sit down. I just got so frustrated that out of the blue I slapped him on the back of the head. Not hard. But it embarrassed him, and he just got up and ran out of the class. It happened only five minutes ago. I can't find him; I am worried about him. I am in a panic. What's going to happen to me? I have never laid a hand on a student in all my years of teaching. Am I going to be fired?"

"Just calm down and go back and finish teaching your classes. Let me do a little looking around and see if I can find Jesse. I will get back to you before the day's end. When your class is over, come on back," said Principal Johnson.

After Martha left, Principal Johnson called in his vice-principal and asked him to get information on Jesse Slocum, whom he did not know.

The vice-principal did know him and filled him in quickly. Jesse was not a bad kid, but he was rambunctious and something of the class clown; he pushed the rules to the limit.

No sooner had he finished talking with his vice-principal and less than ten minutes after Martha went back to class, Johnson's secretary informed him that Mr. Slocum, the boy's father, was on the phone.

Slocum's father yelled, "What the hell is going on at that school? My son just called and said that a teacher slapped him on the head without any provocation."

Principal Johnson asked, "Did your son get hurt?"

"That's not the point," responded the father.

Johnson asked, "Where is your son?"

"He is in school where he should be. He called me on his cell phone two minutes ago. I am going to have this teacher's job. No teacher can be permitted to treat students this way."

"Look, you only have one side of the story, and I need to talk to both your son and the teacher."

The father said, "I will call him on his cell phone and tell him to come and see you, but the teacher ought to be fired. I want to talk to you face-to-face, but I can't come right now because I am at work. I will be there with my son tomorrow morning first thing."

"I'll see you then," said Principal Johnson as the last bell of the day sounded. School was over.

Martha Hildebrand arrived back at the principal's office almost immediately after the bell. She was still visibly shaken and distraught. "Am I going to lose my job?" she asked.

"Calm down," said Johnson. "Everyone makes mistakes."

Hildebrand sat down and began to collect herself. The principal got up from his desk and walked around to where she was sitting. "Martha, slap me the way you slapped Slocum."

She slowly got up and stood behind Johnson and gave him a light brush with the back of her hand.

Johnson said, "I can't tell you that something bad is not going to happen. But I can tell you that I would never support your dismissal based on this incident."

A little relieved, Martha Hildebrand sat back down and sighed.

As Johnson looked at Hildebrand, he was truly sorry to see her in this situation because there was no question that Martha Hildebrand was a conscientious teacher who liked kids and treated them all with respect and they liked her.

"We have a meeting tomorrow morning at 7:30 with the parents. Now go home and don't worry. I will be here with you. The least we're going to get away with is an apology to the father and son."

To which Martha responded, "I have no problem with an apology. I made a mistake. I brought this on myself."

After Hildebrand departed, Principal Johnson began to think about what was going to transpire at 7:30 tomorrow morning. He would have to defuse the situation, calm down the parents, and work toward satisfying them with an apology. Martha did make a mistake and she was willing to apologize. Martha did not hurt the student; she simply embarrassed him. Seventeen-year-old Jesse was at least a foot taller and sixty pounds heavier than the teacher. On the other hand, the father was angry and that would have to be dealt with. Finally, teachers should not hit students.

In the meeting the next morning, will the father be calm enough to accept a heartfelt apology from the teacher, Martha Hildebrand?

Discussing the Case

- If the apology is not sufficient, then what?
- What should the principal's position be?
- What are the principal's goals in the conference?
- What are the elements of a good solution for everyone? Is that possible? If not, why not?
- If such a solution is possible, what is your plan to achieve it?
- Should Martha Hildebrand be punished? If so, how?
- How can the principal prevent this incident from escalating?
- Develop a detailed strategy and plan for the meeting.

CASE 5.11

Low Expectations, Poor Performance

Magnet schools are in all sorts of districts, but a magnet school in a hitherto underserved area of a large urban setting is extremely welcome. Parents line up around the school to get their children admitted to Magnet School 1881. While the school's name doesn't inspire awe, a tour of the building does. In the midst of high density and poor housing, this brand-new elementary school rises five stories. The interior of the building is spotless and inviting. The corridors are lined in tile, and examples of student work decorate the walls. There are no graffiti in PS 1881 and the students want to keep it that way; they are proud of their school.

Because it is new construction, PS 1881 has civilities unknown in other district schools. There are several elevators that students may use. Hallways and stairways are well-lit and easy to navigate. There are no dark and forbidding recesses about the building. The classrooms are often a stark contrast to the unlit and crowded housing that the students know only too well.

These students are fortunate to be in 1881. Many of them are recent immigrants from a variety of cultures. A few have even come from cultures that do not have the concept of school as a place set aside where adults and children engage in formal education. They come from cultures in which education was a day-to-day socialization into the ways of the tribe.

Most students are selected for PS 1881 by lottery. A few more enter on a first-come, first-served registration basis. Once a year, for one day, parents in the area are permitted to register their children for school. Registration begins at 8:30 A.M., but parents begin lining up the night before to insure a place in the school. The first 200 parents who register are guaranteed admission. The remainder are selected by lottery. The school's enrollment is capped at 800 students. Needless to say, the students want to be at 1881.

The teachers recognize the cultural adjustments that their students must make. About a third of the students have been in the country less than three years, and the majority of these recent immigrants come from Mexico, Bolivia, Honduras, and the Dominican Republic. In fact, three-quarters of the students at 1881 are of Hispanic origin and most of the rest are African American. The faculty finds ways to nurture these students. Many of the students live in one-family apartments that actually house two and three families. Often, the children come to school hungry. Many teachers bring cereal, fruit, and milk to help them start the day. Most students generally get a free lunch; in fact, less than 3 percent do not.

A few years ago, the faculty chipped in and bought a washer and dryer for the school. They keep a "slop chest" of clothes that children can wear while their dirty clothes are being washed. The faculty doesn't provide a complete laundry service, of course, but for some special cases the teachers are ready to help. It would be difficult to think of a more concerned faculty.

In spite of the caring faculty and the selective student body, student achievement is not as good as it should be; indeed, it seems to be dropping, as indicated by the fourth-grade achievement scores. A year ago, about half the students were meeting state standards in mathematics and science. The most recent test data were sharply down; only one-quarter of the students met those standards.

Juan Diaz, the principal at 1881 for the past three years, views the recent drop with alarm. Mr. Diaz is working on his Ph.D. in educational administration at City University. He has discussed the drop in academic performance with some of the faculty and a few of his fellow students. He even did a case study to focus on possible causes for the drop. He is still perplexed. The teaching staff has not changed much and the composition of the student body remains stable. The district has given the school more resources than other schools in the district, so why is the school not performing as well as it might?

Could the test scores be a mistake? Diaz thought this was a possibility, but after talking with state and city officials, he was assured that the problem did not lie with the data. The teachers told him that they thought the students were working as hard as they could. Moreover, the teachers claimed that the new fourth-grade proficiency tests were unreliable.

Regardless of the cause of the sudden decline in scores, Diaz asserts that things must get better and the scores must rise. His teachers, however, are skeptical. They believe the students are doing about as well as they can. After all, the parents really can't spend a lot of time helping their kids at home because of their long hours of work and commuting. Many of these families are hard-pressed economically and struggle to put bread on the table. The teachers feel that the students are under enormous pressure as it is and increasing demands on them will simply make their lives more difficult.

As a first step in trying to understand the dynamics of this school, Mr. Diaz asked his teachers to respond to several survey instruments to gauge the climate of the school. The results were intriguing. The teachers described the principal as supportive, fairly directive, and collegial in his interactions with the teachers, and described their interactions with colleagues in much the same way. Parents were seen as noninterfering with the educational program in PS 1881. In spite of the mandatory participation of parents in school governance, parents defer to the teachers. Teacher morale is high. The faculty like their school, their colleagues, their principal, and their students. In fact, the only downside to the climate analysis is the academic emphasis of the school.

Academic emphasis refers to the school's press for achievement. Teachers expect their students to work hard, to be cooperative, to achieve, and to respect those who excel. In this school, academic emphasis is low. Teachers do not expect their students to do exceptionally well, and, as a consequence, they do not pressure their students for achievement. Rather, they accept the fact that the economic and social circumstances of the students simply make it impossible for the vast majority of them to reach high levels of academic achievement. The community forces clearly disadvantage these poor students. Faculty members often say, "These are good kids, but they can only do so much, and they are doing it."

Juan Diaz is determined to improve his proficiency scores. He does not share his teachers' view that there are too many obstacles to achievement. Diaz believes that he and his teachers have the capability to plan and execute behavior that will improve instructional performance and student achievement. He believes that he and his teachers can overcome the difficulties of the students' environment. He needs to motivate his teachers. He needs to take action, and he needs a plan.

Discussing the Case

- What decision-making model would you use for this case?
- How would you conceptualize the problem?
- What are the crucial facts?
- Do these teachers have a self-defeating attitude?
- Is this a case of a self-fulfilling prophecy?
- What is teacher efficacy? Is it relevant in this case?
- Is this a case for restructuring, for climate building, for improving teacher and student motivation, or for political action on the part of the principal?
- Are there other important measures of effectiveness that should be used to evaluate progress in this school?

CASE 5.12

Kinky Hair

Bob Tancredi gathered his papers together and looked forward to a pleasant meeting with the parent advisory team of Hillside Elementary; he liked this group and they worked well together. This afternoon he was introducing Sal Espinoza as the new assistant principal.

Espinoza was a favorite of the community. He grew up in a neighborhood close to the one served by Hillside. It, too, was large, urban, and a sometimes unsteady mix of African American and Hispanic families. Hillside had the list of ills that describe inner-city schools, but it also had a dash of optimism. Hillside celebrated the close of the twentieth century by retiring its coal-fired heating system and putting in a new oil system.

Today, Tancredi was a bit surprised at the large turnout of parents, about forty as opposed to the usual fifteen or so. As Tancredi called the meeting to order, several parents had their hands up. He called on the first one.

"We are bothered by this talking about Black hair by Ms. Cohen. She has no right to talk about our kids' hair. We want you to stop her."

A second parent yelled out, "No, just get rid of her. Now." And forty parents voiced agreement.

Tancredi exclaimed, "I don't know what you are talking about. Settle down, and one person tell me what's happening."

Mrs. Johnson stood up and said to Tancredi, "My daughter, Taisha, is in Cohen's class and she came home with a book titled *Nappy Hair*.[5] I took a look at it and I was horrified by what I saw. I found the pictures offensive. What kind of hair Black people have is no concern of Ms. Cohen. She should stick to teaching what she knows about. She is not entitled to discuss Black problems because she just can't know what we know. She has no right." Everyone shouted agreement and applauded.

Tancredi responded, "Every book that a teacher uses at Hillside has been approved by the board and the superintendent. I tell the teachers never to use any materials that are not on the approved list unless they have cleared it with me." His statement was met with jeers.

What occurred next was a tirade from at least a dozen of the parents, all objecting, and interspersed with cheers from the audience every time there were calls to get rid of Ms. Cohen and to ban the book. Emotion got the upper hand and the group turned mean. They yelled such racial epithets as "cracker bigot" and "Jewish bitch" as well as threats to Ms. Cohen—"We are gonna get that cracker bitch" and "Fire her ass before we do it."

It was clear to Tancredi that he was rapidly losing control of the meeting, and he couldn't reestablish order. After twenty minutes of people venting hostility and frustration, he called the meeting to an end by promising that he would look into the matter and act. Espinoza followed him out of the room, never having been introduced and visibly taken aback himself.

The parents were not happy, and, even though Tancredi left the room, they continued to complain and yell for at least another half hour.

Discussing the Case

- What decision-making model would you use for this case?
- What should you do first? What is the problem?
- Are the parents correct? Are there some things that white teachers shouldn't talk about to Black children?

- How much discretion should teachers have in what they teach?
- Do parents have a right to dictate the curriculum? Ban books?
- As principal, what would be the short-term strategy? Long-term?

CASE 5.13

The Reluctant Assistant

You have just been hired as the new principal of the Coastal Regional High School located along the seacoast in New Jersey not too far from the Pine Barrens. The school has nearly 1,800 students from across the socioeconomic status (SES) spectrum. The students represent not only the expected variety of a big school but the unexpected tension between such decidedly regional groups as the surfers, who represent the higher SES group, and the piners, who represent the established poor and working class locals. As a result, the culture of the school is bipolar with the dominant extremes occupied by surfers and piners. Nevertheless, the school has a good reputation and most parents are supportive of the administration. All parents want the very best schools for their children.

Two weeks into the new academic year, the principal of Coastal abruptly resigned and headed south to Florida for his retirement. His departing words to the superintendent were "I've had it. The school is yours." A week later he was gone. And one of his assistants, gauging the situation, announced that he would retire at the end of the semester (December 31). The superintendent commandeered the remaining assistant principal to fill in while the board searched for a permanent replacement. Everyone assumed that Victor Beecham would effortlessly become the new principal and that the search would turn into a quest for two new assistant principals, whom Beecham would hire.

Much to the surprise of assistant principal Victor and his faculty, the board of education hired you, an experienced outsider with five years experience as a vice-principal in a suburban high school one hundred miles to the north. The word was out: Victor Beecham was passed over for the principalship, but he would be your assistant. In spite of your misgivings and expressions of them to the board, the superintendent insisted that Victor would be a loyal and helpful assistant. The job was attractive and a promotion, and after the superintendent and board agreed that you could conduct a search for another assistant principal, who would begin next July, you agreed to accept the challenge. The board had wanted to hire another assistant immediately, but you convinced them to let you hire a new assistant principal. With that understanding, you were appointed principal of Coastal High School on January 1.

Before you arrived on the job in January, you met with the superintendent about the delicate situation of an acting principal passed over for someone whom no one knew, namely, you. The superintendent has already changed his tune. He warns you that Victor is upset and resentful. You insist on meeting with Victor as soon as possible to discuss the transition. You arrange to meet Victor in the conference room at school, and as you enter the room, you greet him with a smile and friendly, "Hi."

His response was an apathetic shrug with no eye contact. You decide to plunge ahead, "I need you. I understand how you feel; they picked me instead of you. So, you have some right to feel resentful. But, I didn't do the picking; the board did. Give me a chance. We can work together."

To which Victor said, "If you are finished, I have work to do in the office."

Discussing the Case

- Do you have something to say right now to improve the situation?
- Should you wait and give Victor some breathing space? If so, how long?
- What is your short-term strategy?
- What is your long-term strategy?
- What do you do if Victor really doesn't work out?
- Remember, you really do need Victor. You are one vice-principal short, and Victor knows the lay of the land, and you would like his help.

CASE 5.14

The Set Up[6]

Tim Dixon was in his first year as principal at Oakmont High School, a relatively high-performing urban school of approximately 900 students and forty-two licensed teachers. One of seventeen public high schools in a city school district of 62,000 students, Oakmont attracted students from all over the metropolitan area hoping to participate in one of its highly successful athletic programs and to benefit from the rigorous college prep curriculum for which it was known.

Because it was the newest of the high schools in the schools system, it was only one of two that was handicap accessible and complied fully with the Americans with Disabilities Act. Consequently, the school also housed more than 100 special education students in ten different special education units. The mainstreaming of such a large number of students with special needs into regular education classes created unique dynamics throughout the school among various student subgroups, between special education teachers and regular education teachers, and oftentimes between special needs students and regular education teachers, some of whom were not adequately trained to serve them.

First-year teacher Margaret Huber was assigned to one of the two high incidence resource rooms located in a large "flexible space" classroom divided by a moveable partition. A no-nonsense classroom manager, Ms. Huber was observed on many occasions and in different settings by Principal Dixon as being abrupt, harsh, and inflexible with students, parents, and even colleagues. Repeated conferences and formative strategies seemed to help little in changing Ms. Huber's temperament. She simply was a difficult personality who seemed unwilling to change.

Many of Ms. Huber's students were street-tough, growing up amidst difficult circumstances of violence, crime, and substance abuse. One such student was Angie Cleveland. Although Angie was in her third year of high school, she had earned only four credits toward graduation. Raised in a single-parent home, Angie entered the juvenile justice system at age thirteen and over the next few years amassed a long list of offenses including theft, breaking and entering, delinquency, and felonious assault. During the previous school year, Angie faced multiple disciplinary actions, including an expulsion from Oakmont for allegedly assaulting her teacher.

Returning to Oakmont the following year, Angie was scheduled in Ms. Huber's resource room for math and science as specified in her Individualized Education Plan (IEP). However, the promise of a new school year and new teacher failed to yield the fresh start Angie's mom had hoped for. A growing number of discipline referrals from Ms. Huber citing insubordination, classroom disruption, and disrespect toward other students and staff landed Angie in detention and in-school suspension. A fight resulted in an out-of-school suspension and assault charges being filed against her.

Tensions between Angie and Ms. Huber slowly and steadily escalated until one morning when Ms. Huber reported to the assistant principal that Angie had threatened her and that the teacher no longer felt safe with Angie in her classroom. The district's "zero tolerance" policy on threats to staff and students called for the student's immediate removal and subsequent hearing at the expulsion office. Ms. Huber alleged that Angie told her, "get the f--- out of my face or I am going to have my people come up here and beat your ass!" Angie maintains that Ms. Huber called her "stupid" and chided that she would "never amount to anything other than a felon." The student was no stranger to trouble. She feared little and forthrightly confessed without remorse to Dr. Dixon for each of her previous code-of-conduct violations, but she vehemently denied threatening Ms. Huber. No other students or staff witnessed the altercation, and the situation before the principal was truly the word of the staff member versus the word of the student.

At the mandatory expulsion hearing, Angie was placed on forty-five days of home instruction during which a tutor came to her house to assist her with her schoolwork for at least one hour per day. Following her expulsion, Angie was to return to Oakmont High School to resume her educational program as written in her IEP. Furious with the prospect of Angie returning to her classroom, Ms. Huber pressed the issue through the teachers' union filing a grievance against the district and building administrators. She also exhibited her displeasure through the juvenile court system. She persuaded the police department to file menacing charges against the student and lobbied a magistrate for a restraining order prohibiting Angie from coming within 100 feet of the teacher.

Discussing the Case

- What if Angie was right and the teacher made up the story just to get her out of her classroom?
- Could Angie be right? Was she being set up by Ms. Huber?
- Does Ms. Huber have a genuine fear for her safety?
- Is it the school's role to keep them apart?
- What is the appropriate role of the principal in this case?
- What if Angie returns to Ms. Huber's classroom and is baited into a conflict that results in injury?
- What options does the principal have to modify an individual student's IEP to preserve the educational climate of the school?
- Does the student's right to a free public education supersede the teacher's contracted rights to a safe work environment?
- Are there options to accommodate the needs of both the student and teacher?
- The forty-five days will soon be up. Assume the role of principal and develop a plan of action.

CASE 5.15

Dropped for a Loss[7]

"You could plant potatoes in that frown!" was what Grandma Andreoni used to say, Principal Jim Clark recollected, as he wilted into his less-than-favorite office chair and gazed out at Skip Tucker Memorial Stadium. Grandma had gotten it right and his expression showed it. Clark heaved a heavy sigh, took a long draw from his coffee cup, and wondered how such a good thing could have "gone south" so quickly.

Just two years ago, Jim Clark felt like the world was his oyster. An opportunity to become the principal of Hansbrough High School came out of nowhere when Superintendent Dwight Strasburg, his longtime friend and mentor, encouraged him to apply for the high school principalship. After a series of interviews with various school constituencies, Clark was hired. The first several years had gone better than expected; he had earned the respect of students, faculty, and the community. A romantic encounter between a star athlete and another high school student, however, had complicated the administrative landscape.

Edgewater, Florida, had seemed like the ideal spot for Principal Clark when he moved his family there seven years ago. A growing town of 85,000, Edgewater was undergoing rapid change. Several new businesses had surfaced due to the area's temperate climate, cheap labor, and enticing tax abatements. Most notable among the new businesses were a large auto manufacturing plant and a semiconductor research and development facility. This mix of blue- and white-collar jobs had brought in outsiders to Edgewater and enriched the diversity of the community but at the price of conflicting values and expectations. But if there was one thing that united this unsteady mix, it was the local football team. And my, what a ride they had been on this year.

The Hansbrough Hurricanes had only been a Division I football team for two years, but this year they were unstoppable. With eighteen seniors in starting positions and an electrifying junior running back, this was the year that the Hurricanes would win the state championship. And they were now only one game away. Principal Clark, a former athlete, had always enjoyed the camaraderie of the team and its dedication to excellence in performance. On the team, it didn't matter that the nose guard was Anglo, the quarterback was Hispanic, and the star running back was African American. The only colors that mattered were crimson and cream, the team colors. It wasn't just the football team that had the school colors running through its veins. Judging by the signs gracing storefronts and car windows, just about everyone in Edgewater had been swept away by Hurricane fever.

Maybe DeShawn Franklin, the star running back, had begun to feel like the invincible hero who was above the rules. Or maybe he was just a regular kid who hadn't really done anything wrong at all, but was caught in a web of innuendo and assumption. In any event, DeShawn was in trouble and Clark was cast into the roles of judge and jury. The initial principals of the case were DeShawn, Ashley Vasquez, and her father, Rene, who was the assistant principal at Hansbrough, but the plot was beginning to cascade out of control.

Rene Vasquez was a good assistant principal, and a better friend; in fact, Rene was the first person that Clark had hired after being appointed principal. He had proved to be a loyal and valued colleague whose steady judgment smoothed out many administrative problems. On Friday night after the game Vasquez had cornered Principal Clark and was fuming, "That punk really crossed the line. There's no way that kid is going to get away with taking advantage of my daughter. I caught him dead to rights . . . on school property to boot. And to top it all off, he took a shot at me! I'm suspending him, Jim, you've got to back me on this one." Principal Clark had never seen his assistant so enraged, but he managed to calm him down a little. "OK," he told Vasquez, "we will take care of this first thing on Monday. Just calm down and don't cause a scene."

By Monday morning things had escalated. Rumors in the community were rampant. Moreover, DeShawn Franklin's version of the events of Friday night was quite different. Franklin openly admitted to Principal Clark that he and Ashley had been doing a little more than kissing. But when pressed, he had flippantly replied, "So what? She was cool with it." According to DeShawn, Mr. Vasquez had discovered them under the bleachers after the game making out and he "flipped out and started dissin Ashley, getting all up in her face, and pushing her around." DeShawn claimed he stepped between them and accidentally bumped the principal as he was trying to separate father and daughter. DeShawn ended up on the ground with a pounding, headache and a bloody lip. He explained his injuries to his parent by saying, "It was a tough game and we won. That is all that matters." His father was proud.

It was only 9:00 A.M. when Clark's secretary interrupted his reflection. She informed Clark that Misty Duchamps, the sports director of WXOX-TV, was waiting outside and would like to talk to him about the assault Friday night after the game. Clark was on the hot seat. Misty wanted the facts before she aired her five o'clock sports program. The Hurricanes were on their way to a state championship and nothing could stop them unless their star was dropped for unnecessary roughness.

Discussing the Case

- What are the crucial facts of the case? Who are the major players?
- What decision-making model is most appropriate for this case?
- What is the potential role of politics in this case?
- What are the priorities? What must be done immediately? What can wait?
- What are the consequences if the principal ignores political pressure? Acquiesces to political pressure?
- Develop a strategy to deal with this problem if you were the principal.

ENDNOTES

1. We are indebted to Professor Megan Tschannen-Moran of the College of William and Mary for her idea of the SMART case brief, which we think is a useful tool of analysis.
2. "Discord and Disharmony" was written for this text by Nancy Nestor-Baker at the University of Cincinnati, and is used by permission.
3. "Sour Notes" was written for this text by Nancy Nestor-Baker at the University of Cincinnati, and is used by permission.
4. "Zero Tolerance" was written for this text by Michael DiPaola at the College of William and Mary, and is used by permission.
5. The book, written by a Black Writer, Carolivia Herron, is a coming-of-age story about a Black girl who is ridiculed about her kinky hair.
6. "The Set Up" was written for this text by Thomas Reed at Ohio State University, and is used by permission.
7. "Dropped for a Loss" was written for this text by Sean Kearney and Page Smith at the University of Texas, San Antonio, and is used by permission.

CHAPTER SIX

SHARED DECISION MAKING
A Comprehensive Model

Shared decision making has taken on added importance as reformers advocate teacher involvement in decision making. Always involving subordinates is as short-sighted as never involving them. Participation in decision making can improve the quality of decisions and promote cooperation if the right strategy is linked to the right situation. That is, the decision to utilize subordinate involvement is best made using a contingency model.

There is ample evidence of the desirability of involving subordinates in decision making in business as well as in educational organizations (Allutto & Belasco, 1973; Heller, Pusic, Strauss, & Bernhard, 1998; Hoy, Newland, & Blazovsky, 1977; Mohrman, Cooke, & Mohrman, 1978; Moon, 1983). The effects of teacher participation in decision making, however, are neither simple nor clear cut (Aditya, House, & Kerr, 2000; Bachrach, Bamberger, Conley, & Bauer, 1990; Conley, 1990; Conway, 1984; Imber & Duke, 1984; Vroom & Jago, 1988).

Popular exercises in administrative and teacher training include the NASA Moon Problem, the Desert Survival Problem, and Lost at Sea. These games require players to rank the importance of various items needed to cope with challenging environments. Individual and group rankings are compared to each other and to expert rankings (Lafferty & Eady, 1974). Typically, groups outperform individuals, a finding that may be interpreted to demonstrate the superiority of group decision making; however, Vroom and Jago (1988) suggest a more appropriate interpretation is that *under some circumstances* groups outperform some individuals. It is just as wrong to conclude that autocratic decisions will always be inferior as to believe that they will always be superior.

There are times when participation improves the quality of the decision, as well as times when participation impedes effective decision making (Brickley, Smith, & Zimmerman, 2001; Vazquez, 2004). The critical question is: Under what conditions should subordinates be involved in decision making? Two models of shared decision making are useful in addressing this question: one based on a comprehensive set of decision rules (Vroom & Yetton, 1973) and the other on a simple set of three criteria—expertise, relevance, and trust in subordinates. Both models are designed to enhance the acceptance and quality of decisions (Bridges, 1967; Hoy & Miskel, 2001; Hoy & Tarter, 1992, 1993a, 1993b; Tschannel-Moran, 2001).

Thus, there are two primary reasons to involve others in decision making—to lower the resistance to decisions and to improve the quality of decisions.

MANAGING PARTICIPATION: ENHANCING QUALITY AND ACCEPTANCE

Victor Vroom and Phillip Yetton (1973) proposed a model of shared decision making that develops two sets of rules from the extant empirical evidence. Clearly, it is the best-known model of management of participation in organizations; in fact, after reviewing research evidence on normative leadership theories, Miner (1984, 1988) concludes that no leadership theory surpasses the Vroom-Yetton model in either its validity or usefulness. In its latest version, Vroom and Jago (1988) identify a set of problem properties that should influence subordinate participation in decision making in a variety of situations. These properties are defined by a set of decision rules and their operational questions.

The essence of this model is a contingency approach that matches participation in decision making with the nature of the problem and situation. Four rules enhance the quality of decisions.

1. *The Quality Rule (Quality Requirement).* Only use a unilateral approach (a) if the quality requirement is low and the matter unimportant to subordinates, or (b) if the quality requirement is low, the decision is important, and it will be readily accepted by subordinates.

> *Operational Questions:* How important is the quality requirement of the decision? Does the decision have a strong technical component, or is the situation relatively trivial? What is difference for the organization of a wise decision compared to an unwise one?

2. *The Leader Information Rule (Leader Information).* Do not make a unilateral decision when the quality of the decision is important and you do not possess sufficient information and expertise to solve the problem alone. To do otherwise risks a low-quality decision.

> *Operational Questions:* Does the leader have sufficient information to make a high-quality decision? Does the leader have the necessary expertise to solve the problem without subordinates?

3. *The Trust Rule (Goal Congruence).* Make a unilateral decision when the quality of the decision is important and you cannot trust subordinates to decide on the basis of the organizational goals. A lack of control over the decision may jeopardize its quality.

> *Operational Questions:* Do subordinates share organizational goals; that is, can they be trusted to make decisions in the best interests of the organization? Are solutions preferred by subordinates likely to violate organizational interests?

4. *The Unstructured Problem Rule (Problem Structure).* Involve knowledgeable subordinates to collect relevant information when the quality of the decision is important, the problem is unstructured, and you lack sufficient information or expertise.

> *Operational Questions:* Does the problem have a well-defined goal and set of alternatives? Does the problem have a standard set of solutions?

Four rules enhance the acceptance of decisions:

1. *The Acceptance Rule (Acceptance Probability).* Involve subordinates when their acceptance of the decision is critical for effective implementation and when you are unsure of their acceptance of an autocratic decision. Denying their participation in decision making risks acceptance.

> *Operational Questions:* Is it likely that an autocratic decision will be accepted by subordinates? How likely is it that the superior will be able to sell his or her solution to subordinates?

2. *The Conflict Rule (Subordinate Conflict).* Involve subordinates when there is conflict, acceptance of the decision is critical, and an autocratic decision is unlikely to be accepted. Structure the situation and provide information so that subordinates can resolve their differences. Subordinate conflict differs from goal congruence as means differ from ends. Subordinates can share goals with the organization, but disagree among themselves over the means to achieve the ends.

> *Operational Questions:* Is conflict likely among subordinates over preferred solutions? Is the decision problem controversial?

3. *The Commitment Rule (Subordinate Commitment).* A group decision should be made even when the quality of the decision is not important, but its acceptance is critical and problematic. A group decision will likely generate more acceptance and commitment than a hierarchical one.

> *Operational Questions:* How important is subordinate commitment to the solution of the problem? How important is the willingness of subordinates to make the decision successful?

4. *The Subordinate Information Rule (Subordinate Information).* Subordinates should not be called on to make a decision for which they have insufficient information or expertise.

> *Operational Question:* Do subordinates have the necessary expertise to solve the problem?

In addition to these eight rules, there are a number of constraints on the process. We consider two constraints, minimizing the time to make the decision and maximizing the opportunities for subordinate development. These two constraints are formulated as two additional rules:

1. *The Time Rule (Motivation–Time).* Time is not free. The amount of time used in making a decision is a cost expressed in terms of the loss of attention to other activities.

   Operational Questions: How important is the press of time on the decision? How important is the cost of time for making decisions?

2. *The Development Rule (Motivation–Development).* Decision making is a learned skill developed through practice. To empower teachers means to give them the skills and opportunities to make important decisions.

   Operational Questions: How important is the broadening of your subordinates' skills and cooperation in problem solving? How important is the opportunity for growth and development?

DECISION-MAKING STYLES

Vroom and Yetton (1973) make a distinction between individual problems and group problems. An individual problem is one that has the potential to affect one and only one person. A group problem, by contrast, has effects on more than one individual. We begin our discussion of decision processes by examining five alternative decision styles that are applicable to group decision. The styles are modified from Vroom and Yetton (1973) and arrayed along the following continuum from autocratic to group participation:

- *Autocratic (A):* Solve the problem unilaterally using the available information.
- *Informed-autocratic (IA):* Solve the problem unilaterally after obtaining necessary information from subordinates. Subordinates may or may not be told the purpose of your questions, but they do not play a role in either defining the problem or generating or evaluating alternative solutions.
- *Individual-consultative (IC):* Share the problem with subordinates, soliciting their ideas individually without forming a group. Then make the decision, which may or may not reflect the influence of subordinates.
- *Group-consultative (GC):* Share the problem with the group and solicit their ideas and suggestions. Then make the decision, which may or may not reflect the influence of subordinates.
- *Group-agreement (GA):* Share the problem with subordinates as a group. Together generate and evaluate alternatives in an attempt to reach consensus. Act as the chair of the group, but do not press the group to accept your solution. You are willing to accept and implement any group decision.

We can illustrate each of these five decision styles with an example. Suppose you are the principal of a large high school. The problem is to develop a plan to provide a new instructional program in AIDS prevention as instructed by the superintendent and the board of education. In the *autocratic* style, you simply formulate a plan based on available knowledge. You might, for example, schedule the instruction as a three-week unit in the existing health and physical education program. On the other hand, you might solicit information from the health teachers about the difficulties of implementing such a plan before issuing any directive—an *informed autocratic* style.

Upon reflection, you might decide on a consultative strategy. In the *individual-consultative* style, you would check with a key individual or two, soliciting their ideas and suggestions individually before deciding. Or you might bring a group of health teachers together for the same purpose—a *group-consultative* style.

Finally, if *group agreement* were sufficiently important, you would share the problem with subordinates as a group, seek their views, have them generate and evaluate alternatives, and then make a democratic decision. You act as the moderator of the group—accepting, supporting, and implementing group decisions.

DECISION-MAKING TREES

Decision effectiveness depends on the quality, acceptance, and timeliness of a decision (Vroom & Jago, 1988). The key to maximizing effectiveness in a decision is to match the appropriate decision style with the decision rules. The answers to the rules define situations that call for one of the five decision styles. There is no simple way to use the model, and even though there are only ten rules, the analysis can be intimidating.

The use of decision trees is helpful in this regard. A decision tree is a graph that traces the possible decisions that arise when one follows decision rules. Four decision trees grow out of the Vroom-Yetton model; two are for group decision making—one for development (Figure 6.1) and the other under the pressure of time (Figure 6.2). Likewise, there are two trees for individual decision making—one for development (Figure 6.3) and the other under pressure of time (Figure 6.4). Figure 6.1 is a decision tree in which we have illustrated the appropriate paths for each decision style under the constraint of maximizing teacher development. Eight decision rules are used to plot differences among the decision-making situations. Take a few moments to study Figure 6.1. The decision tree is given for group decision making. The rules have been stated as questions. First is the technical requirement question; it has two branches, high or low, and each branch leads to the next question (How important is subordinate commitment?), which in turn defines two new branches, and so on. The branches of the decision tree eventually lead to the appropriate decision-making style.

When is an autocratic decision appropriate? According to the model in Figure 6.1, if the technical quality requirement is low and the issue is unimportant to subordinates, an autocratic decision is desirable. Or if the technical quality is low, but the issue is important to subordinates, then use an autocratic approach only if it is likely that subordinates will accept an autocratic decision. The decision

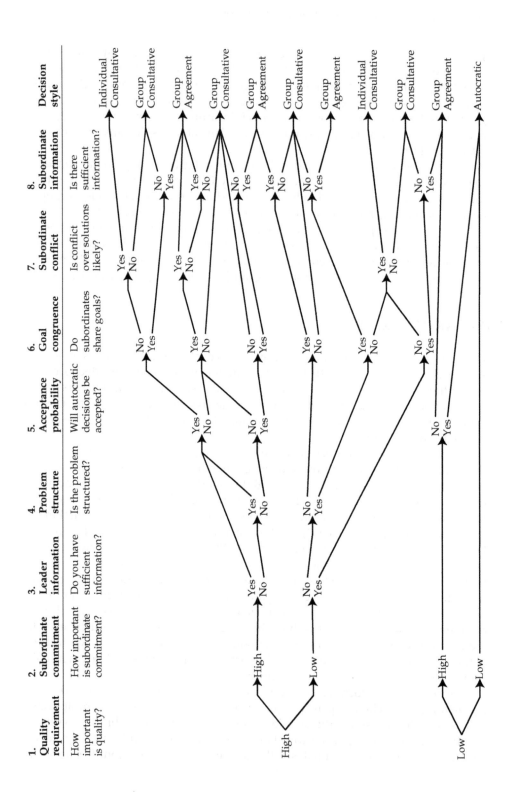

Decision-Making Styles for Group Problems

Autocratic (A)   Solve the problem unilaterally using the available information.

Informed-autocratic (IA)   Solve the problem unilaterally after obtaining necessary information from subordinates. They may or may not be told the purpose of your questions, but they do not play a role in either defining the problem or generating or evaluating alternative solutions.

Individual-consultative (IC)   Share the problem with subordinates, soliciting their ideas individually without forming a group. Then make the decision, which may or may not reflect the influence of subordinates.

Group-consultative (GC)   Share the problem with the group and solicit their ideas and suggestions. Then make the decision, which may or may not reflect the influence of subordinates.

Group-agreement (GA)   Share the problem with subordinates as a group. Together generate and evaluate alternatives in an attempt to reach consensus. Act as the chair of the group, but do not press the group to accept your solution. You are willing to accept and implement any group decision.

FIGURE 6.1 Decision Tree for Group Decision Making for Development

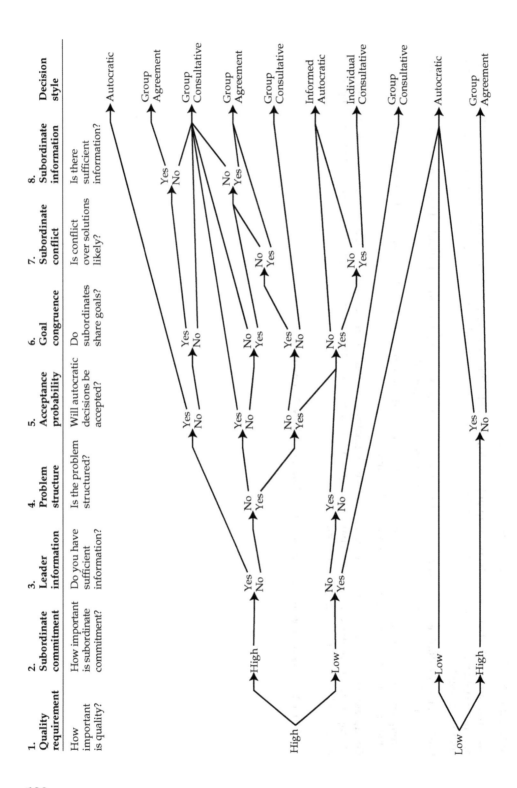

Decision-Making Styles for Group Problems

Autocratic (A)   Solve the problem unilaterally using the available information.

Informed-autocratic (IA)   Solve the problem unilaterally after obtaining necessary information from subordinates. They may or may not be told the purpose of your questions, but they do not play a role in either defining the problem or generating or evaluating alternative solutions.

Individual-consultative (IC)   Share the problem with subordinates, soliciting their ideas individually without forming a group. Then make the decision, which may or may not reflect the influence of subordinates.

Group-consultative (GC)   Share the problem with the group and solicit their ideas and suggestions. Then make the decision, which may or may not reflect the influence of subordinates.

Group-agreement (GA)   Share the problem with subordinates as a group. Together generate and evaluate alternatives in an attempt to reach consensus. Act as the chair of the group, but do not press the group to accept your solution. You are willing to accept and implement any group decision.

FIGURE 6.2 Decision Tree for Group Decision Making under Time Pressure

129

style and the problem properties are combined through a series of complex equations (Vroom & Jago, 1988; Vroom & Yetton, 1973), which are beyond the scope of our current presentation. The decision tree in Figure 6.1, however, is one solution to those equations.

A good exercise to familiarize yourself with the model is to choose one of the five decision styles and walk through the decision tree. For example, when is it appropriate to use an *individual-consultative* style, (that is, share the problem with subordinates, soliciting their ideas individually without forming a group, and then make the decision, which may or may not reflect the influence of subordinates)? There are four paths:

- **First:** *a high-quality requirement*, high subordinate commitment, sufficient leader information, high probability of acceptance; *subordinates do not share goals, and conflict is high.*
- **Second:** *a high-quality requirement*, high subordinate commitment, insufficient leader information, a structured problem, high probability of acceptance; *subordinates do not share goals, and conflict is high.*
- **Third:** *a high-quality requirement*, low subordinate commitment, insufficient leader information, structured problem; *subordinates do not share goals, and conflict is high.*
- **Fourth:** *a high-quality requirement*, low subordinate commitment, sufficient leader information; *subordinates do not share goals, and conflict is high.*

In brief, an *individual-consultative* style is called for when a high-quality decision is required, subordinates do not share goals, and conflict is high.

There is no question that the model is complex, but so, too, is decision making. It may not seem so at first blush, but the model actually simplifies the process. The research suggests that the questions proposed by Vroom and his colleagues are critical ones that influence the effectiveness of leadership and decision making. In the model pictured in Figure 6.1, there are thirty-two appropriate paths to the five decision styles, but that number pales by comparison to the myriad of paths that are possible using all eight criteria.

To illustrate the model, we begin with an actual administrative problem for a principal to solve.

CASE 6.1

The Curriculum Dilemma: A Group Problem

Your school's social studies department is highly regarded for its innovative approach to teaching.[1] The program is oriented toward inquiry as a process, rather than the retention of historical fact. Typically, curriculum is made by the department as different concepts are developed. The teachers are enthusiastic about their program, and it is well received by the students. You respect all the members of the department and see it as one of the strongest departments in the school. You do not always agree with the direction of the curriculum, but there is little question that this is a highly skilled and professional group of teachers whom you respect.

Recent reform in the state has argued for back-to-basics and the use of curricular materials that stress recall of specific persons, places, and events in state and national history. The reform is supported by a battery of state tests, which have been used to compare the effectiveness of schools across the state. Although the state maintained that no invidious comparisons would be made, your community has made them. The superintendent has his feet to the fire on this issue, and now you are feeling the heat. Recent test scores show that your students are not doing nearly as well in history as they are in science and mathematics. The superintendent has "requested" that you integrate the state curricular materials into the history program to correct the current deficiencies. Your history faculty, on the other hand, claim that this is exactly the wrong tack to take to develop inquiring minds. They are not overly concerned with the students' performance on the state tests because they claim the tests measure the wrong thing. There is strong pressure in the community, however, to do well on all tests. Parents cannot understand why their children are not doing as well in history as they are in math and science; in fact, at the last board meeting the superintendent promised under pressure that the scores would rise.

There is no question that you as principal must help realign the history curriculum. You are troubled by the current state of affairs, but decisions must be made.

ANALYZING THE CASE: THE CURRICULUM DILEMMA

If you were the principal of this high school, what decision style would you use to deal with the case? Use the decision tree in Figure 6.1 to determine the strategy that is suggested by the Vroom-Jago model. Start with the problem and ask the first question: How important is the technical quality of the decision? Then work your way through the other seven questions, moving from left to right along the appropriate branches in the decision tree. Eventually, you will arrive at the appropriate decision style, given your answers to the eight questions. We used the following logic to determine the appropriate decision style for this curriculum problem:

1. *How important is the technical quality of this decision?*   High
   Curriculum choices are a critical aspect of schools. A wise
   decision will benefit the operation and goal attainment
   of the school.

2. *How important is subordinate commitment to the decision?*   High
   The teachers must implement the decision. Without their
   support, it is doubtful that any decision can be successful.

3. *Do you have sufficient information for a quality decision?*   No
   The principal in this case is not an expert in social studies
   curriculum.

4. *Is the problem well structured?* It is not clear specifically what   No
   needs to be done to raise the scores while at the same time
   promoting critical thinking. This is not a routine problem
   for which there are standard solutions.

5. *Will an autocratic decision be accepted?* Teachers will likely   No
   resist an autocratic decision by the principal because they
   believe they, not the administration, have the expertise
   in this area.

6. *Do subordinates share organizational goals?* Teachers prefer   No
   their own solutions to instructional problems. Although they
   are committed to what is in the best interests of the students,
   they disagree strongly with the administration's acceptance
   of a fact-driven social studies curriculum. The goals in this
   instance are not shared because the teachers' preferred solutions
   are likely to violate district objectives (high scores on the
   standardized test).

7. *Is subordinate conflict over solutions likely?* There is little conflict   No
   among teachers. They believe they have a strong program.
   And they are united in their conviction that inquiry education
   is superior to drill and rote memory.

8. *Do subordinates have sufficient information to make a high-quality*   *Yes*
   decision? The teachers have a high degree of expertise in both
   the content and the pedagogy of social studies.

Now let us follow the path of the tree with our answers. The requirement for high technical quality leads to the demand for subordinate commitment to the decision, which raises the question of the leader having sufficient information. The lack of information elicits the question of how well the problem is structured. In this case, it is unstructured and prompts the question of whether an autocratic decision will be accepted. The answer is probably no. Therefore, the path moves to the issue of goal congruence—do the teachers share the organizational goals? This is a complicated issue. One could argue that the teachers and administrators are in agreement on the school goal—to provide the best possible education for students. There is disagreement, however, in terms of the meaning and strategy for achieving the best possible education. Thus, if you believe there is goal congruence, then the question becomes, Is there a conflict among the teachers? In this case there is not. But do subordinates have sufficient information to make a high-quality decision? They do. Therefore, the appropriate decision strategy is *group-agreement*—that is, you share the problem with the teachers as a group, and together you generate and evaluate alternatives as you attempt to reach consensus. Your role is to insure that all the issues are thoroughly aired as the group decides. You are committed to the group decision. If, on the other hand, you decide that the goals are not shared by teachers (the burden of evidence does support the view that there is conflict in the goals of teachers and administrators), then the decision calls for a *group-consultative* style, not group-agreement. You share the problem with your history teachers in a group meeting, obtain their ideas and suggestions, and then you make the decision, which may or may not reflect their ideas.

Recall that the decision tree in Figure 6.1 operates under the constraint of teacher development. Suppose the major constraint is time rather than development. Then Figure 6.2 depicts the paths to an appropriate style of decision. The decision questions are the same, but the path is slightly different. The ends remain the same. If you believe there is goal congruence, then the appropriate decision strategy is *group-agreement*—that is, you share the problem with the teachers as a group, and together you generate and evaluate alternatives as you attempt to reach consensus. Your role is to insure that all the issues are thoroughly aired as the group decides. You are committed to the group decision. If, however, you decide that the goals are not shared by teachers, then the decision calls for a *group-consultative* style, not group-agreement. You share the problem with your history teachers in a group meeting, obtain their ideas and suggestions, and then you make the decision, which may or may not reflect their ideas.

In the current instance, the decision style of the principal will be the same regardless of time. That is not always the case. Compare Figures 6.1 and 6.2. When time is a constraint, it is more likely that unilateral decisions will be made; but when subordinate development is the constraint, group agreement is more likely.

INDIVIDUAL PROBLEMS

Not all problems are group problems; some issues affect only one person. These individual problems elicit a different approach to shared decision making; they should be handled individually (Likert, 1961). Vroom and Yetton (1973) propose the following slightly different set of decision-making styles for individual problems, which we have modified. The first three styles are the same for group and individual problems, but two new individual styles, consensual and delegative, replace group-consultative and group-agreement. The individual styles are defined as follows:

- *Consensual (C):* Two people—you and your subordinate—form this group. Share the problem with the subordinate and solicit ideas and suggestions. Then develop a mutually satisfactory solution in an open manner; knowledge drives the decision, not status or authority.
- *Delegative (D):* Delegate the problem to a subordinate. Give the person any relevant information you have and then free rein to solve the problem. Support any decision your subordinate reaches.

Bringing a group together to discuss an issue that affects only one individual in the group is typically not a good idea (Vroom & Jago, 1988). Instead, develop a mutually satisfactory solution with the individual involved *(consensual)* or delegate the solution to the person most appropriate *(delegative)*.

Figures 6.3 and 6.4 represent the decision trees for solving individual problems under the constraints of maximizing subordinate development (Figure 6.3) and minimizing time (Figure 6.4). Again, take a few minutes to familiarize yourself with each figure. For instance, when is a delegative situation appropriate if the constraint is development? Walking through the model in Figure 6.3 shows that when the quality requirement is low, subordinate commitment is high, and an autocratic decision will be resisted, a delegative strategy is best. The superior simply delegates the problem to the subordinate by giving him or her the relevant information and free rein to make a decision, which the superior will support. When time pressures constrain the decision, the leader is more likely to make unilateral decisions or delegate; there simply is not time for subordinate development. Thus, there is much less consultation when time is a problem.

We recommend a developmental model for both individual and group problems when time permits because ultimately we want subordinates to initiate their own leadership acts and accept responsibility. Here is an individual problem for you to solve. Use both the developmental and time decision trees (Figures 6.3 and 6.4) to develop your strategy of action.

CASE 6.2

The Secretary's Office: An Individual Problem

You find yourself in an unusual, but fortunate, situation. The superintendent has informed you that there is some extra money in the budget that must be spent in the next three months. He remembered your complaining about the shabbiness of your secretarial suite. There is enough money for replacing the carpet and repainting.

As a first step, you have contracted with a painting and carpeting company to do the job. They have sent over some paint and carpet samples for your selection. They all look reasonable. You have examined the samples and made an initial selection. As you are walking out the door, you are struck by your insensitivity to your secretary. You haven't even told her about the redecoration. You rationalize that you are going to surprise her. But then you think that she may not be pleasantly surprised if she doesn't like the colors you have chosen. But then again, she probably will. Why not ask her? Should she be involved in this decision? Should you start over?

ANALYZING THE CASE: THE SECRETARY'S OFFICE

The eight decision properties remain the same. Thus, we analyze the case by asking the same questions in the same order, following the decision tree in Figure 6.3 and then in Figure 6.4.

1. *How important is the technical quality of the decision?*   Low
   How important is it which course of action is adopted?
   In this instance, the color of the walls or the pattern
   of the carpet is not critical to the organization. You are
   relatively indifferent to the solution; this is a minor if not
   trivial situation.

2. *How important is subordinate commitment to the decision?*   Probably
   How critical is it that your subordinates buy into the   Low
   decisions? Although it would be nice for the secretary
   to be pleased with the color of the walls and the general
   decor of the office, the final decision seems unlikely to be
   resisted over the long term. There is a possibility that some
   secretaries would really be put off by your selection,
   in which case the morale of the office could be seriously
   affected.

3. *Do you have sufficient information for a quality decision?*   Yes
   You believe that you have the information you need to make
   a good decision. Although you are not an expert in interior
   design, you feel comfortable making the decision.

4. *Is the problem well structured?* This problem is structured   Yes
   because the objectives are clear and the means to achieve
   them are familiar.

5. *Will an autocratic decision be accepted?* If you decide to   Yes
   make a unilateral decision, the secretary will probably
   accept the decision because this is likely to be viewed as
   an organizational prerogative.

6. *Do subordinates share organizational goals?* You can trust your   Yes
   secretary to make a decision that is in the best interest
   of the organization. She is a dedicated team player.

7. *Is conflict over solutions likely?* You judge that it is unlikely   No
   that your secretary will be upset with your decision.

8. *Do subordinates have sufficient information to make*   Yes
   a high-quality decision? You judge that your secretary has the
   knowledge to make a reasonable decision. She is neat and
   presents herself well.

Let us go through the decision tree in Figure 6.3. Because the quality requirement is low and strong commitment is not required, this decision should be made
unilaterally by the principal. However, if the principal judges that not involving
the secretary in the process will seriously affect morale (subordinate commitment
is desired), the decision should be delegated to the secretary on the assumption
that the secretary will resist an autocratic decision. Figure 6.4 shows that the constraint of time does not change the decision-making style in this case.

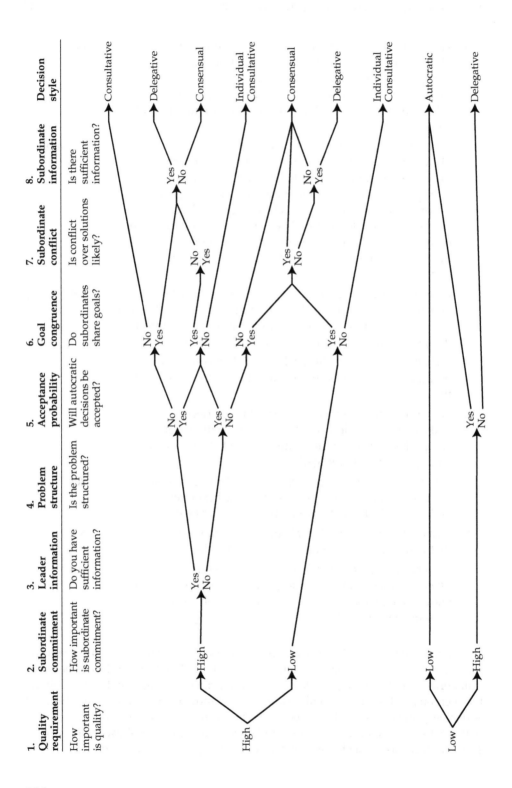

Decision-Making Styles for Individual Problems

Autocratic (A)   Solve the problem unilaterally using the available information.

Informed-autocratic (IA)   Solve the problem unilaterally after obtaining necessary information from subordinates. They may or may not be told the purpose of your questions, but they do not play a role in either defining the problem or generating or evaluating alternative solutions.

Individual-consultative (IC)   Share the problem with the relevant subordinate, soliciting his or her ideas. Then make the decision, which may or may not reflect the influence of the subordinate.

Consensual (C)   Two people—you and your subordinate—form this group. Share the problem with the subordinate and solicit ideas and suggestions. Then develop a mutually satisfactory solution in an open manner; knowledge drives the decision, not status or authority.

Delegative (D)   Delegate the problem to a subordinate. Give the person any relevant information you have and then free rein to solve the problem. Support any decision your subordinate reaches.

FIGURE 6.3 Decision Tree for Individual Decision Making for Development

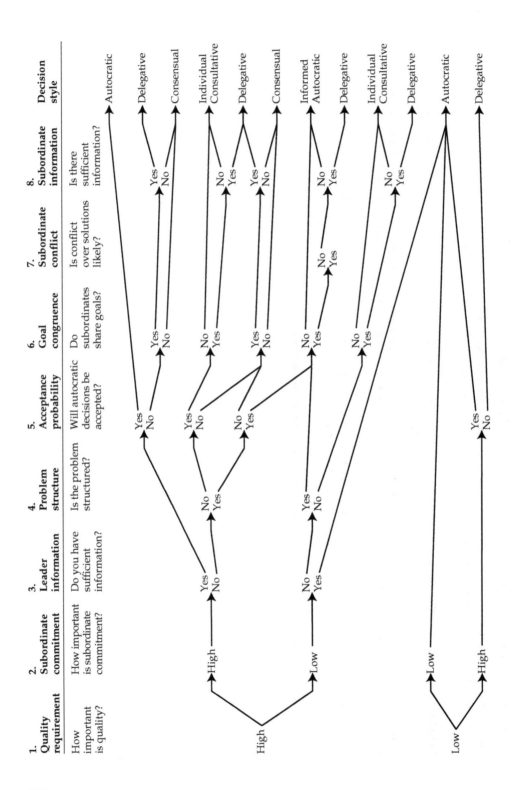

Decision-Making Styles for Individual Problems

Autocratic (A)   Solve the problem unilaterally using the available information.

Informed-autocratic (IA)   Solve the problem unilaterally after obtaining necessary information from subordinates. They may or may not be told the purpose of your questions, but they do not play a role in either defining the problem or generating or evaluating alternative solutions.

Individual-consultative (IC)   Share the problem with the relevant subordinate, soliciting his or her ideas. Then make the decision, which may or may not reflect the influence of the subordinate.

Consensual (C)   Two people—you and your subordinate—form this group. Share the problem with the subordinate and solicit ideas and suggestions. Then develop a mutually satisfactory solution in an open manner; knowledge drives the decision, not status or authority.

Delegative (D)   Delegate the problem to a subordinate. Give the person any relevant information you have and then free rein to solve the problem. Support any decision your subordinate reaches.

FIGURE 6.4   Decision Tree for Individual Decision Making under Time Pressure

SUMMARY AND CAUTIONS

There is no question that the Vroom-Jago model is a powerful tool that guides participation of subordinates in decision making. We have presented four versions of the model. The answers to each question have been dichotomized to make the model usable without a computer. Even with this simplification, however, the analysis is so complex and intimidating that, without decision trees, most leaders simply ignore the procedure. Nonetheless, the model is widely used in the training of managers in the corporate sector of the United States and, in fact, in most of the developed nations of the world.

There are several important points to keep in mind. First, the model is not a panacea; it is only as strong as the accuracy of the leader's perceptions. Second, the model is only a guide to action; it suggests the appropriate strategy for participation of subordinates in decision making. Third, the model does not solve the specific problem; it does not guarantee a good solution. Fourth, there is no substitute for reflective thinking and skillful interpersonal relations; the model is not mechanistic. Finally, the model forces one to consider the important requirements of quality and acceptance of decisions; it raises critical questions that should be addressed before rendering any decision. Like all theoretical models, this one requires practice; hence, we conclude with another actual administrative problem for practice.

CASE 6.3

Parking Lot

You have just been appointed principal of an expanding senior high school. In three brief years, enrollment has grown from 800 to 1,200 students. The building has too many students for its size; in fact, to open school next month, three temporary structures that will house six more classrooms are near completion. The expanding student population and the new construction have produced a host of dilemmas, including parking problems.

Yesterday you received from the builder a final set of plans for the addition of the temporary classrooms. For the first time, you realize that the new construction has reduced the parking spaces for the administrative staff. There had been thirteen spaces immediately adjacent to the principal's office intended for staff and visitor parking. In the past, a minimum of eight spaces had been reserved for the administrative staff (the principal, three vice-principals, five traveling supervisors). School policy mandates a minimum of three spaces open for parents and visitors. The new plans show that no more than ten spaces are possible. There is no way to increase the total number of spaces, given the new construction. The faculty and student parking lots are overcrowded. In fact, by 8:00 A.M., fifteen minutes before the beginning of school, the lots are filled.

As the new principal, you have been working with the administrative staff in forging a team approach. You have been emphasizing that all members of the team are important elements in the effective administration of the school. You have been treating each individual as a colleague, avoiding status distinctions among the team members. To be sure, there are salary differences among the vice-principals and supervisors, but team spirit prevails. Each, however, expects the reserved parking privilege that has been the practice in the past. Experience shows that people feel strongly about status. Thus far, you and your staff have crystallized as a team and you are reluctant to take any action that might jeopardize this relationship.

Discussing the Case

- Is the parking problem in this case a trivial issue?
- Is this a case for developmental decision making?
- How significant is the pressure of time?
- Are the actions to be decided of any real consequence?
- Is this a case for a decisive action to forestall bickering?
- Or is it a time for deliberative involvement of the administrative staff?
- As principal, what do you consider a good outcome?
- Develop a decision strategy for action as the principal.

ENDNOTE

1. The shared decision-making cases were inspired by our students and are attempts to pattern the illustrative cases used by Victor Vroom and Arthur Jago in *The New Leadership: Managing Participation in Organizations* (1988).

CHAPTER SEVEN

SHARED DECISION MAKING
A Simplified Model

Participation and teacher empowerment are increasingly fashionable as school site management becomes popular. Should teachers be involved in decision making? Of course! The question, however, is misleading because it allows only a yes-or-no response. Teachers should be involved in some decisions, but which ones and how? The Vroom-Jago perspective provides one answer to these questions, but because their model is formidable, its utility is limited. A more user-friendly model is needed to encourage administrators to involve teachers in decision making.

Applying theoretical concepts from Chester Barnard (1938), Herbert Simon (1947), Edwin Bridges (1964, 1967), and Wayne Hoy and Cecil Miskel (2001), we propose a simplified normative model of shared decision making.[1] It suggests under what conditions subordinates should be involved in decisions and the frequency, nature, purpose, and structure of their involvement. Further, the framework specifies different roles of the administrator, depending upon the situation.

ZONE OF ACCEPTANCE

There are some decisions that employees simply accept because they are indifferent to them. As Barnard (1938, p. 167) observed there is a zone of indifference "in each individual within which orders are accepted without conscious questioning of their authority." Simon (1947) prefers the term *acceptance* rather than *indifference*, but they are used interchangeably in the organizational literature (Bridges, 1967; Hoy & Miskel, 2001). Bridges (1967) was first to develop a model of shared decision making using the zone of acceptance. Although his formulation was developed for use by school principals to involve teachers in the decision-making process, it is a good general perspective. We cannot overemphasize the importance of the zone of acceptance—it drives shared decision making. Understand the concept and the model will be yours. The zone of acceptance enables you to identify specific situations that call for different strategies of involvement.

Drawing on the work of Barnard (1938) and Chase (1952), Bridges (1964, 1967) advanced two propositions:

1. As subordinates are involved in making decisions located in their zone of acceptance, participation will be less effective.
2. As subordinates are involved in making decisions clearly outside of their zone of acceptance, participation will be more effective.

There are, however, decisions that fall neither within nor outside the zone of acceptance. In other words, there are marginal cases; the boundaries of the zone are blurred. Subordinates are often uneasy about a pending decision. In such situations, it is difficult for an administrator to determine whether the decision is inside or outside the acceptance zone. For example, teachers may be concerned about a proposed change in the payroll system, but their involvement could complicate the issue as they attempt to protect their own interests at the expense of the welfare of the organization. Clearly, we need a more precise definition of the zone of acceptance.

Mapping the Zone of Acceptance

How does an administrator know if a decision is inside the zone, outside the zone, or a marginal case? Guidelines are required. Two decision rules have been developed for this question (Bridges, 1964, 1967): the relevance rule and the expertise rule.

- *The relevance rule:* Do subordinates have a personal stake in the decision outcome?
- *The expertise rule:* Do subordinates have expertise to contribute to the decision?

These two rules define four discrete decision situations, as shown in Figure 7.1. The zone is a two-dimensional construct defined by relevance and expertise. When subordinates have both expertise and a personal stake, then the decision is clearly outside the zone of acceptance. But if subordinates have neither expertise nor interest, then the decision is inside the zone. Now we can more precisely define marginality. There are two distinct types of marginality, each with different decisional constraints. When subordinates have expertise but no personal stake, or they have a personal stake but no particular expertise, the situations are marginal and participation is problematic.

This mapping of the zone of acceptance suggests two additional theoretical propositions:

3. As subordinates are involved in making decisions for which they have minimal expertise, their participation will be marginally effective.
4. As subordinates are involved in making decisions in which they have minimal interest or stake, their participation will be marginally effective.

**Do Subordinates Have
Personal Relevance?**

	Yes	No
Yes	Outside zone of acceptance (definitely include)	Marginal with expertise (occasionally include)
No	Marginal with relevance (occasionally include)	Inside zone of acceptance (definitely exclude)

Do Subordinates Have Expertise?

FIGURE 7.1 **Zone of Acceptance and Decision Situations**

If we apply proposition 3 to our previous payroll example, we see that involving teachers in the decision about the accounting system would be marginally effective because they have only interest without the relevant knowledge to inform the decision. An example of proposition 4 occurs when administrators exploit the expertise of subordinates. An administrator who needs expert advice often encounters resentment and even alienation when he or she forces subordinates to participate in problems they do not care about. The biology department may resent being asked to suggest office plants to decorate the foyer, or the math department may chafe at being forced to make decisions about the layout of the landscaping for the new administration building.

One more consideration is necessary to apply our model to actual problems. *Trust* of subordinates may affect their appropriate degree of involvement. When subordinates' personal goals conflict with the organizational goals, it is ill-advised to delegate the decision to them. For example, a high school principal with a limited budget for supplementary instructional materials would be unwise to delegate the decision completely to teachers if they have vested interests in enhancing their own departments at the expense of the overall welfare of the school. Thus, the appropriate level of participation is mediated by trust in faculty. To gauge subordinate trust, we propose a final consideration:

- *The trust consideration:* Can subordinates be trusted to make decisions in the best interests of the organization?

If the decision is outside the subordinates' zone of acceptance and if they share the aims of the organization, then participation should be extensive. But if there is little trust, then participation should be restricted; to do otherwise invites moving the decision in directions not consistent with the organization's goals. Mintzberg (1989, p. 183) explains that strong personal needs can be sufficient for employees to displace legitimate goals.

If the decision is inside the zone of acceptance, trust is not an issue because subordinates will not be part of the decision. In the two marginal situations, subordinate trust is seldom a consideration because participation is already limited by either lack of expertise or lack of interest.

PARTICIPATION

Participation is not simply a yes-or-no decision; it varies along a continuum from extensive to limited. Extensive participation involves individuals in the process as early and as long as possible. To illustrate, let us conceive of the decision-making process as a seven-stage cycle:

1. Define the problem.
2. Diagnose the problem.
3. Develop alternatives.
4. Consider the consequences.
5. Evaluate alternatives.
6. Select an action strategy.
7. Implement the strategy.

To maximize involvement, subordinates are included in the process as early as possible. They share in the definition and elaboration of the problem, and then are involved in each successive step of the cycle. But participation is limited when involvement occurs only in the later steps of the process. For example, if the problem has been defined, reasonable alternatives identified, and the consequences specified, then participation is restricted only to evaluating, selecting, and implementing a strategy for action. On the other hand, if teachers are provided data, are asked to define the problem, and are involved in each subsequent step of the decision-making process, then their participation is extensive.

In practical terms, involvement in the decision-making process depends on more than the subordinates' zone of acceptance. Involvement is also constrained by the area of freedom granted to the administrator by the district. Administrators cannot delegate authority that they do not have. It is important to make clear to subordinates the boundaries of their authority and the area of freedom to decide (Bridges, 1967).

Situations for Participation

The initial formulation of decision situations contained four types of collaborative opportunities—outside the zone, marginal with relevance, marginal with expertise, and inside the zone (see Figure 7.1). The commitment rule elaborates situations outside the zone of acceptance. Subordinates may have expertise and a personal stake in the decision outcome but not be committed to the aims of the organization. Therefore, the area outside the zone of acceptance can be divided into situations with committed and uncommitted subordinates. When subordinates are committed, the resolution of the problem may require total consensus rather than a simple majority. Unlike previous analyses (Bridges, 1967; Hoy & Miskel, 1991), which fail to consider these subtleties, these variations outside the zone of acceptance are identified as important constraints. Thus, five decision situations are defined as follows:

1. A *democratic* situation occurs when the decision falls outside the zone of acceptance (participants have interest and expertise) and the teachers are committed to the aims of the school. The only issue here is whether the decision should be a product of consensus or a simple majority. However desirable, consensus is not usually realistic. When the decision requires total acceptance (by law or for successful implementation), an administrator must hold out for unanimity. These situations are rare. More commonly, teachers and administrators seek a majority solution.

2. A *conflictual* situation occurs when the decision is outside the zone of acceptance but is one in which teachers' personal agendas are different from the school's goals; that is, the teachers are not committed to the goals. Here, teachers cannot be trusted to make a decision in the best interests of the school. There is likely to be conflict between administrators and teachers. In these conflictual situations, unrestricted participation is counterproductive. Still, effective decision making requires using teachers' expertise while allaying their anxieties about the consequences of the decision.

3. A *stakeholder* situation is a marginal one in which teachers have a personal stake in the outcome but no expertise to contribute. Regardless of teacher commitment, unrestricted participation is dangerous because it may frustrate teachers as they are asked to do a job for which they are ill prepared.

4. An *expert* situation is a marginal one in which teachers have expertise but no special interest. Again regardless of the degree of trust, teachers routinely involved in these decisions come to feel exploited by their superiors.

5. A *noncollaborative* situation occurs when teachers have no expertise and no personal stake in the outcome; the decision is in their zone of acceptance. They have neither the inclination nor the skill to inform the decision. These five situations for collaborative decision making are summarized along a continuum in Table 7.1.

TABLE 7.1 Situations for Collaborative Decision Making

	DEMOCRATIC	CONFLICTUAL	STAKEHOLDER	EXPERT	NONCOLLABORATIVE
Relevance?	Yes	Yes	Yes	No	No
Expertise?	Yes	Yes	No	Yes	No
Trust?	Yes	No	Yes/No	Yes/No	NA

Matching the Situation with Participation

When the decision is *outside the zone*, subordinates should be involved in the decision-making process (Bridges, 1967; Field, 1982; Hoy & Miskel, 2001; Vroom & Jago, 1988) because they have the knowledge and skill to improve the decision and because they have a personal stake in the outcome (Alluto & Belasco, 1972). Subordinate involvement is appropriate, and it should be extensive in the *democratic* situation. However, when subordinates have both a stake and expertise but are not be committed to the aims of the organization, the situation is *conflictual* and participation must be sharply limited.

In the *stakeholder* situation, the subordinate has a personal stake but not expertise; involvement should be limited. Subordinate participation is dangerous because it leads to frustration when teachers must do a job for which they are ill prepared (Imber & Duke, 1984; Mulder, 1971). Involving teachers who lack expertise may reduce their resistance, but it cannot inform the substance of the decision. The administrator who makes a show of soliciting opinion that is subsequently ignored gives the appearance of manipulation and game playing and eventually produces teacher hostility (Bridges, 1967; Duke, Showers, & Imber, 1980; Mintzberg, 1983; Mulder, 1971). Occasionally teachers must be brought into the process to gain acceptance of the decisions, but only when the teachers know at the outset that their role is advisory. The role of the administrator is clearly educational, a point to be developed later.

In the *expert* situation, subordinates have expertise but no personal stake; involvement should also be limited. Teachers forced into these decisions may feel that they are merely being used by their superiors (Bridges, 1967; Duke, Showers, & Imber, 1980; Mintzberg, 1983; Mulder, 1971). They are indifferent to the decision because they are unaffected. Initially, they may feel a sense of worth as they participate, but that quickly passes as they labor. Alienation is the long-term consequence. Teachers wonder aloud, "What does the principal get paid for doing?" and "What is my payoff?" No payoff, no personal stake, and no motivation produce eventual resentment and alienation. Nonetheless, we argue for occasional involvement because sometimes it can improve the quality of the decision without producing alienation among subordinates.

Finally, teachers should not be involved in decision making when they have neither the inclination nor the skill. This is a *noncollaborative* situation requiring unilateral administrative decision making (Vroom & Jago, 1988; Vroom & Yetton, 1973).

Structuring Participation

Participation in decision making is now defined in terms of five structural arrangements, appropriate matchings between administrative delegation and actual teacher involvement. Administrative delegation is the extent to which administrators give teachers the authority to make decisions. Teacher involvement is the degree to which teachers actually participate in decision making. Group consensus is the most extensive involvement and delegation possible within an organization,

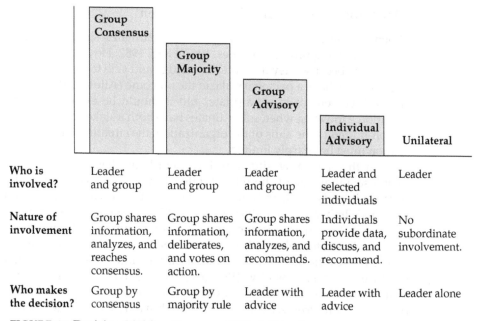

	Group Consensus	Group Majority	Group Advisory	Individual Advisory	Unilateral
Who is involved?	Leader and group	Leader and group	Leader and group	Leader and selected individuals	Leader
Nature of involvement	Group shares information, analyzes, and reaches consensus.	Group shares information, deliberates, and votes on action.	Group shares information, analyzes, and recommends.	Individuals provide data, discuss, and recommend.	No subordinate involvement.
Who makes the decision?	Group by consensus	Group by majority rule	Leader with advice	Leader with advice	Leader alone

FIGURE 7.2 Decision-Making Groups and Their Functions

while unilateral decision making marks the least involvement and delegation. There should be a congruence between teacher involvement and administrative delegation; in fact, we conceive of the structures (see Figure 7.2) of participation arrayed along the following continuum:

1. *Group consensus:* The administrator involves participants in the decision making, then the group decides. All group members share equally as they generate and evaluate a decision. Total consensus is required before a decision can be made.

2. *Group majority:* The administrator involves participants in the decision making, then the group decides using parliamentary procedures. All group members share equally as they generate and evaluate ideas and attempt consensus. Ultimately, though, a decision is usually made by the majority.

3. *Group advisory:* The administrator solicits the opinion of the entire group, discusses the implications of group suggestions, and then makes a decision that may or may not reflect subordinates' desires.

4. *Individual advisory:* The administrator consults individually with relevant subordinates who have expertise to inform the decision and then makes a decision that may or may not reflect their opinion.

5. *Unilateral decision:* The administrator makes the decision without consulting or involving subordinates in the decision.[2]

Matching Situations with Structures of Participation

Thus far, we have defined five situations and five structures for participation. The successful use of these decision-making structures is contingent upon the situation. Recall that there are two situations outside the zone of acceptance—the democratic and conflictual. Most frequently, a group-majority decision is made in the democratic situation. That is, each individual, including the administrator, has an equal voice as a majority decision is reached. Occasionally, a regulation mandates consensus, or the implementation of the decision requires consensus. In these relatively rare instances, group consensus is the necessary structure.

In the conflictual situation, in which employees are not committed to the organization and the decision is outside the zone, subordinate involvement is limited and the structure of the decision making is group advisory. Here, the administrator solicits opinions as the group is educated to the problem at hand, but eventually the administrator must act for the group. In these instances, the administrator explains at the outset that he or she has the final responsibility for making the decision.

When subordinates have a stake but no expertise—a stakeholder situation—the structure of decision making should be group advisory. The administrator requests opinions from the group, discusses the implications of group suggestions, then makes a decision that may or may not reflect subordinate desires. If subordinates take such participation as tokenism, however, there is a danger of backlash.

When subordinates have expertise but are unaffected by the decision—an expert situation—the structure of decision making should be individual advisory. The administrator consults individually with subordinates who have expertise to inform the decision and then makes a decision that may or may not reflect their opinion.

When the decision is inside the zone of acceptance—noncollaborative—the administrator uses existing information to make the decision alone; a unilateral decision is made.

DIRECTING PARTICIPATION: ADMINISTRATIVE ROLES

Thus far, our analysis has focused on the subordinates in decision making. Let us turn to the role of the administrator. How well do groups function when the administrator is a group member? A study by Bridges, Doyle, and Mahan (1968) deals directly with this question in the context of public schools. In an experimental study of twenty groups of administrators and teachers, groups without administrators were significantly more productive, efficient, and showed a greater propensity for risk taking than those groups in which an administrator was a member. In this particular study, a group mode of decision making was used; such other modes as consensus, group advisory, and individual advisory were not examined.

Administrative involvement in group decision making may have some dysfunctional consequences. The introduction of hierarchy into a group may complicate the social interactions by making subordinates reluctant to disagree with superiors (even if they are wrong), by fostering a desire for consensus at the expense of the divergent idea, and by nurturing competition for managerial favor rather than group respect (Blau & Scott, 1962; Bridges, Doyle, & Mahan, 1968; Mulder, 1971). As early as 1955, Torrance found suggestions that lower-status group members were often ignored, even when lower-status members had correct solutions more frequently than other members of the group. This research is not cited to suggest that administrators should avoid involving either subordinates or themselves in decision making but rather to identify effective roles to improve decisions.

We conceive of the following five effective administrative roles for shared decision making:

1. The *integrator* brings subordinates together for consensus decision making. Here the task is to reconcile divergent opinions and positions.
2. The *parliamentarian* facilitates open communication by protecting the opinions of the minority and leads participants through a democratic process to a group decision.
3. The *educator* reduces resistance to change by explaining and discussing with group members the opportunities and constraints of the decisional issues.
4. The *solicitor* seeks advice from subordinate experts. The quality of decisions is improved as the administrator guides the generation of relevant information.
5. The *director* makes unilateral decisions in those instances in which the subordinates have no expertise or personal stake. Here the goal is efficiency.

Principals lead using all five roles (see Table 7.2), but an effective strategy for collaborative decision making involves matching each role with the appropriate situation. If consensus is required, then the group probably can best achieve

TABLE 7.2 Administrative Roles for Decision Making

ROLE	FUNCTION	AIM
Integrator	Brings together divergent positions	To achieve consensus
Parliamentarian	Facilitates open discussion	To support reflective deliberation
Educator	Explains and discusses issues	To insure acceptance of decisions
Solicitor	Solicits advice from teachers	To improve quality of decisions
Director	Makes unilateral decisions	To attain efficiency

consensus by itself, that is, without the active intervention of the leader. If, however, *consensus* does not emerge, then the administrator functions as the *integrator* who brings together divergent positions. Divergent alternatives are integrated into still another proposal that includes the best of the competing views. If such accommodation fails, the administrator may either suggest experimental trials of the divergent approaches or continue to work with the group on decreasing the obstacles to consensus. The challenge one faces is in overcoming likely polarization within the group and bringing the group together.

If a *group majority* is required, then the appropriate administrative role is that of *parliamentarian*. The parliamentarian of the group guarantees open communication by protecting the opinions of the minority from a tyranny of the majority. Premature decision making reduces the quality of decisions (Barnard, 1938; Nitzan & Paroush, 1984). The administrator must insure that different ideas, regardless of the personalities holding them, get a thorough airing.

If a *group advisory* is desired, then the appropriate role of the administrator is one of *educator*. The purpose of participation in this case is to reduce resistance to change by educating the teachers or other administrators to the need for the decision. There are two situations when the administrator acts as educator. In the conflictual situations, subordinates have both expertise and a personal stake but do not share goals with the organization. Here the leader supplies information to reduce resistance to change. In the stakeholder situation, subordinates have a personal stake in the outcome of the decision, but, by definition, they do not have the expertise to make the decision. The administrator makes the case by stipulating the problem, examining the difficulties, reviewing the opportunities and constraints, and developing the rationale for the final decision. The role is clearly educational.

If an *individual advisory* is required, then the administrator is a *solicitor*; advice is solicited from experts. The purpose of involvement in this case is to improve the quality of the decision by using the skill of organizational members. Here the challenge is to overcome the reluctance of faculty and staff to criticize the status quo. The free flow of communication is nurtured by focusing on problem solving, risk taking, and divergent ideas.

If *no participation* is required, the administrator as a *director* simply makes the decision. From integrator to director, the role of the manager varies according to leadership function, purpose, and appropriate decision-making arrangement (see Figure 7.3).

USING THE MODEL

Principals are too often exhorted to involve teachers in all decisions. The more appropriate tack is to determine when others should be involved in decision making. We have proposed a model that answers this question. The model has several advantages: It is built upon sound organizational theory and research, its internal logic is clear, its applicability is extensive, and it is easy for administrators to use.

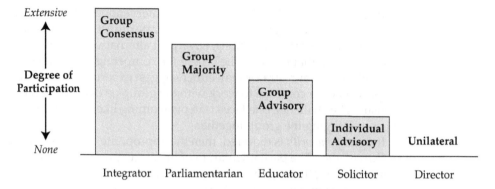

Administrative Roles

FIGURE 7.3 Matching the Administrative Role and Situation

The key concept in the model, drawn from Barnard (1938) and Simon (1947), is the zone of acceptance. There are some decisions that subordinates simply accept and, therefore, in which they should not be involved. The administrator identifies those situations by asking two questions:

1. *Relevance question:* Do the subordinates have a personal stake in the outcome?
2. *Expertise question:* Can subordinates contribute expertise to the solution?

If the answer to both these questions is yes—the subordinates have both a personal stake in the outcome and expertise to contribute—then the situation is outside the zone of acceptance. Subordinates will want to be involved, and their involvement should improve the decision. However, one must next evaluate their trust in the organization by asking the following question:

3. *Trust question:* Can subordinates be trusted to make a decision in the best interests of the organization?

If they can be trusted, their involvement should be extensive as the group tries to develop the best decision. In the process, the role of the administrator is to act either as an integrator (if consensus is essential) or as a parliamentarian (if a group majority is sufficient). If subordinates cannot be trusted (conflictual situation), their involvement should be limited. In this situation, the administrator acts as an educator, and the group serves to advise and identify pockets of resistance.

If, however, subordinates have only a personal stake in the decision, but no expertise to contribute (stakeholder situation), their involvement should be occasional and limited. Subordinates are interested in the outcome, but they have little knowledge to bring to bear on the decision. The reason for occasional involvement in this situation is to lower resistance and educate participants. If the involvement is more than occasional, the danger is alienation, as teachers feel manipulated because their wishes are not met. At the outset, all parties know that the group is clearly advisory to the leader. The administrator's role is to decide and educate.

If subordinates have expertise but no personal stake (expert situation), their involvement should also be occasional and limited as the administrator attempts to improve the decision by tapping the expertise of significant individuals who are not normally involved in this kind of action. At first blush, one might think that expertise should always be consulted in a decision, but if workers have no personal stake in the outcomes, their enthusiasm will quickly wane. They may well grumble, "This isn't my job."

In noncollaborative situations, the teachers have neither the interest nor the expertise to contribute to the decision. Yet there is such a strong norm about involving teachers in all sorts of decisions that school administrators often feel constrained to involve teachers regardless of their knowledge or interest. Such ritual is dysfunctional and illogical. Why would you involve someone in a decision when that person does not care and cannot help? Our model proposes that administrators make direct unilateral decisions when the issue is within the zone of acceptance of subordinates. The entire model is summarized in Figure 7.4.

Although our discussion has focused on matching the appropriate decision style with each situation to maximize effectiveness, the framework also has a developmental component. Ultimately, the goal of shared participation is to involve teachers in as many decisions as is realistically possible. To increase effective subordinate involvement sometime requires education. Such education is appropriate when subordinates lack expertise or cannot be trusted. That is, professional development sometimes is a matter of fostering trust between superiors and subordinates, and at other times, it is mastering the knowledge and skills necessary to confront and solve the problem. In the final analysis, shared decision making is collaboration to gain greater cooperation from those affected by a decision and to improve the decision by bringing expertise to bear on the process.

To illustrate the use of the model, we will apply it to several cases. We begin with a reanalysis of the curriculum problem we examined in the last chapter.

CASE 7.1

The Curriculum Dilemma: A Group Problem Revisited

You are the principal, and your school's social studies department is highly regarded for its innovative approach to teaching. The program is oriented toward inquiry as a process, rather than the retention of historical fact. Typically, curriculum is made by the department as different concepts are developed. The teachers are enthusiastic about their program, and it is well

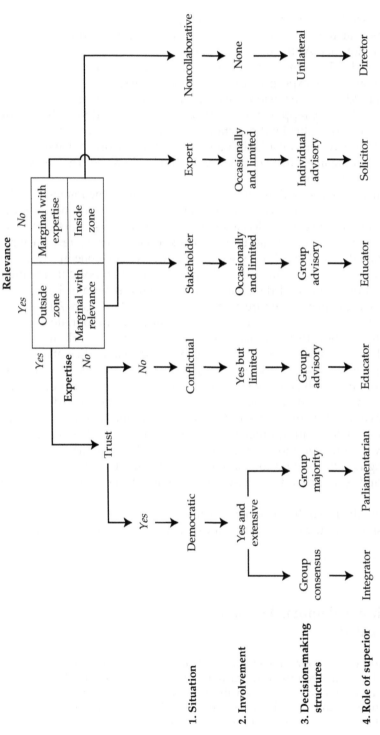

FIGURE 7.4 A Normative Model for Participative Decision Making

received by the students. You respect all the members of the department and see it as one of the strongest departments in the school. You do not always agree with the direction of the curriculum, but there is little question that this is a highly skilled and professional group of teachers whom you respect.

Recent reform in the state has argued for back-to-basics and the use of curricular materials that stress recall of specific persons, places, and events in state and national history. The reform is supported by a battery of state tests, which have been used to compare the effectiveness of schools across the state. Although the state maintained that no invidious comparisons would be made, your community has made them. The superintendent has her feet to the fire on this issue, and now you are feeling the heat. Recent test scores show that your students are not doing nearly as well in history as they are in science and mathematics. The superintendent has "requested" that you integrate the state curricular materials into the history program to correct the current deficiencies. Your history faculty, on the other hand, claim that this is exactly the wrong tack to take to develop inquiring minds. They are not overly concerned with the students' performance on the state tests because they claim the tests measure the wrong thing. There is strong pressure in the community, however, to do well on all tests. Parents cannot understand why their children are not doing as well in history as they are in math and science; in fact, at the last board meeting the superintendent promised under pressure that the scores would rise.

There is no question that you as principal must help realign the history curriculum. You are troubled by the current state of affairs, but decisions must be made.

ANALYZING THE CASE: THE CURRICULUM DILEMMA

In this case, the principal must determine whether the faculty has expertise and interest in the issue. Without question, the social studies teachers have a personal stake and expertise to contribute. The decision clearly falls outside of the zone of acceptance; they should be involved. Are the teachers committed to the aims of the school, and can they be trusted to work for the best interests of the school? As we saw in the last chapter, this is not a simple issue. One could argue that the teachers and administrators are in agreement on the school goal—to provide the best possible education for students. There is clearly disagreement in the meaning and strategy for achieving the best possible education.

If the principal judges that the social studies teachers can be trusted to work in the best interests of the school, then the model tells us that the teachers should be involved extensively because they have a personal stake and expertise and are committed. The purpose of their involvement is to improve the quality and acceptance of the decision. The manner of their involvement is also suggested by the model. The principal must work with teachers, first trying to integrate and achieve consensus and, if unsuccessful as a parliamentarian, helping the group realize a majority decision. The process can be summarized as follows:

Expertise	Yes
Relevance	Yes
Trust	Yes
Situation	Democratic
Involvement	Yes and extensive
Structure	Group consensus or majority
Role of Leader	Integrator or parliamentarian

On the other hand, if the principal sees the faculty as uncommitted to the overall goals of the school, a different plan is necessary. What is the administrative response to this uncommitted and recalcitrant faculty? This is a conflictual situation and the model suggests more limited involvement in which the administrator seeks to reduce resistance to change by explaining and by cajoling the faculty. The principal will use the advice of the faculty, but it is the principal who must control and make the final decision. The challenge is clear: to use the expertise of the teachers to develop a solution acceptable to both the teachers and the superintendent. The process can be summarized as follows:

Expertise	Yes
Relevance	Yes
Trust	No
Situation	Conflictual
Involvement	Yes, but limited
Structure	Group advisory
Role of Leader	Educator

DISCUSSION: A PREFERENCE FOR ACTION

In "The Curriculum Dilemma," there is a conflict over the definition of the goal. The administration and faculty both agree that the organizational goal is providing students with the best possible education. But the faculty and administration disagree over the appropriate means to achieve the goal. The administration argues that raising the scores on the state test is evidence of instructional effectiveness, and the faculty disagree. We argue that the group with the expertise is in the best position to determine the means to goals; moreover, their cooperation is essential to the success of any plan to implement teaching and curriculum change. The faculty has both expertise and a personal stake in the outcomes, and can be trusted to make a decision in the best interests of the school. Therefore, we recommend a democratic strategy, moving the group toward consensus, and if total consensus fails, the majority rules. Is this too simple a solution to a complex problem? It is not a solution. It is a strategy of action to solve the problem, one that emphasizes teacher–administrator collaboration under several different assumptions.

Still, this strategy can be used to weave a solution. Consider the following actual scenario:

The dilemma faced by the principal is this: The superintendent has given the marching orders—raise the test scores—but the faculty is adamant in its insistence that the test measures the wrong outcomes. Moreover, any change in the curriculum depends on the willingness of the faculty to implement the changes in good faith. Telling the faculty what to do, that is, imposing change, seems doomed to failure.

Nonetheless, a history faculty meeting is called with the principal presiding. The faculty members at first threaten to make a mockery of what they feel is the superintendent's order to teach facts. There are many suggestions—to make up a fact sheet to be distributed to all classes to be memorized, but continue the inquiry-driven approach; to devote five minutes of each class to memorizing facts for the test; to send home a long list of facts to parents to help them quiz their children. After a bitter hour of acrimony, in which the faculty vent their hostility, calmer heads prevail. The principal gets the faculty moving in an inquiry-driven mode toward an answer to the dilemma. The group begins to understand that the superintendent is really saying "Get the test scores up," and she does not care how it happens. The principal makes it clear that the superintendent is not usurping their professional role, but rather is seeking their help. She is defining an end product that is endorsed by the community and asking the professional staff to develop an effective plan to achieve that end. Thus, what the group needs is a set of options (alternatives) that will raise the test scores while preserving the benefits of the existing program.

After much discussion and debate involving several meetings, many compromises, and a few false starts, the faculty agrees on the following course of action:

1. A faculty committee is appointed to examine what is being measured on the tests—the specific kind of factual information needed to do well.
2. Each faculty member will develop a fact sheet for each unit and then integrate the facts into a inquiry-driven approach—that is, more emphasis will be placed on facts in developing arguments and defending positions.
3. The faculty also will develop a jeopardy type of game in which the students write questions from the areas measured by the state test for a schoolwide contest.

The assumption is that the effort will elicit student activity on historical facts in a way that students will find interesting. History classes at each level will be responsible for developing a pool of factual questions for each unit. Then a contest will be structured to give as wide an opportunity as possible for student participation. There will be a series of eliminations before the championship round, which will precede the state tests by two weeks.

We conclude with an individual staff problem rather than a group faculty example to demonstrate the general applicability of the framework. Our model works with individuals as well as groups; the focus merely changes from the group to the individual. Let us illustrate.

CASE 7.2

The Secretary's Office: An Individual Problem Revisited

You find yourself in an unusual, but fortunate, situation. The superintendent has informed you that there is some extra money in the budget that must be spent in the next three months. She remembered your complaining about the shabbiness of your secretarial suite. There is enough money for replacing the carpet and repainting.

As a first step, you have contracted with a painting and carpeting company to do the job. They have sent over some paint and carpet samples for your selection. They all look reasonable. You have examined the samples and made an initial selection. As you are walking out the door, you are struck by your insensitivity to your secretary. You have not even told her about the redecoration. You rationalize that you are going to surprise her. But then you think that she may not be pleasantly surprised if she does not like the colors you have chosen. But then again, she probably will. Why not ask her?

ANALYZING THE CASE: THE SECRETARY'S OFFICE

Once again the model provides direction. We first ask the question, "Does the secretary have expertise in the decision area?" In all likelihood, the secretary has no special expertise in interior design or color coordination. However, it is also obvious that the secretary, who works in the room every day, has a personal stake in the outcome. Thus, the decision is a stakeholder situation. The model suggests that some involvement is appropriate provided that it will not lead to alienation or backlash, a reasonable assumption in this case. Ultimately, however, you will make the decision after deliberation with the secretary; a discussion should produce for both parties a better understanding of the constraints. We suspect that in most cases principals will affirm the wishes of their secretaries, but they do hold a veto over the final decision. Of course, if the answer to the expertise question is yes, that is, the secretary does have expertise in color selection, then the decision falls outside the zone of acceptance, and the decision should be delegated to the secretary.

We repeat: This model does not solve problems. It is no substitute for clear and reflective thinking. However, the model is a guide to participative decision making. Note that in the examples given above, no solutions are offered, for good reason. The framework simply addresses the following questions:

1. Under what conditions should subordinates be involved?
2. To what extent should they be involved?
3. What is the purpose of their involvement?

4. How should the process of decision making be structured?
5. What are the administrative and subordinate roles in the process?

A COMPARISON

Our model is more parsimonious and, therefore, easier to use than the Vroom-Jago model. In both of the problems used to illustrate the models, the "Curriculum Dilemma" and the "Secretary's Office," the strategies to involve subordinates are essentially the same. Elsewhere we examined the potential utility of our model by applying it to other comparable cases presented by Vroom and Jago (1988) and compared our decisions with theirs. Assuming that the manager has sufficient time to involve subordinates in the group decision process, our resulting strategies are virtually the same. In those decisions that affect only one subordinate (individual problems), our model is more likely to call for a different decision than found with the Vroom-Jago procedure.

The two models of shared decision making, ours and the Vroom-Jago model, complement each other. Ours is a simple but heuristic model that can be used quickly and efficiently. The Vroom-Jago model is much more time consuming. It involves a series of eight sequential questions and the elaboration of complex decision trees. Our advice is to use the simpler model routinely and, when time permits, use the more complex model to validate and refine actions derived from our simple model.

ANOTHER APPLICATION

We have used the simplified model presented in this case with hundreds of students and administrators to test its utility. It takes about twenty hours of training and practice for individuals to become proficient in its use. Learning the model is not sufficient. Students can learn specifics of the model in a few hours, but it takes practice with actual cases and extended discussion with others before students begin to use the model with skill. We conclude this chapter with another case that is used in the training of administrators. Although there is no best solution to the case, there are a number of satisfactory decisions. First we present the case, and then we provide two analyses done by beginning principals trained in the use of the model.

CASE 7.3

Computer Purchasing Problem

You are the principal in a school that was one of the first to implement a comprehensive computer technology program for students. You have three highly competent computer teachers who are doing an outstanding job with their students. In fact, your school computer program is a model for others in the region. Teachers from other districts have visited, and the program has been showcased by the state. There is little question that you have three of the most knowledgeable computer people in the district. They have a love affair with computers.

You have seen the success of computer applications and are convinced of their usefulness to both instruction and the general clerical operation of your office. You are a Mac devotee and have Macs in your school and home offices. Your staff, however, is split. Some use Macs and others have PCs. All are competent, loyal, and highly motivated, but they cling to their biases, which often cause compatibility problems. For the first time in five years, money is available to upgrade the services of your office, but you must move quickly. You are perplexed by the diversity of computer equipment and services offered by such strong companies as Apple, Hewlett Packard–Compaq, and Dell. Salespeople have developed extensive proposals, all of which sound good to you. The superintendent said that she will support any reasonable decision you make.

You have a window of opportunity to improve the technical support for your school. Clearly, there are a number of problems that need attention if you are to succeed. What problems should you address first, and how? These are the questions running through your mind as you drive home Friday afternoon.

ANALYZING THE CASE: A THEORY-DRIVEN STUDENT ANALYSIS

A student, we will call her Cheryl, provides a good example of a skillful application of the model.[3]

Analysis

Cheryl divided the problem into two questions: (1) purchasing appropriate equipment and (2) training the office staff to use the equipment. She outlined the two phases of the problem as follows:

- *Phase 1:* Determine which of the many equipment and service packages offered will be most appropriate for the needs of the school.

Participants	Three computer teachers and the principal
Expertise	Yes
Relevance	No
Situation	Expert
Involvement	Limited to improve decision
Structure	Individual advisory
Role of Superior	Solicitor

- *Phase 2:* Decide on the new system to be used and plan for the training of staff.

Participants	Office staff and principal (with computer teachers as consultants)
Expertise	No
Relevance	Yes
Situation	Stakeholder
Involvement	Limited to increase acceptance
Structure	Group Advisory
Role of Superior	Educator

Rather than paraphrase Cheryl's analysis, we will quote large sections of it to retain the sense of her working through the problem. Cheryl writes:

> There is a twofold problem in this case, requiring a two-part solution. The principal is faced with the decision of choosing an appropriate computer system for the office and the task of convincing a hesitant office staff that the decision is not only a good one but one that creates a program they can master and use efficiently.
>
> Though the principal has some knowledge of computers, he would be unwise to try to choose a system alone when expertise exists in his building. The three computer teachers certainly have technological knowledge or expertise. The decision made would not be all that relevant to them, as it will mainly affect the office staff at this time, though their interests may indirectly be served by moving the staff forward. Therefore, the principal should involve them in an individual advisory capacity using the expert strategy. With their help, the principal can eliminate those systems that would be of least use in the school.

Once the choices have been narrowed, the principal can move to phase two. In this step, the principal involves the office staff. They are the ones who will most definitely be affected by the change; therefore, they have a personal stake in the decision. They have some knowledge of computer systems and what they can do, and are somewhat anxious about changing to an unfamiliar computer; the Mac people want a Mac system, and the PC people want a PC system. They are all competent and dedicated. The principal will use the stakeholder strategy at this point by educating the staff and lowering their resistance to the change, while gathering their input and ideas as to the best approach for implementation.

Solution Strategy

The principal has a school with a model computer program, one that has been showcased by the state. It is understandable that when the superintendent gives him the go-ahead to upgrade the services of the office, along with support and money, the principal is eager to move forward. The choices facing him, however, are confusing due to his somewhat limited knowledge, and he knows that although he must move quickly, he needs to be sensitive to the concerns and anxieties of his office staff if he hopes for the new program to be accepted and effective. He decides to move forward—now he needs help in choosing the system and convincing his staff.

During the weekend, the principal phones several of his colleagues in other districts who he knows have upgraded their offices. He speaks with them informally about the pros and cons of the various systems in use in their schools and gathers data to help with his decision.

On Monday morning, he meets with the three computer teachers. He explains the opportunity facing him and asks for their help in narrowing the choices of systems. Two of the teachers immediately begin praising the new Apple line. The third offers her opinion on the Dell system used in her previous district. As the principal shares the various proposals, the discussion becomes more focused. It becomes apparent to all that several of the proposals can be eliminated—they just do not make sense for the school. The group studies the last five proposals and narrows them down to the three that sound least complicated, appear most effective, and require only a reasonable amount of hardware (remembering the superintendent's words about a reasonable decision).

On Monday afternoon, the principal meets with his office staff, telling them that the superintendent has offered them the opportunity to upgrade the office. He explains that their tasks will become easier with a new system, but they will require initial training. He encourages them to share their concerns and assures them that they will be involved not only in the decision of choice of system but also in the planning of their own training. He ends the meeting explaining that he will meet tomorrow with them and the three computer teachers to devise a plan.

On Tuesday, the combined group of staff and computer teachers meets with the principal. At first, staff members are hesitant to speak, fearful of what is coming, and somewhat intimidated by the knowledge of the computer teachers. However, as the meeting continues, they realize that the principal is eager to involve them in the changes that will affect them and willing to provide both support and time to help them make the transition. Together the group formulates a list consisting of specific office needs to be addressed by the new technology (staff) and requirements of the new equipment and system (computer teachers). Once they have decided what they want the new office to be able to do and what type of equipment seems most appropriate, they agree on the following next steps:

1. Companies offering the top three proposals will be asked to send a representative to visit the school as soon as possible to give a minipresentation to the group.
2. The group members will do any outside research they can do quickly on other systems used in other school offices. The principal will provide released time, if necessary, for members to visit other schools to see systems in operation.

3. A report will be given by staff as to which of the three proposals seems most compatible with their office procedures. (Get information from computer teachers, if necessary. All input will be due to the principal within ten days.)
4. The principal will make the decision and inform the superintendent in two weeks.
5. Following the superintendent's approval, the group will meet again and develop a plan for training the office staff.

Cheryl used the model to offer a well-conceived plan and strategy for action. A central issue addressed in her response is the question of involvement of subordinates. The purpose of involvement is to improve the quality and acceptance of whatever plan does evolves from their shared deliberations. The strategy outlined here is intended to solve the problems of computer acquisition and training. There is no guarantee that the proposed strategy will solve all the issues without any hitches, but it is a reasonable beginning.

Another student, Fred, developed a slightly different strategy.[4]

Analysis

This situation calls for a two-pronged approach. There is the problem of selecting the appropriate computer system and the problem of introducing a new system to the office staff. The first instance, choosing the system, represents an expert situation. Several computer teachers have expertise but little personal stake in the kind of computer equipment used in the office. Consulting these experts (individual advisory) should be useful in making the decision, but the administrator must be careful not to take advantage of the situation. Situations of this type call for occasional involvement but not routine involvement because enthusiasm will quickly wane. Clearly, the purpose of the involvement is to improve the quality of the decision by tapping the skill of organizational members. Selecting the equipment underscores the potential problem of staff resistance to change. The staff has a personal stake in the decision but no expert knowledge in computer systems, a situation that calls for a group advisory decision with the explicit purpose of educating and lowering resistance. Here, the principal is the educator.

Solution Strategy

As principal, I would first talk individually to each of the three teacher experts. Assume that two of the three teachers are intrigued by the problem and agree to help formulate a plan. I would meet with the two teachers and identify the problems in the workplace that the computer system could address. Specifically, I would want to streamline general office work, that is, reduce incompatibilities among the computers, increase efficiency in letter writing, filing, report writing, and record keeping. The current office equipment is a hodgepodge of different computers, monitors, and printers. After soliciting proposals from all interested vendors, I would meet with the two computer teachers to go over the proposals made by the salespeople. I would ask them to rate each proposal on the following rating scale:

	APPLE	H-P–COMPAQ	DELL
Ease of use			
Completeness of system			
Expandability of hardware			
Ability to use required software			
Life expectancy			
Compatibility with other equipment			
Compatibility with knowledge of school experts			
Cost			

OVERALL EVALUATION

After a week, the teachers would come back with a report and recommendations. I would accept the report in which they had described the problem. The PC proposal is less expensive than the Apple proposal, but the equipment is considered more difficult to use, especially for the secretaries who are Mac users. In addition, the central office already is using some PCs and the computers in the school lab are PCs. Apple, however, offers the advantage of user-friendliness; that is, their computers are easy to use, and there is a minimal amount of time required to learn. Both systems can meet office needs. The problem seems to boil down to one of the following choices:

1. Purchase a PC system, with its price advantage on equipment and compatibility but its disadvantage on learning cost.
2. Purchase an Apple system, with its learning advantage but its price and compatibility disadvantages.
3. Purchase a combination of both systems, and hire a networking expert to make the two systems compatible on one network.
4. Postpone upgrading the office system until a clear systemwide choice is made.

Given this information, I would decide not to entertain a combination of both systems because incompatibilities between PCs and Macs will inevitably emerge. Further, I see no advantage to postponing the decision. The money is here now and I have been given the go-ahead. This is no time for indecision.

I would call the office staff together to inform them of the opportunity to improve office work and conditions. I would tell them that I must make a decision, but because they will be affected by the decision, I want their opinions. I would review the background to the recommendations and the four alternatives. I would explain why alternatives 3 and 4 were eliminated. My goal would be to allay their anxieties and get their support for the final decision. I would have decided that either system would accomplish the work of the office in a more efficient fashion once it was embraced by the staff. I really would not care whether it is a PC or an Apple system. What I would care about is the willingness of the staff to use the new equipment expeditiously. After listening to staff misgivings about different systems and seeing that they have no sound basis for a preference, I would suggest a compromise proposal: request enough equipment to give each system a trial use in the office. I would agree to accept whatever decision the staff makes after a trial of the equipment for each system.

In the event that I could not get enough equipment for the test, I would make the decision. It is likely that I would select the Apple system because of its friendliness and short learning curve. I believe that, within the criteria of effectiveness, cost, and ease of learning, Apple represents a more satisfactory choice. One could make the case for the PC selection by anticipating the negative consequences, that is, anticipating the difficulty of the staff learning the system and addressing this difficulty directly with a training program for the staff funded by the money saved on the PCs.

Both Fred and Cheryl have reasonable solution strategies to the computer purchasing problem. Both show an easy application of the model, and both seem to have a good sense of the organization. They both asked the right questions; the model is especially useful in this regard. Their facility in using the model no doubt stems from practicing with it. In fact, it is usually the case that after using the model to direct decision making on three or four cases, students become quite proficient.

SUMMARY AND CAUTIONS

There is no question that teachers should be involved in decision making. But the important considerations are how and when. We propose a simplified model to address the frequency, nature, purpose, and structure of subordinate participation in decision making. One concept, the *zone of acceptance*, guides participation. The zone of acceptance is determined by the expertise and personal stake of subordinates.

If teachers are not interested in the decision and have no expertise in the question, the decision falls inside their zone of acceptance and they should not be involved; this is a *noncollaborative situation* in which subordinates do not participate—the administrator acting as a director makes a unilateral decision.

If teachers are not interested in the decision but hold expertise in the question, the decision rests on the margin of the zone and there may be some occasions for inclusion; this is the *expert situation* in which the administrator occasionally solicits advice from expert individuals before making a final decision.

If teachers are interested in the decision but have no expertise in the question, the decision again rests on the margin of the zone, and there will be times when subordinate participation is useful; this is a *stakeholder situation* in which the administrator seeks group advice and attempts to educate and lower resistance to the decision.

If teachers have both interest and expertise in the question, the decision falls outside the zone of acceptance, and they should be involved. Degree of trust, however, moderates the extent of the participation. Where there is no trust, we have a *conflictual situation* in which the administrator seeks group advice and attempts to educate and lower resistance to the decision. But if teachers can be trusted to make a decision in the best interest of the school, we have a *democratic situation* in which the administrator acts as a parliamentarian and integrator to reach a majority decision and, if necessary, consensus.

As we examined a variety of school problems confronted by the principal, we were struck by the difficulty of finding decision areas where the principal should make unilateral decisions. Because the principal is a key figure in the organization, virtually every decision he or she makes affects someone. Clearly, it is not possible for all subordinates to be involved in all decisions. Nor should subordinates be involved in the same ways. The model deals with these questions. However, time forces administrators to make unilateral decisions, thereby increasing the risk of a poor decision or a decision that will not be readily accepted by subordinates.

Some may object to the fact that the principal, rather than teachers, decides expertise, personal stake, and trust of the teachers. In fact, the *Canadian Administrator* published an exchange in which we defend the authenticity of the model in promoting teacher–principal collaboration (Hoy & Tarter, 1992, 1993b). The decisions we are considering are problems the administrator must solve as part of the job. The model is an administrative tool. Its use can be no better than the skill, perception, and sensitivity of the administrator. We assume that when administrators have questions about the criteria of inclusion, they will consult with subordinates.

We have described the properties of our model as categorical variables to keep it simple. Each variable may be conceived as continuous; of course, there are degrees of expertise, relevance, and trust. The press of practice frequently requires timely decisions, hence our simplified and direct approach. The model is a helpful tool that can be mastered with practice. Thus, we conclude with another actual administrative problem.

CASE 7.4

Teacher Tardiness

The official policy of the school is that if a teacher is going to be absent or late, he or she must notify the office. For some years, however, the social studies department has followed an unofficial policy of covering for faculty who are late to school. If the teacher does not call and is late, the department assumes that the teacher has simply been delayed and whoever has a free period covers the class until the teacher arrives. The policy has worked smoothly and no teachers abuse it.

Some disgruntled students have come to you, the principal, to complain about this policy. They know the department covers for their tardy colleagues, and the students are offended by this apparent double standard. Students who are late don't have anyone to cover for them; they must suffer the consequences. In fairness, they argue, teachers should also bear the consequences of tardiness. You have carefully avoided any official recognition of this departure from standard procedures. The students have now complicated the matter, and, much to your chagrin, you have found there is also some carping about the matter among other teachers not in the social studies department.

You are undecided on what to do. Clearly, you could simply enforce the established policy and end the unofficial policy. You could change the policy. Or you could open the question of policy to the faculty at large. All have advantages and disadvantages. Perhaps if you do nothing, the issue will subside. After all, the unofficial practice of the social studies department has worked well for years, and it is May and the complaining students will soon graduate. You are confident that the authority to make and implement such policy rests with you, but the question of how to make it is vexing.

Discussing the Case

- Is this a case for simply enforcing the policy?
- Can you ignore this problem?
- Should others be involved in the solution to this problem?
- Use the simplified decision-making model to decide who should be involved and the form of their involvement.
- If you are feeling venturesome, also use the Vroom-Jago model to develop a strategy of action. Compare the actions suggested by the models.

ENDNOTES

1. An earlier version of the simplified model appeared in the *Journal of Educational Administration* (Hoy & Tarter, 1993a).
2. Our framework for distinguishing decision-making arrangements is similar to Vroom and Yetton's (1973) management decision methods; however, we distinguish between consensus and majority rule because some situations require consensus, but we do not distinguish between sharing and obtaining information.
3. We thank Cheryl Moretz for permitting us to use her case analysis.
4. We thank Fred Reiss for permitting us to use his case analysis.

CHAPTER EIGHT

DECISION MAKING
Final Cases

The last two chapters have extended our discussion of decision making to include two models that involve subordinates in problem solving. Although the models are distinct, they are variations of the more general frameworks presented in Chapters 2 through 5. We conclude our discussion of decision making by reviewing, comparing, and contrasting the Vroom–Jago comprehensive model of managing participation with our original and simplified model of shared participation.

SUBORDINATE PARTICIPATION: A COMPARISON

The two shared decision-making frameworks are dramatically different in their degree of complexity. The Vroom and Jago (V-J) framework is clearly more complicated than our model (H-T). Even where questions are answered categorically, as yes or no rather than along a Likert scale, the sheer number of criteria in the V-J model is formidable; in fact, the V-J model is difficult to use without the aid of decision trees (see Figures 6.1, 6.2, 6.3, and 6.4). The decision trees certainly help, but they themselves can be intimidating, especially to the neophyte.

One clear advantage of the H-T model is its simplicity. There are only three criteria for including subordinates in decision making—expertise, relevance, and trust, which produce six paths to subordinate participation. The criteria are intuitive and easily remembered. In contrast, the V-J model employs eight criteria and two additional constraining factors that produce four variations on the general perspective. The paths to subordinate participation are consequently complex and varied; in fact, there are thirty-two recommended paths to consider in the complex model as well as significant differences between individual and group problems. In brief, our simplified model (H-T) has three criteria and six paths to consider, while the comprehensive (V-J) model has eight criteria and a myriad of decision paths.

Ease of use is another important consideration in comparing the two frameworks. Ease of use is closely related to complexity; the more complex the model, the more difficult it is and the less inclined managers are to use it. As we have just seen, the H-T simplified model is easier to use than the V-J comprehensive one. Is ease of use a compromise with effectiveness? Usually not. Our systematic study of the solutions to problems posed by Vroom and Jago (1988) demonstrated that most of the time the decision strategies are the same. In fact, when they vary, the differences are subtle and tend to be those of emphasis and style. In these cases, we suspect that empirical data will reveal no significant differences in effectiveness.

Scope distinguishes the two perspectives. Without question, the V-J model has broader scope. It specifically deals with individual as well as group problems and with subordinate development as well as time constraints. Our simplified model does not specifically deal with the issues of development and time. Ease of use is the tradeoff for broad scope.

Research support for the V-J model is more extensive. The V-J model is a direct extension of the original Vroom-Yetton model developed in 1963, for which there has been ample validation evidence (Vroom & Jago, 1988). Miner (1984, 1988) concludes that the Vroom-Yetton model is unsurpassed as a contingency approach to leadership in both its validity and usefulness. The current V-J version also has some empirical support (Vroom & Jago, 1988). Our simplified model is grounded in a strong theoretical tradition (Barnard, 1938; Bridges, 1964, 1967; Simon, 1947) and is supported by indirect empirical evidence (Duke, Showers, & Imber, 1980; Hoy & Tarter, 1993a; Mulder, 1971; Schneider, 1984). Although both models need further empirical validation, the V-J model has a stronger empirical base.

Both models have practical *utility*. Both models are widely applicable to practical administrative problems. Both provide guidelines to help administrators manage participation in decision making in ways that are effective. Practitioners find in both models useful tools for problem solving in their daily work. Our experience in classes over the past twenty years has reconfirmed our sense of the utility of each of the models, and there is ample evidence to suggest that both are widely used (Hoy & Miskel, 2001; Vroom & Jago, 1988).

It is in the question of *parsimony* that the difference between the two models is perhaps most stark. The simplified model of Hoy and Tarter is much more parsimonious than the comprehensive models of Vroom and Jago. As we have demonstrated, the number of questions and constraints of the V-J model lead to many more competing decision paths and considerations than the H-T model.

In sum, the differences in the two models along the six criteria of complexity, ease of use, scope, research support, utility, and parsimony are summarized in Table 8.1. The V-J model is more complex, has a broader scope, and has more

TABLE 8.1 A Comparison of the Vroom-Jago (V-J) and Hoy-Tarter (H-T) Models of Shared Decision Making

CRITERIA	V-J	H-T
Complexity	High	Low
Ease of Use	Low	High
Scope	Broader	Narrower
Research Support	Extensive	Limited
Utility	High	High
Parsimony	Low	High

empirical support, but it is more difficult to use and less parsimonious than the simplified H-T framework. Both models have high utility (see Table 8.1).

WHICH MODEL?

There are benefits and costs for using either of the shared decision making models. Ultimately, the administrator will decide. A major consideration for most will be the importance of the problem at hand. The costs of the V-J model are clear—time and effort. It is difficult initially to learn the model, and then it is challenging to apply it. As we have suggested, and others have confirmed, either a decision tree or a computer is necessary for its effective use. This impediment limits the attractiveness of the model. What administrator wants to carry a decision tree around in his or her pocket? The use of either a tree or a computer gives the impression of a merely mechanistic approach to human problems.

On the other hand, the simplified H-T model requires neither a pony nor a computer. The model is an in-the-head tool that administrators can easily carry around with them at all times. It is easy to learn, easy to apply, and is highly flexible; it is a guide to action. Further, it can easily be combined with the satisficing, mixed-scanning, and incremental models that we have already discussed. However, the simplified model pays a price for its simplicity. It may not be as well suited for exceedingly complex problems as the comprehensive formulation of Vroom and Jago.

Our advice in selecting a model is straightforward. *Use the H-T model routinely and flexibly. On important problems, when you have time, check the validity of the H-T strategy with the V-J model.* Important problems demand the careful analyses provided by the Vroom-Jago perspective to support the tentative strategy developed using the simplified approach. It is easy for us to make such recommendations, but it is another matter for students and administrators to accept them. Only when individuals are convinced of the power and practical utility of such frameworks will they become part of their conceptual repertoire and standard behavior. We believe the best way for individuals to routinely use the models is to find through practice that, indeed, the models work. Thus, we conclude with a series of case studies and problems that lend themselves to shared decision making. Practice developing strategies for each case using both models. You will decide when to use each model and how each fits into your administrative practice in general and decision making in particular.

CASE 8.1

Administrative Communication

You are the superintendent of a K–12 district with 4,000 students. You have good relationships with the board of education, your administrative staff, and the teachers in the district. Recently, however, you have felt that the board has become too narrowly focused in such technical activities as investment decisions, purchasing agreements, and negotiations. You are afraid that the board members are losing touch with the more important educational activities you have been initiating throughout the district. You feel that the board is not only missing the forest, they may be looking at the wrong trees.

You sense that the board views you as an efficient manager rather than as an educational leader. That makes you uncomfortable. You are justly proud of your managerial prowess, but your primary concern as an educator has always been broad educational matters rather than bureaucratic efficiency. Your board is composed of professionals including four middle-level managers from Exxon, AT&T, Xerox, and Merck. They like the administrative efficiencies that you have introduced to the district, but you feel that there has been an overemphasis on these matters at the expense of some of the more important educational issues. It is time to address this problem, a problem that you believe will be solved by routinely informing the board of the educational initiatives that are currently underway in the district. It is a problem of information and communication, not one of change and new directions.

You feel constrained to act, that is, to inform your board about exciting and challenging educational initiatives that you have first-hand knowledge of in the district. Basically, this is your problem, one of improving communication with the board.

Discussing the Case

- Is this a personal problem that requires no consultation?
- Should you involve the board in this problem? How?
- Should you involve your staff in this problem? How?
- Is this simply a problem of communication?
- Is this an issue for incremental decision making, or should the shared decision-making models be used?
- Develop a decision strategy for action as the superintendent.

CASE 8.2

Principal's In-Service

You are a high school principal who has done quite well in the administration of a large comprehensive high school. As both reward and part of your professional development, the superintendent and the board of education have agreed to send you to a special management training seminar for school principals, sponsored by the Harvard Business School. The seminar will last three weeks and provides participants with five distinct curricular options:

1. coaching
2. information management
3. team building

4. organizational culture

5. organizational design

Each participant is permitted to enroll in two of these elective options. You are excited about the prospect, and you want to get the most benefit possible from the experience. All the options sound intriguing. You have the pleasant task of deciding on your specialty. You have checked with the superintendent, who agrees that any and all of the options are useful and encourages you to make your own decision.

You have decided to participate in coaching and team building tracks. You mentioned what you were going to do to your assistant, who asked you if you had talked to any of the faculty about your choices. You had not even thought about it. Why? Now you are having second thoughts. Do you need to involve teachers in all decisions? Even decisions that are for your own professional involvement? Then again, they may very well be influenced by what you learn at Harvard. What to do?

Discussing the Case

- At first blush, this case seems like a personal professional decision, but it may have consequences for the faculty.
- How sensitive should an administrator be to the consequences of his or her professional decisions?
- Are professional decisions of superiors so connected to the work of subordinates that subordinates should typically be consulted? Or is such consultation usually unnecessary? Where should the line be drawn?
- What about this case? Should the teachers be consulted? Why or why not?
- Develop a decision strategy for action as the principal.

CASE 8.3

Parent Complaint

You are the principal of a K–8 school, and you have been working to develop harmonious relations between the school and the community. Thus, you were dismayed when several parents dropped by your office, ostensibly to talk about parents' night but actually to complain about Mr. Jones. All three claimed that their children are terrorized by his loud manner and aggressive tactics. Mr. Jones has taught in the district for five years and has always been respected and admired by kids and teachers alike.

In the past, Mr. Jones has taught sixth and seventh grade and coached the soccer team. Jones, who lettered in two sports in college, was a physical education minor. He is one of only five men in this elementary school of twenty-six teachers. This year he was assigned to third grade, which he welcomed. You thought it would be useful to introduce a male role model earlier in the school program. Jones agreed; he likes kids. You have observed him in the classroom more than a dozen times during his tenure and there is no question in your mind that he is a knowledgeable and skillful elementary teacher. The kids learn.

As part of a school-based management project started in the district this year, the teachers in your school have elected a supervisory council to improve the instructional performance of the faculty. The council is strictly a teachers' group; the principal is not a member. This is the council's first foray into faculty management; the faculty is eager and well-meaning, but a bit hesitant.

On the one hand, it might be best to handle this matter informally and discreetly. Jones is a popular and easygoing teacher with whom you have good personal and professional relations. On the other hand, you do have a supervisory council to deal with such matters. Your teachers are professionals. They claim they want to be much more involved in the management of the school.

Discussing the Case

- Is this a case in which you initiate teachers in the management of the school?
- Should you talk to Jones about this matter before making any decisions?
- Is this an issue simply among you, Jones, and the parents?
- Is this a case for a mixed-scanning or an incremental model?
- Under what conditions should the teachers of the supervisory council be involved? Are either of the shared decision-making models useful here?
- Develop a decision strategy for action as the principal.

CASE 8.4

The Hiring Problem

You have been a principal for seven years. Your district has finally hired a superintendent who is willing to delegate important professional matters to the administrative staff. At the last administrative council meeting, a monthly meeting of all the principals in the district, the superintendent announced that he was decentralizing hiring procedures. In the future, all principals would be responsible for hiring teachers in their schools. Although the superintendent retained a veto power, it seemed clear to you that finally you would be able to hire the teachers you deemed best for the job.

This morning, one of your teachers walked into your office sobbing. After a few minutes, she calmed down and announced that she had to quit. She found out last week that she was pregnant; she and her husband felt that she should leave teaching for a few years. She is happy about the impending birth, but sad to leave a profession in which she has been so successful. You are a little unhappy, too. There is no question in your mind that she has been a good teacher, and replacing her will be difficult. Fortunately, you will have until winter break (about three months) to hire a new teacher.

This is your first opportunity to use the new hiring policy. There are a myriad of questions to be answered. Should you advertise? Where? How should you screen applicants? How should you interview? How many tiers should be in the interviewing process? How many semifinalists and finalists should be selected? Should there be observations? What other criteria should be used to evaluate applicants? Should the faculty be used in the process? If so, how?

Discussing the Case

- Use the simplified model of decision making to develop a strategy of action.
- Who should be involved? How? What is your role as principal?
- How extensively should the faculty be involved? What should be their role?
- Is this a time for total consensus?
- After you have analyzed this case using the simplified model for shared decision making, use the Vroom–Jago model on the case and then compare your results.

CASE 8.5

The Advisory Council

You are the principal of a high school in a district that has recently settled long-standing union discord. As part of the agreement, the district encourages the principal to consult with an advisory council on questions of curriculum matters, though the contract does not mandate such consultation. The advisory council at your school is made up of elected faculty who represent each department of the school; they number twelve.

The social studies teachers on the council have privately expressed their disagreement with the current curricular emphasis in the department. They consider the program to have too much content and not enough process. You are willing to provide a forum in which a discussion can take place. But nothing is ever as simple as it seems.

You realize that the advisory council's position in the school organization will be strengthened if they are involved in the decision. Yet not all the members have expertise that bears directly on this curricular question. Moreover, in the past there have been acrimonious confrontations between the math and science people, on the one hand, and the social studies teachers on the other. The math and science teachers contend that the social studies program is already too process oriented and is devoid of sufficient content. The social studies teachers scoff at the narrow-mindedness and rigidity of these so-called scientists.

After years of difficult negotiation with the union and with the teachers, you have finally succeeded in producing some harmony in the school. You wish to preserve the harmony, but you realize that in airing the different dimensions of the problem, conflict is inevitable.

As you plan a forum to consider changes in the social studies curriculum, you must decide who should be the players in this decision and what role they should have. Should the council be involved? The department? Only the interested teachers? Everyone?

Discussing the Case

- Use the two shared decision-making models and develop a strategy for action.
- What are the constraints in the problem at hand?
- Can the models be used to overcome sharp professional differences?
- To what extent can curricular decisions be delegated to teachers?
- Is this a problem for the entire advisory council or only the social studies teachers?

CASE 8.6

Student Athletes

Your school has had an increasingly successful athletic program. School teams have acquired a regional prominence, and a new sense of community spirit has emerged, which has produced a level of community support for the school hitherto unsuspected and unexperienced. People in the community like the school, support its programs, and regularly vote for the budget. The students are proud of their school and are quick to say so. They believe their school is the best. Teachers like it, too. It is a great place to teach, a far cry from what it was when you arrived five years ago.

Teachers in the school have been involved in curriculum development and in-service activities since you took over. You and your staff have worked to develop a more professional level of operation. You have seen the school become a more open place to work and to learn. Teachers go about their work with a real enthusiasm, and their commitment to academic performance is shared by the students. There is little question about the improvement of the academic program, but it has been the extraordinary success of the athletic teams that has brought solidarity to the school and community.

You are troubled, however, by recent complaints from the math department that students are often pulled from their last period classes ten minutes early so that team practices can begin on time. As you investigate their complaint, you find that other departments are similarly troubled. In fact, a confrontation between the coaches and the academic departments is brewing. Unfortunately, virtually all the coaches come from the social studies and physical education departments.

You are thinking about simply establishing a policy that would end the practice of students leaving classes early. Although you have the power, and this may be the time to short circuit a conflict, you have earned the reputation of involving teachers in important decisions, and the teachers have responded well.

Discussing the Case

- Is a quick, unilateral decision appropriate here?
- If not, who should be involved and to what extent?
- Who should have the final say? You? Your teachers? Or must there be some kind of consensus?
- Are coaches educators first and foremost? Does the answer affect how they should be involved in the decision?
- Develop a decision strategy for action as the principal.

CASE 8.7

Subversive Web Page

Upper Lebanon (UL) is a suburban community near a large west coast city. The district is fortunate to have one of the wealthiest tax bases in the state. Not surprisingly, Upper Lebanon High School has a reputation of being the best public high school in the state. Some might argue about that conclusion, but virtually no one would dispute the fact that UL is one of the best. Ninety-five percent of its students go on to higher education; last year the high school had forty national merit scholars; and the school routinely has 10 percent of its students accepted to Stanford, Berkeley, and Ivy League colleges.

Students are active in all kinds of intellectual endeavors, and there is a small group of students who get their needs fulfilled by using computer networks in creative ways, including at least a half dozen hackers who are about as good as they come. Given these facts, it came as no surprise to Principal Marian Eaglehof that many of the students had their own web pages, which they maintained and showcased. Some were truly creative. For example, one student had a mix of vacation blogs on the web site that combined still pictures, videos, and commentaries of vacation destinations along with inexpensive travel and accommodation information. Marian had even used the site to plan her summer vacation to Greece, and her husband welcomed the substantial savings.

This morning, however, Principal Eaglehof was acutely aware of a new site that had emerged quickly and without warning. The web page was a critical analysis of the high school and some of its teachers and administrators. There was a buzz among the students about the site, www.realul.com, which promised inside information about the students, teachers, and administrators at UL.

Apparently, this very day there was a lead feature on the site showing a picture of a teacher with her arm around a young student. The caption for the picture read "Hanky-Pank at Upper Lebanon?" The accompanying blog carefully raised the question of inappropriate behavior of Miranda Lee, the social studies department chair. The blog was circumspect and never quite claimed that there was untoward behavior by either the student or the teacher, but it was cleverly enough written to pique one's imagination.

The site went on to promise further and startling disclosures about the social and intellectual life at UL. One future item caught the principal's eye—"Principal Eaglehof to Terminate Teacher." No specific teacher was named, but the principal was caught off guard because it was indeed true that she was not going to recommend reappointment of second-year teacher Bart Mathews. Eaglehof had been quietly compiling a record of class visitations, performance evaluations, and comments from colleagues and parents about the teacher. These were password protected in a special file on her school computer. Some of the information was simply allegation but also included were the actual performance evaluations of Mathews. All the data were confidential and the school had taken some steps to maintain firewalls and state-of-the-art security. The information was collected from department chairs, supervisors, and influential faculty members, some of whom were not particularly careful with sensitive written reports. On more than one occasion, Eaglehof had walked into a supervisor's office to find personnel evaluation forms simply left in view for the most casual observer.

Another item promised a student evaluation of all math faculty, in what was termed "the real skinny," what students really knew about their teachers, from their undergraduate grade point averages (GPAs) to their credit scores and their other institutional affiliations. The motto of the site was "The Truth and Only the Truth: It Will Set You Free." Eaglehof was aghast.

The student or students running the site had not done anything illegal, though they judiciously were walking a fine line. The principal found it especially irritating that the last item on the site was an extensive discussion of the First Amendment and Constitutional guarantees for all people, including students. The discourse ended with a resounding conclusion that students should not fear expressing themselves on all topics, especially controversial ones, provided that it was done within the boundaries of the law.

Discussing the Case

- Is this a case for shared decision making?
- What should Principal Eaglehof do?
- With whom should she consult?
- Should she initiate some preemptive action to nip this in the bud? If so, what?
- Should she informally alert her faculty and staff, or would that simply play into the hands of the students running the site?
- Should she attempt to find the students involved? How?
- What would she do if she found out?
- Is she overreacting? Perhaps, she should just monitor for now.
- Does she need a committee of teachers and administrators to discuss the issue and potential disruption that could ensue?
- Should she touch base with the superintendent? School attorney?
- Should she talk to Bart Mathews? What would she say?
- Should she talk with the social studies chair, Miranda Lee? What would she say?
- Should the school develop a school policy on student web sites?
- Assume the role of the principal of this outstanding school and develop a plan to deal with the situation described in the case.

CASE 8.8

Grading Policy

"It is not fair to have my child in that class, and I want you to do something about it!" the parent screamed at Pat Hempstead, principal of the town's middle school. This parent, louder than most, but echoing the complaint of others, had come to have her child transferred from Joyce Nygren's eighth-grade English class. Nygren's class and her grading policies had become the subject of student and parent concern. Hempstead reflected on the series of events that occurred since the beginning of school.

1. In the third week of school, a sobbing student rushed into his office with a tale of unfair treatment. She had been given an F on her first writing assignment simply because she had left the assignment in her locker and not turned it in on time; the teacher refused to let her go to her locker for the paper. Hempstead calmed the girl and promised to talk to Mrs. Nygren. It was Nygren's position that adolescents should be taught responsibility.

2. It was shortly after the incident of the paper in the locker that three students requested a transfer from Nygren's class. They were all good students and were worried about maintaining their grade-point average. Hempstead told them not to worry about their grades and explained that they were receiving a rigorous educational experience, and they should return to the class and work harder.

3. It was after the first marking period that things started to get out of control. Out of one hundred students, Nygren gave one A, ten Bs, and thirty-nine Cs. Approximately half of the students got Ds or simply failed. Hempstead found out about this grading distribution as parents began calling the principal's office. And it wasn't just Nygren: English grades were down generally.

4. When Hempstead talked with Nygren, she was friendly and not unsympathetic to the problem. However, she argued that these good students needed to be confronted with the rigors of excellence that they would encounter in high school. "After all," she exclaimed, "these grades won't influence college admissions. I'm trying to get these young people used to the harsh realities of the real world. I guarantee that by the end of the year their grades will be up and, more important, they will know the proper use of the Queen's English." She seemed concerned that the youngsters learn as much as possible.

5. Nygren had been on the staff as long as Hempstead had been principal—six years. She had never had any trouble with parents, students, or colleagues. She was well respected by all. Hempstead was puzzled by this sudden turn of events and decided to talk informally with the department chair. The chair told Hempstead not to worry. He explained that the department was raising standards and, in fact, three of the teachers, including

Mrs. Nygren, had taken a special summer workshop, "Excellence for the Twenty-First Century." They had returned with enthusiasm and a renewed sense of mission, determined to improve the quality of instruction and learning in English education.

6. Hempstead's concerns grew when the band director came to complain that a couple of his best students were dropping out of band to devote more time to Mrs. Nygren's English class. The band director said the standards in Nygren's class had become ridiculous. He argued, "After all, Pat, this is a middle school. Students are supposed to explore different areas. This isn't a senior high school. Nygren is frustrating the kids; her work takes up too much of their time. They don't have time to be kids. And it's not just Nygren, you know, it's that whole damn English department. They're nuts. This is middle school. These are kids. Let's lighten up."

7. These were prophetic words, no sooner spoken than a number of complaints about the grading of Henry and Davidson, two other eighth-grade English teachers, began to surface. They, too, were giving what parents claimed to be a disproportionate number of low grades. Only Geoff Spencer in the English department gave what parents (and students) considered to be easy grades. Although Spencer did not have a reputation as a strong teacher, he had become increasingly popular.

8. Hempstead had a somewhat unusual encounter at the meat market when by chance he ran into his friend and superintendent, Chris Butler. The superintendent asked him how things were going. Although Hempstead said everything was fine, the superintendent wished Hempstead good luck with the grading problem. Hempstead left the store wondering how widely the grading problem was known and feeling increasingly uncomfortable.

9. The issue had now come to a head when the screaming woman turned out to be the wife of a board member. "I want my child out of Nygren's class" was the refrain that kept going through his mind. The school year was not even half over and a revolt among the parents and students seemed imminent.

The time to do something is now. You are the principal. If you don't take the initiative, you and your English department will be caught like leaves in the fall wind.

Discussing the Case

- Is this a case for shared decision making?
- Who should be involved? The teachers? The parents? No one?
- Should you take bold action and initiate your own plan to prevent future problems?
- Should you delay any action until you get a better feel for things?
- Develop a plan of action and rationale. Don't forget unanticipated consequences.

CASE 8.9

Honest Reporting?

Students in New Albany High School in upstate New York do not pass through metal detectors. They are not escorted to class by police officers, and their lockers are graffiti free and not routinely searched for drugs. But last month the New York State Department of Education placed New Albany on its first "Watch List of Dangerous Schools." New Albany was listed in the top ten schools in student violence—for weapons possession, assaults, drug arrests, and arson.

New Albany High School is a suburban school nestled in a high-tech campus on a former air force base. Teachers, students, and parents are in agreement "New Albany does not belong on this list."

"Maybe they have been too honest," said Gary Sandioni, the local police chief and the husband of a New Albany High science teacher.

A national list of "persistently dangerous" schools, the most serious category of violent schools, was developed last year. Pennsylvania accounted for one quarter of the total, and New Jersey and New York combined to account for a second quarter, while a majority of the states had no schools on the list.

The bad publicity for the New Albany schools not only is troubling but has the superintendent and school board on the defensive. Although parents don't believe the statistics, they don't like the negative publicity. A few are disgruntled because they fear the value of their homes may be falling. One parent commented, "I don't like the reputation we are getting because it sounds like we are not a good place to live."

At a closed session of the board of education, the discussion of this embarrassing report consumed more than two hours, with everyone agreeing that it was not a fair picture of the schools in New Albany. Sure, they had their fights and drugs in the school, but life in New Albany was relatively safe—students, teachers, and parents were not worried about violence in their schools. There was general agreement that safety in the schools of New Albany was much better than that in New York City, Rochester, and Buffalo; indeed, there was no comparison.

An analysis of the school records supported this conclusion; the data showed that most of the violent incidents at New Albany involved confiscation of penknives (weapons) and fights between students. There were only two cases that led to any serious injury. In the first, a student received medical treatment after a fight on the school bus (a broken nose), and in the second a student got upset and tossed a book over his shoulder striking a teacher in the eye. Both the teacher and the student agreed that the injury was accidental. The latter incident is the kind in which mandatory reporting is required.

The consensus of the board was that violence should be reported the way most other schools reported it, that is, not be so concerned with the letter of the law but rather with the general practice of reporting. For example, Mount Holly, a district not too far removed from New Albany and one with twice as many students, did not report a single assault resulting in physical injury for the last academic school year; New Albany reported more than fifty such incidents. And even if you asked people from Mount Holly about safety in the schools, most would agree that New Albany schools were much safer.

"I think that we are over-reporting our violence," said Donald Garcia, the president of the New Albany Board of Education, "while Mount Holly is under-reporting and it makes us look bad."

To which the superintendent responded, "I am not comfortable with the implied suggestion that honesty is a vice not a virtue."

"We are not suggesting you be dishonest," said the board president, "but rather we want your reporting to be in line with others. The bottom line is that we want our schools and this community to be given due credit for having good and safe schools. We must stop this bad and untrue publicity. The fact is that our schools are not dangerous, and it is dishonest to say they are."

Although the superintendent felt troubled, he realized this was neither the time nor the place to make an issue of honesty. This was a time to be constructive, and the superintendent asked for some guidance.

After another hour of give and take, the board charged the superintendent to develop a plan with the following objectives:

1. to correct the false impression of the schools and community that had been generated by the news media;
2. to be prudent in the reporting of violence at school;
3. to improve safety in the schools.

Discussing the Case

- Is this case for shared decision making? Who should be involved? Assume the role of superintendent.
- What are the short-term and long-term problems?
- Is the board suggesting that you be less than honest?
- Is that what "prudence" means?
- Is this an ethical dilemma for you and your principals? Why?
- What directions should you give principals in reporting incidents of violence? How will they react?
- How should you track violence in schools?
- How can you improve the safety of schools?
- What can you do to correct the false impressions that have been created?
- Outline a strategy of action in response to the board of education's charge.
- Who should be involved in responding to the board's mandate and why?
- How will violence be reported? How can over-reporting be limited?
- Be sure your plan responds to all three objectives of the board's mandate.

CASE 8.10

Double Entendre

Arbor Heights is a suburban community within an easy commute to a major population center, Capital City, where many of the Arbor Heights people work as professionals. The comfort, convenience, and, above all, the excellence of the schools keep the town happy, real estate values high, and the town's children good bets for admission to the best universities. This is a place that takes its educational advantages seriously.

Administering Arbor Heights High School (AHHS) is a negotiated dance between stability to maintain high academic performance and a carefully cultivated freedom for the broadest range of student ideas. There is always a balance between order and freedom, and AHHS is struggling with that dilemma. Students at AHHS seem to push the limits of freedom, while teachers and administrators want to maintain decorum, good taste, and academic performance. This is an academic high school: the students are bright, curious, sophisticated, and adventurous.

One of the issues that risk the delicate balance of order and freedom is the dress of students. The overwhelming majority of students have the resources to dress in current fashion. Designer jeans for the girls at AHHS are the rule, not the exception. Although the jeans are stylish, yet conventional, the accompanying T-shirts are often provocative and loaded with double meanings, forcing administrators and teachers to make fine distinctions over what is acceptable and what is not. For the most part, there is an uneasy acceptance of the dress of students at AHHS. But, without challenge, the T-shirts are getting more risqué and closer to crossing that obscure albeit important line over what is appropriate and in good taste.

Consider the following T-shirts that generally go unchallenged by teachers and administrators. "Your boyfriend is a flirt"; "I'm too hot"; and "Yes, but not U"; "Meet me by the bike racks"; "Trust me, I'm good." These T-shirts have been given a pass. However, when students are wearing shirts that clearly cross the line, they are usually given a school T-shirt to wear for the day or asked to turn their shirts inside out. Administrators claim that evaluating the shirts is awkward in many respects, especially so when the words are printed right over the student's chest. Moreover, students make it difficult by striding past quickly or ducking away and taking evasive actions when they see an administrator in the hall. It is like a game of PacMan. Retailers are not much help. For example, when asked about the messages his company markets to teenagers, a vice-president for corporate communication at an upscale clothing chain explained, "Our t-shirts are sometimes controversial, which we are fine with." He declined further comment.

Parents are concerned about what their kids wear. In fact, they generally oppose racy shirts, but they either don't know what the students actually wear to school or just give in. For example, Marianne Dooley ordered her daughter, Tina, a seventeen-year-old senior, to return a T-shirt that said "Yes, but not U." But Tina insisted and the mother caved in. "I have to pick my battles," the mother said. "OK, I don't like it; but she's wearing it and it could be worse."

When the assistant principal challenged another senior with a provocative and sexy shirt by asking her, "Why would you wear something like that?" She retorted, "I don't know, but my dad knows I wear it."

When the assistant principal called the dad, his response was that he had no idea that his girl had such a shirt and he bluntly said, "Just throw it away."

In this context, the principal found himself on the defensive when a social studies teacher was unhappy about one of his student's T-shirts, which proclaimed, "I support the oral tradition."

When the principal asked the teacher, "Did you ask her what it meant?" the teacher responded with exasperation, "Yes, I made that mistake. The student told me that I ought to know she was referring to the oral rather than the written tradition in history. It is your job to keep the lid on this stuff and it is getting out of hand. I know that both Aurelio Sanchez and Grace Fletcher feel the same way."

The principal knew that the Spanish teacher and English teacher were close friends of the social studies teacher. Up till this point there was a little conversation, mostly joking, about the T-shirts, but more important, were things getting out of hand? As he thought about the current state of affairs, he mulled on a number of questions.

Discussing the Case

- Is this a case for shared decision making?
- How widespread was faculty concern on this issue?
- Was it time to develop a more specific student dress code?
- How should the students be involved?
- Is this one of those issues that might better be left alone?
- To what extent do the parents know what their children wear to school? Do they care?
- Is it the school's responsibility to tell the parents about the dress of their children?
- Is this really a problem? If so, will it take care of itself?
- Assume the role of principal in this school and develop a plan of action. Be sure to anticipate in your plan the potential negative consequences that could occur, and address the question of whether your actions are worth those outcomes.

CASE 8.11

Special Education: Successful Collaboration?

"Why me?" asked Nancy Chow.

"Because," answered Principal McGurren, "you are a good English teacher, the kids like you, and your colleagues respect you. I think you are a good candidate to help us work out a collaborative program mainstreaming a special education student. It will really help the student and I would appreciate your giving us a hand here."

McGurren was relieved with Chow's agreement. McGurren, who had been principal at Suburban High for six years, was also happy to report to the superintendent's office that he had found a reliable teacher to help satisfy the board's request for inclusive teaching at the high school. While McGurren didn't know much about special education, he was in basic agreement with the board's policy to foster inclusion for the sake of No Child Left Behind (NCLB) scores and he genuinely believed that most special education kids reap a long-term benefit from inclusion.

Chow, who taught sophomore English, met later that month with Julia McMahon, a special education teacher designated to work as a partner. The meeting went well as McMahon described the student, Stephen Jenkins, who would be in Chow's class. Stephen had been diagnosed as borderline attention deficit disorder and had difficulty keeping on task. McMahon reassured Chow that the behaviors shown by Stephen were controllable and would not disrupt the class. The student's Individual Educational Program (IEP) was amended to include regular sophomore English.

About three weeks later, Nancy Chow was in the principal's office expressing doubts about the collaboration effort. Chow taught composition and had a long-standing rule: *No student paper could pass with more than 5 grammatical errors.* The course focused on writing and rewriting, and students had conformed to her expectations in composition over the years. Stephen Jenkins, Chow suggested, should be sent back to special education classes; he could not pass her requirements for the course and changing the course would not serve anybody's interest. Jenkins often did not pay attention in class and was sometimes a disruption to the other students.

It was Julia McMahon's turn the next day to talk to the principal. "Look," said McMahon, "if Stephen accomplishes, say 80%, of the IEP in English, that is significant. He has not been in inclusion courses and needs more time for accommodation. I tried to explain to Nancy that behavior changes take some time. In fact, I wrote up my rationale for treating Stephen a little differently and she had the nerve to send my memo back to me with the grammatical mistakes circled in red! Give me a break! I've been teaching special education for ten years and I have seen this sort of insensitive behavior on the part of regular teachers for every one of those years. I respect her command over the niceties of language, but she shows no respect for my knowledge of the behavior of these kids. She complains because Stephen is a little spontaneous and thoughtless in his actions. Believe me, as special education kids go, he is a peach."

Discussing the Case

- Is this a case for shared decision making?
- Is there a difference between mainstreaming and inclusion?
- What is your strategy? Bring the teachers together for a conference?

- Should you involve the district special education coordinator?
- Is this an issue for which school policy should be developed?
- Should the superintendent be advised or consulted?
- Just what is the problem and how do you frame it?
- Develop a plan of action.

CASE 8.12

Just Charge It

Linda Owens, a thirteen-year veteran, has been principal at M. L. King Middle School for the past five years. M. L. King is located in the heart of a large urban school system in the Midwest. She has been pleased with her progress. Since she became principal, the low state proficiency test scores have risen slightly but consistently for the past four years. She credits much of the improvement to new relationships that have been forged between her teachers and the parents. One of the mechanisms to involve teachers has been the parent–teacher organization (PTO), which has grown both in membership and in engagement. Meetings of the PTO are marked by a spirit of give and take but a coming together once a decision has been made. Although Principal Owens seldom misses a meeting, two nights ago was the exception. She was surprised when the president of the PTO, Denise Johnson, scheduled a meeting to see her first thing Monday morning to discuss what Denise called a "brilliant idea." Linda wondered what the "brilliant idea" was and she was about to find out.

Denise was excited and exuberant as she entered the office and gave the principal a big hug. "We had a wonderful meeting," Denise exclaimed. "And we developed the best idea that I have heard since I have been a member of the PTO—the Panther Parent Credit Card."

"So, tell me what is the Panther Parent Credit Card?" asked Principal Owens.

"Well, it is not a real credit card, but here is how it would work. Parents can earn credit card points by volunteering to help out around the school. And then those points can be spent in a number of ways including free admission to athletic events, free food at Parent-Teacher Conferences, or a free Panther tee shirt. Later in the year, parents will be allowed to pass on points to their children, who can buy forgiveness."

Owens asked, somewhat startled, "Buy forgiveness?"

"Yes, suppose a student has forgotten her homework; 50 points might give the student a chance to bring it in the following day. Or, suppose you get an F on a test, maybe 50 points would bring up your score to a D, or a 100 points to a C."

The PTO president continued her explanation, "The credit card program isn't meant to let students wiggle out of their academic responsibilities, but rather to urge parents to get involved in helping their kids succeed. Parental involvement can benefit students' grades a lot more than the occasional quiz-score boost. Think of the possibilities: We might give points for good behavior, or maybe to buy special privileges, school spirit shirts, or snacks at the school cafeteria. We haven't worked out the details of the program yet, but we are excited about the possibilities."

Taken aback, Principal Owens responded, "This is an intriguing idea, but we need to think it through a little more."

Denise responded, "We can get parents to monitor school bus areas during arrivals and departures, monitor the school lunch room, monitor study halls, and even monitor school detention. What we think will happen is that kids will save up their volunteer points for a "rainy day" and use them only in a pinch. What a terrific way to get parents involved!"

Principal Owens haltingly commented, "I am not sure what teachers will think of using points to get out of homework or using points to raise grades."

To which Denise explained, "We won't allow that to happen very often, but I am sure the teachers will join with the parents and work out the details. In fact, we will even get the students involved in determining legitimate uses for volunteer points. I see this as a win-win-win situation. Students win, parents win, and teachers win."

With that the principal rejoined, "This sounds like a good idea, but before we get too far down the road, let me run this by my teachers and my boss."

"They'll love it," Denise said with conviction and pride as she left the principal's office.

Principal Linda Owens sat back in her chair and reflected on what had just happened.

Discussing the Case

- Where should Principal Owens begin?
- The research is clear—parental involvement makes a difference in the academic success of students. Is this a good way to get such involvement?
- Is this intrinsic or extrinsic motivation? What are its consequences?
- The parents are excited, but what will the teachers think? Her superiors?
- What are the possible negative consequences of such a plan?
- What are the costs compared to the benefits?
- What is the likelihood of success? What is success?
- The principal needs a plan. Assume the principal's role and develop a specific strategy of action.

CASES IN HIGHER EDUCATION

Increasingly, students in educational administration classes are interested in working in higher education. The frameworks that we have described and demonstrated are useful in that context as well; in fact, the models have general applicability beyond schools.

CASE 8.13

Appropriate Attire

Greenlawn College is a strong regional college located in the heart of one of the largest cities in the United States. The college was founded by a religious order and continues a tradition of service to those in need; however, the college has taken on a distinctly sectarian tone in recent years. Its 17,000 undergraduates follow a number of majors and the school of education gets a large percentage of young people interested in teaching as a career. Often, these students are the first in their family to go to college. The college is sensitive to the problems of these students and has an extensive program teaching study habits, library skills, and offering math and writing labs.

Before students begin student teaching, they take a couple of courses that teach them how to observe what is going on in a school, including how to interview for a job in the schools. Some of these prospective teachers need advice and role models on such basics as what to wear on the job and to the interview. Occasionally, a student will indignantly argue that he should be judged by what he knows not by how he dresses.

"You not only have to be good; you have to look the part of a professional," says the department chair, Professor Pat Cotter, who has been serving as a successful administrator for the past decade. Cotter is responsible for supervising a faculty of twelve professors, seven senior professors, and five junior faculty. One of those faculty members is Roberta Vagas, a first-year hire from the University of California. Vagas was a real addition to the department because she brought a strong research background but, more important, the skill and enthusiasm of an outstanding teacher. Not only was she a good teacher, she modeled good teaching.

She didn't model good teaching enough Cotter opined, who thought that she dressed inappropriately for the classroom, especially as a university supervisor of student teachers on-site in local schools. All of Vagas's colleagues, male and female, young and old, dressed formally when visiting the schools. The men wore jackets and ties and the women wore either dresses or pantsuits. Not Vagas, who invariably wore jeans and a jacket. On the one hand, she looked fine; on the other, she was not modeling the kind of attire that the department required of its student teachers when they were in public school classes. In fact, one of the cooperating teachers mentioned to Cotter that Vagas looked too much like the high school students and not enough like a university professor. It irked Cotter that Vagas persisted even after it was broadly hinted that she might not be setting the proper example for the student teachers. Vagas was blithely indifferent to the situation. It especially bothered Cotter because appropriate attire had never been a problem in the department. The entire faculty dressed professionally, and there was never a need for a dress code. One of the hallmarks of Cotter's style was a caring informality. Cotter believed that the fewer rules, the better; professional judgment was the guide to behavior, not bureaucratic rules.

It was clear, however, that Vagas had not gotten the message on appropriate attire when visiting the local schools. A few of the student teachers, in fact, had made comments about the double standard in dress. Cotter believed he had to do something, but was this a problem of individual preference or the tone of the program? Should others be involved in the matter, or should it be kept strictly personal? Make no mistake about it, Professor Vagas was a talented young teacher educator, and Cotter, who saw the chair's role as supportive, not judgmental, was a bit hesitant in moving too quickly.

Discussing the Case

- Is there a problem here? If so, how would you frame it?
- Does the department head have an obligation to guide new professors?
- Should other members of the department be enlisted to help?
- At what point should the informal process yield to the formal one?
- Is this a case for participative decision making? If so, who should be involved and why?

CASE 8.14

Professional Dilemma

You are the associate dean of academic affairs at a graduate school of education in a major state university. Your school has seventy-five professors and nearly 2,000 students, most of whom are part-time. As associate dean, your role is to monitor the integrity of the academic programs, coordinate class scheduling, monitor the development and approval of new courses, maintain a quality doctoral program, serve as liaison between students and faculty, and occasionally adjudicate disputes between faculty members.

Henry Washington, a fifth-year Ph.D. student, arrives in your office Monday morning at 9:00 A.M. with a serious look on his face. Although he had no appointment, you fortunately had time to see him.

"Dean," he says, "we have a problem. I would like to speak to you in strict confidence. Will you agree to that?"

"Of course," you respond.

"Last Saturday morning, seven students from Educational Psychology sat for the candidacy exam. The exam was, in my view, unfair and bogus. I can tell you with certainty that at least half of the people cheated."

"How do you know that?" you immediately respond.

"A group of students got together and hired a hacker who got into the departmental secretary's files. At least, that is what I assume. What I know is that more than one person had a copy of the exam and had answers prepared. I really didn't know what to do, so I had a long talk with my minister yesterday to clear my mind and figure out what I should do. I believe the right thing for me to do is to ask that the entire exam be invalidated and that there be another test administered."

"Who were the cheaters?" you ask.

"With all due respect, Dean, I cannot in good conscience give you any names. In fact, I expect you to be true to your promise of confidentiality."

"Well, Mr. Washington, I can keep your name confidential, but I must act on this information."

"I was hoping you would do something, sir. Are you going to invalidate the exam?"

"I can't do that until I get more information and talk to the faculty in the Educational Psychology Department. But I am glad you came in, and be assured we will move on this information. Is there anything else you can tell me that might be useful?"

"No, sir, but I am relieved that you know of the foul play and are going to do something about it. Thank you for seeing me and listening to my grievance. And, please do as you promised. Keep our conversation confidential."

With that comment, Mr. Washington arose and departed.

You sit back in your chair to contemplate what has just transpired. What a mess!

Discussing the Case

- Is this a case for strong leadership?
- Is it time for a centralized policy on candidacy exams?
- Is this a schoolwide problem or a departmental problem?
- Does the school need an explicit policy on candidacy exams and cheating?
- What is your role in this problem? Should you attempt to resolve this issue?

CASE 8.15

Intellectual Property?

Professor John Knight was a full professor in the Department of Educational Psychology at a large East Coast university. He was a thirty-year veteran, a "full bull" as he described himself, and inclined to be cantankerous. Graduate students complained that his tests were twenty years old, and, indeed, there was some merit to their complaints. He always gave two examinations, a midterm and a final. The exams were always structured identically—fifty multiple-choice questions and one long essay.

The midterm of the fall semester found Professor Knight returning his examinations. His loyal graduate assistant, Jayne, sat in the back of the room observing her mentor. Knight dutifully went over the correct answer to each question and outlined what he had expected in the essay exam. After about fifteen minutes of questions and discussion, he asked the students to return all the papers, explaining that they were required to establish norms for future examinations. Although many of the students thought the real reason for returning the exams was that the same questions would be used on all future midterms, they didn't object.

The students obediently complied, and the papers came to the front of the room, that is, except for the paper of Lisa Pagan, who paid no heed to the directions. Much to his chagrin, Professor Knight repeated the directive and waited for the paper, but it was not forthcoming.

"Ms. Pagan, please pass your paper forward," he said harshly.

She responded, "No, Professor Knight, this is my paper, not yours. Indeed, it is my intellectual property and you are not entitled to it."

Knight was nonplused. Turning bright red, he exclaimed, "This is the last time I am going to tell you to turn in your paper!"

To which Pagan responded, "Yes, it is my paper, my intellectual property, and I am going to keep it. My score, if you don't have it recorded, is 78. The score is yours, but the paper is mine," she said as she folded the paper and put it securely in her purse.

Professor Knight, trying to maintain his composure, directed Jayne, his graduate assistant, to call campus security hoping that the threat would loosen the hold Ms. Pagan had on the paper. Jayne left the room; all were frozen in place watching the developing scene.

The standoff continued for another ten minutes before Officer Mazza appeared in class and inquired as to the problem.

"No problem here," said Professor Knight, "this student (pointing at Ms. Pagan) refuses to return my examination paper. Get it back."

To which the student indignantly responded, "This is my paper, my intellectual property, and I will not return it. It even has my name on it."

Officer Mazza thought to himself, "this is bizarre." Never had he encountered such a situation. But these people were serious. After another fifteen minutes of bickering, a compromise was agreed on. Ms. Pagan would surrender her paper to Officer Mazza, who would give her a receipt for it, and he promised to lock it in the vault at campus security. The dean would adjudicate the question when she returned to campus early the following week.

You are the dean and, much to your consternation, Monday morning you get a call from campus security; they explain the situation to you and ask if it is all right to bring the paper in question to your office. You tell security you will get back to them shortly.

Discussing the Case

- What are you going to tell security?
- Do you want this exam paper in your office?
- Do you want to talk to the protagonists?
- Should you get the department chair involved?
- Is this really a problem?
- Who should be involved in making this decision?
- Are you the final arbiter? What is your role here?
- Do you want to be the final arbiter?
- Are there legal implications to your action?
- Do you want to involve the university lawyer?

CASE 8.16

Grade Change

Dr. Margo MacDermott is the Assistant Dean for Student Affairs in the College of Education of State University. She has been in this position for five years and has a reputation among students and faculty as being judicious and fair. She is the go-to person for faculty and students alike. Her range of activities includes course adjustments, room scheduling, registration problems, roster issues, problems with international students, student record questions, staff relations, preparation of the student and faculty handbooks, and grievance procedures. In brief, she is a reservoir of knowledge about people and procedures. Therefore, it was not surprising for her this Friday afternoon to be listening to Freda Armstrong's complaint of an unfair grade. Freda was visibly agitated as she complained angrily about her recent grade in philosophy of education.

"This is a disgusting grade and ruined my 4.0 grade-point average," Freda protested. "I have never gotten a B in any of my classes. A B is not a grade I am satisfied with and all the work I have gotten back from Professor Shields was graded A. How can he possibly give me a B?"

"Maybe it's a mistake. Have you talked to Professor Shields about your grade?"

"Of course. All he said was, 'You got the grade you earned.' There's just no reasoning with the man. I think bright, aggressive women threaten him. I am willing to do anything I have to do to get this grade changed. I will go directly to the president and sue if I have to."

Dean MacDermott promised to look into the problem and get back to Ms. Armstrong in a timely fashion. As Freda Armstrong left the office, she seemed a bit more composed than she had been throughout their meeting, but her parting comment was, "I don't want this issue to languish in some faculty committee. I know you will help me Dr. MacDermott."

During the next two days, the assistant dean was able to garner the following facts:

1. The professor in question had given her an A on the only written assignment that was graded and returned, which he readily admitted.
2. When asked why the student had gotten a B when her only grade was an A, he said, "That's what she deserved."
3. He concluded the interaction by saying, "I gave her a B and I stand on my decision. If you want to change the grade, go ahead, but I am not going to. Let me give you a piece of advice: if you get into the grading business, all the students will want their grades changed, and there will be no end to it."
4. Although Professor Shields had made other written assignments and had provided feedback to the students, only one of Freda Armstrong's papers had been formally graded.

5. Other students in the class had received several grades on written assignments.

The information that was gathered led to the conclusion that the student might have a legitimate point. Fortunately for Assistant Dean MacDermott, there was a Faculty Committee on Student Complaints to which she turned over the information. Their deliberations moved surprisingly swiftly. When the chairman of the committee approached Professor Shields, he haughtily retorted, "I gave the right grade. I don't care what you do, to tell you the truth. But, if you want to grade, I'll send all my papers to you and the committee. Good luck."

The chair of the committee scheduled an open hearing and invited both the student and the professor to attend at different times. The student was there to tell her story and presented a graded paper. An hour later, Professor Shields was a no-show and could not be found in his office. When approached the next day, Shields's position was that he was too busy to be involved is this charade. "Read her paper, and you will see that she is not an A student. This is the thanks I get for trying to encourage a weak student with positive feedback. Never again. I'll just flunk them."

The committee believed that they had no other choice than to uphold the student's petition for an A, but they were reluctant to change the grade themselves. A memo to that effect went to Assistant Dean MacDermott, so the ball was in her court. In her five years as assistant dean, she had never changed a grade against the wishes of any professor, and she was hesitant now, especially because Professor Shields was already making noises about the infringement of his academic prerogatives, and his position was not without faculty sympathy. The word was out that he was hoping the administration would change the grade so he, no fan of the dean, could demonstrate once and for all the ineptitude of "power-hungry bureaucrats" who make decisions without full information. Moreover, MacDermott had briefed the dean on the matter and the dean's response was a terse, "I don't want to be involved in this matter, so take care of it. But, be careful."

Discussing the Case

- What is Dean MacDermott's next step?
- Does she have the authority to change the grade?
- Should she talk to Professor Shields again?
- Should she involve the fairness committee further?
- Should she get the committee and Professor Shields together to initiate a plan of action? What if Shields won't attend?
- How can MacDermott prevent this from dragging out and infuriating the student?
- Should she involve the university lawyer?
- How can the assistant dean get the school dean to act?

CASE 8.17

The Staffing Problem

This is your second year as dean of the College of Education. Your predecessor had built a strong college of education during his twelve-year tenure at Oakmont University, in large part by bold and unilateral actions. The dean appointed search committees, named the chair (someone he could depend on), and invariably chose the new faculty member, which was always supported by the committee. Make no mistake, the new hire was the dean's choice.

Because of your belief in collegial governance, you want to open up the process and give faculty major influence in recruitment and hiring decisions. Oakmont University's College of Education has thirty-eight full-time faculty members organized into five departments: Educational Leadership, Teacher Education, Curriculum and Instruction, Educational Psychology, and Foundations of Education. The enrollments have leveled off and the college has been in a steady state for the past three years. The president and the provost believe that the school is about the right size. No further enrollment growth is planned. The president, however, has kept his hiring promise to you of adding two new faculty lines to improve the quality of your school. In addition, you have gotten the go-ahead to hire three people to replace the three retirements that are occurring this year. You can hire five new professors.

As dean you would like to delegate the hiring and recruitment to your faculty, but they have little experience in making such decisions. As a first step, you invite recommendations for hiring from each of the five departments. To your chagrin, each department proposes three new hires, fifteen candidates for five slots. Clearly, these requests are unrealistic and smack of departmental empire-building.

One thing you know for certain: the lines should not be distributed equally with one in each department. The challenge here is to hire the best people for the school and not let departmental politics and rivalries displace responsible faculty hiring. How can you nurture a recruitment, selection, and hiring procedure that will maximize the likelihood that strong professors will be hired to the benefit of the school? To the immediate point, how can you avoid parochial departmental decisions?

Discussing the Case

- Use the simplified model of decision making to develop a strategy for action.
- Who should be involved? How? What is your role as dean?
- Is the faculty ready to be given the power to make such decisions?
- How extensively should the faculty be involved? What should be their role?
- Is this time for consensus, or simply majority rule?
- Should the dean be prepared to exercise a veto in any recommendation of the faculty?

CASE 8.18

New Department Chair

You have just been recruited from the Midwest and hired as chair of a fifteen-member Department of Educational Policy and Leadership at a large western state university. The department is composed of three full professors, six associate professors, and six assistant professors. The dean's mandate to you when she hired you was to "get these professors on the same page. All they do is fight and play political games; that is a shame because this is a talented group." You readily accepted the challenge and guaranteed the dean that you were "up to the task."

You soon discovered that you would get no help from the two most senior professors in the department who, along with you, comprised the complement of full professors; in fact, you quickly concluded that these two senior professors themselves fomented most of the department problems. They were bullies. They ruled by intimidation and ruthless power. They frequently reminded the nontenured professors that no one had been granted tenure in the department in the last ten years. On more than one occasion they had threatened one or more junior professors that they would not get tenure. They were on all of the important department committees and, until your arrival this year, either one or the other had chaired the department for the past twelve years. They greeted you with a "friendly embrace" and assumed that you would get with the program. The only change in their eyes was that there were now three "full bulls" to keep the others in line.

Your hopes of including the two senior professors in any plans to bring the department together into a cohesive group of professionals engaged in collegial governance was quickly dashed by their dogmatic belief that junior professors "had to make it on their own" and "demonstrate their worthiness and loyalty." There was no helping each other in this department; the senior professors frowned on supporting junior faculty. Moreover, the two fulls had most of the associate professors convinced that the only way they would ever make full was by loyalty to them. You had a sense of how they ruled because shortly after you arrived they took you to lunch to discuss things. Much to your chagrin, the lunch was all about school and department politics and, in the end, you were surprised and nonplussed when they told you, in so many words, "Look, you are either with us or against us; make up your mind." They had threatened you.

You have a number of points of leverage at your disposal. You are responsible for appointing all the departmental committees; you are in charge of a sizable budget for travel, supplies, new equipment, and the hiring of adjunct professors (five or six are hired each year); you have significant responsibility for determining merit raises, and you have the full cooperation of the dean, who is committed to change in the department. On the other side of the ledger, you have two senior professors who have controlled everything in the department for more than a decade, and they did it with power politics. They created a culture anchored in subordination, loyalty, dependence, and fear. Your job is to change that culture; at least, that is what you have promised the dean.

Discussing the Case

- Where do you begin?
- Who should be involved in making departmental decision? When? How?
- Can you use a democratic approach in this situation? Why?
- What are your constraints and opportunities?
- Develop a short-term plan to deal with your immediate problems.
- Develop a long-term plan to change the culture of the department.

CASE 8.19

Assistant Dean

You are the Assistant Dean for Student Affairs in the College of Education at a large state university. The administration of the college consists of the dean, an associate dean for research, an associate dean for programs, and an assistant dean for student affairs, which is your position. All of the administrators in the college are line administrators; that is, they have direct authority through the dean's office. All the administrators have doctorates; you have a Ph.D. in administration and higher education. What makes your position distinct is that you are the only one on the administrative team who does not also have a faculty appointment. You are a full-time administrator with a five-year contract, and you serve at the discretion of the dean. You are in the third year of your contract and you have a good relationship with the dean. She is supportive, grants you autonomy, and has full confidence in your work; indeed, you have great rapport with your dean, and she delegates many important projects to you.

The faculty in the College of Education is a diverse group, and most are nice people even when their philosophies and ideologies clash. You have just arrived at your office early Friday morning and are reviewing your calendar for the day. You note that your first appointment is with Tawanna Jackson, a third-year Ph.D. student, who is scheduled to arrive in another five minutes. You are surprised as you glance out the door and see Tawanna and four other students enter the outer office. You walk out to greet Tawanna. She smiles and says, "I hope you don't mind that I have brought my friends along. We all have the same problem."

"Not at all," you respond. "Come in and sit down. Can I get anyone a cup of coffee?"

After the introductions and a little small talk, Tawanna began: "Dean, we have a problem that we need your help with. This is a delicate situation, so I hope we can count on your confidentiality in the matter. We are students and we are vulnerable."

"Of course," you respond, and then listen as Tawanna and her classmates describe their problem.

The story that unfolds is troubling. They all were in a graduate seminar in ethics, taught by a senior professor with tenure. Each student confirms the complaint, namely, that the professor was unfair, harsh, treated women as second-class citizens, made disparaging remarks about their abilities in class, and was aggressive in his interactions with them. You listen carefully as, one by one, each student recounts an incident or two involving the ethics professor. Apparently, what has brought this group to your office is that they are dissatisfied with their grades and treatment in the course. Tawanna is the most outspoken member of the group and she accuses the professor of sexism and racism.

"Nine people in the class," she noted, "four As and five Bs. Guess who got the Bs?" she exclaimed, and then answered her own query. "All the men got the As and all the women got the Bs."

All five women told similar stories. The seminar was one in which students read assigned articles on ethics, which were then discussed in class. Each student described an incident in which her ideas were belittled by the professor in class. "It got so bad," one said, "that I simply stopped talking midway through the course." The grade in the course was based on a final paper. Each student made an appointment with the professor to insure that the topic of the paper was acceptable. The five women claimed similar experiences with the professor; he was condescending, harsh, and questioned their ability to take his "high-level course." Tawanna claimed that he not only was nonsupportive and insulting, but he made inappropriate pronouncements about the role of women; his was a traditional perspective of women. He had made the same comment to several of the students: "You are an attractive woman. Why are you bothering to get a doctorate? You'll just get married and stay home with the kids."

Moreover, all of the women asserted that at some time during their appointment and discussion of the paper that the professor had subtly suggested that "with a little cooperation" an A was easily had. Tawanna and one other student described the professor's invitation to continue their meeting at his apartment later in the evening, an invitation that they both declined.

What did these five students want? Nothing for themselves. They realized that little could be done to change their grades, but they wanted to protect other women from this "sexist bigot." They wanted someone in authority to know what was going on in his seminars. They wanted his sexism to cease; they wanted fairness and ethical professional behavior, an irony that was not missed by you or the students.

As you think back about your own interactions and observations of the professor in question, you do recall what you also considered sexist and racist remarks on his part. Further, there have been rumors that this professor was "hitting on" women faculty members, but there never had been any actual complaints from the woman professors.

Discussing the Case

- Is action called for? If so, what?
- Who should be involved in dealing with this issue?
- Should the allegations of racism and sexism be pursued? If so, how?
- How should the rights of both students and the professor be protected?
- What is the role of the assistant dean in this situation?

- Should the assistant dean touch base with the dean before taking action?
- What model of decision making seems most appropriate for this case?

CASE 8.20

The Dean's Advisory Council

You are the new Dean of an education school with forty-three full-time faculty members. The school had been in chaos the last several years as the faculty and your predecessor worked through a contentious and divisive restructuring of the school. The new configuration of the school has four departments: Teacher Education (16 faculty); Foundations and Educational Administration (12 faculty); Educational Psychology (8 faculty), and Cultural Studies (7 faculty). There remains rivalry and bickering among the departments as they try to form new identities. You believe that the units are much more alike than different, and you have been trying to get the departments to cooperate and come together as a cohesive whole, the School of Education. To that end you have established a Dean's Advisory Council to help make schoolwide decisions, which is composed of you, your associate dean, and the four departmental chairs.

You have just received a complaint from a student who claims that she is being systematically excluded from cultural studies courses simply because she is a Ph.D. student in educational psychology. The reason she has been given for her exclusion is that the courses are fully subscribed by cultural studies majors and there is no room for "outsiders." She counters that there are plenty of graduate students from Educational Administration and Teacher Education in the cultural foundations courses, and they never encounter difficulty in registering for those classes. She argues that she is being discriminated against because she is in Educational Psychology and professors in Cultural Foundations just don't like the professors in Educational Psychology. You have asked your associate dean to investigate the matter, and the report strongly confirms the student's claims.

Discussing the Case

- Is this a case for the Advisory Council or only for the two departments involved?
- Does this problem call for strong, direct action on your part?
- Who should be involved in this decision?
- What are your short- and long-term goals?
- Develop a plan for action.

CHAPTER NINE

PUTTING IT ALL TOGETHER

*Decision makers tend to exaggerate their control over their environment,
overweighting the impacts of their actions and underweighting the impact
of other factors.*
—James G. March, *A Primer on Decision Making*

We conclude this text with a comprehensive case called "Redistricting." Like all of the cases in this book, there is no one correct course of action for addressing the problems presented, but, make no mistake, this is an important case with a host of critical issues that must be addressed. The case is a complex one that requires careful analysis, planning, consideration of long-term as well as short-term consequences, and cooperation and communication with many different constituents. We believe that a group approach to this case is useful; in fact, we recommend that the case become a group project extending over several class periods. We have a few suggestions in that regard, but first the case.

CASE 9.1

Redistricting[1]

At one time, Clifton was a small town, comfortably distant from its big-city neighbor twenty miles down the road. But times changed. The urban neighbor grew, sprawling across farmlands, packing in housing and strip malls and gas station mini-marts. Highways were built to zip traffic from town to city and back again. It became difficult to tell where Clifton's boundaries began and where the city's boundaries ended. Like other towns that were once well removed from the big city, Clifton became a teeming first-ring suburb in a large metropolitan area.

Within three decades, Clifton's population grew tenfold. To the amazement of residents who have lived in Clifton many years, the population is now approximately 78,000. Like its burgeoning neighbor to the south, the city of Clifton annexed farmland, developed new housing areas, and created office parks and industrial zones. Apartment complexes and densely populated subdivisions are located in Clifton's southern areas while the northern subdivisions are upscale "golf course communities" with lower population densities and higher income. The center of Clifton holds the nineteenth-century historic district where boutiques and antique stores occupy storefronts that once housed grocers and buggy makers. Victorian and early twentieth-century houses surround the town center, providing a glimpse of Clifton's past and an identity for many of those who choose to move to this community. Its southern and western borders hold the majority of its commercial and industrial growth. A number of buffer zones consisting of lower-priced houses and multifamily units separate these businesses from the nineteenth-century district and from the upscale subdivisions.

With growth has come greater population diversity. At one time 98 percent Caucasian and almost exclusively middle class, the composition of Clifton is now as follows:

Ethnicity (percent of population)

Caucasian	65%
African American	16%
Latino/a	9%
Asian/Pacific Islander	5%
American Indian	3%
Other	2%

Household Income Levels (percent of population)

Above $200,000	6%
$199,000–100,000	16%
$99,000–75,000	19%
$74,000–50,000	20%
$49,000–25,000	16%
$24,000–15,000	16%
below $14,000	7%

Many local corporations recruit Mexican workers for entry-level jobs, giving Clifton a growing population of Mexican immigrants. Most of these immigrants live in the southern end of Clifton or in the buffer zone near the commercial areas. The southern end of Clifton is also home to a growing population of immigrants from war-torn African countries. The influx of these immigrants has resulted in a growing Muslim influence, although the majority of Clifton's population is still Christian. There are several nondenominational Christian fundamentalist churches, numerous mainline Protestant churches, a large Catholic parish, and a Greek Orthodox cathedral. No temples or mosques have heretofore been located in Clifton. Though outwardly tolerant of religious diversity, private comments from some Clifton citizens suggest growing discomfort and resentment.

The following stories illustrate these feelings:

- Overheard at a local barber shop: Why should *we* always have to bend over backward for *them?* We used to call it Christmas vacation and we used to sing Christmas carols at work and the schools took off on Good Friday. Whatever happened to the way the other immigrants did things when they came here: worked hard, learned our customs, didn't expect a handout? I know it must be tough, but I've got rights, too, you know, and I was here first. It just doesn't seem fair.

- A high school sophomore tells her mother: They won't even dress for gym class. How can dressing for gym be bad? They wear those scarves and long dresses. The teachers all say to smile and try to be helpful. I do, too, but I feel like they think I'm an infidel or something.

Even though Clifton has many new residents, there are plenty of "old timers," people who have lived here many years and have clear memories of the days before big-city growth came to town. These long-time residents are concerned about the changes in Clifton. New developments, increases in taxes to pay for services, immigrant influx, and urban encroachment are issues that alarm them. Over the past few years, the membership roster of the Clifton Preservation Society has swelled with long-time residents who fear that their community's culture will deteriorate as the area continues to grow.

Typically, key leadership positions are held by people who have lived in Clifton for at least a decade or longer. Stability is valued. Conservatism is respected. The City Manager has held his position for eighteen years. The former school superintendent held office for twenty years before his retirement two years ago. His replacement came from a different district and is new to Clifton. Although respected, the superintendent is often referred to as "the new guy." City Council and school-board members generally hold their offices for several terms and are rarely thrown out of office; they are reelected until they choose not to run anymore. Three veteran school-board members chose not to seek reelection this past year. Their replacements, all long-time community members, ran on platforms of "open and honest dialogue and community participation." They were sworn in only a few weeks ago. Thus, with two veterans and three newcomers, the board is relatively inexperienced, and big changes are on the horizon. It is time to redistrict.

As the community of Clifton has grown, so have the schools. Over the past thirty years, several new schools have been built, existing schools have been expanded, and student populations have been assigned and reassigned to adjust to available classroom space. There are currently sixteen elementary schools, five middle schools, and two high schools in operation. The three smallest elementary schools are magnets, drawing selected students from across the district to take part in a curriculum delivered with special foci. There is a mathematics magnet, a fine and performing arts magnet, and a global languages magnet. Some of the schools are woefully overcrowded. Portable classrooms are used at some locations to accommodate the student populations.

Four years ago, the school board changed school attendance boundaries in an effort to stave off the need to construct more buildings. At that time, the board and superintendent asked for volunteers from the Clifton community to serve on an ad hoc committee to make boundary recommendations. Anyone who wanted to volunteer was welcome. Forty-eight citizens stepped forward to serve on the committee. All were Caucasian. Three-fourths of the committee members lived in the central and northern portions of the district. The superintendent placed several district administrators on the committee, including the Director of Planning, to help insure that the committee members had useful information about the school's capacities and the student numbers.

For three months, the committee toiled. Committee members learned quickly that carving the district into manageable pieces was not an easy task. Subdivisions did not come in conveniently sized parcels. Schools were not necessarily located where the children were. Adjoining neighborhoods wanted to "stay together." But the committee worked diligently, eventually coming up with three possible configurations that were presented to the board. Two examples reflect the community reaction:

■ From the newspaper editor's commentary at the time: The Clifton community owes a debt of gratitude to the Redistricting Committee members and a nod of approval to the Board of Education. The large committee, working with unwieldy data, brought forth well-conceived suggestions for elementary school boundaries while the board provided extensive public opportunities for the greater community to influence the deliberations. No redistricting plan can please all the people all the time. And no mere shuffling of student bodies can truly address the rampant overcrowding in Clifton's school buildings. But it is clear that the open and aboveboard efforts put forth by all involved led to a plan that is acceptable to a large majority of those affected.

■ A committee member speaks up: I worked my tail off on that committee. Nights, weekends, we were at it all the time. And then, when we made our presentation, the board started asking a lot of pointed questions about why we did this and why didn't we do that and what were we thinking and so on. Oh, I know, they've got the right to ask questions. But it still made me mad. When we created the plans, we figured they'd look at them, listen to some comments, and pick one. I guess they didn't see it that way. There were all these self-congratulatory little comments and reports in the newspaper when they made their decision. All this stuff about thanking the committee and how they'd taken the committee's work and "adjusted it" to get the final plan, and talking about how successful the process had been, and blah, blah, blah. You know what I think happened? They had these plans out there and people started griping and coming to the board meetings to complain and arguing about why the plans weren't right. Where were they when we were doing all the work? I remember this one meeting where they had about 500 parents there, most of them upset about where their kids were going to go. It went on for hours. So the board made their "adjustments" because of the pressure, and then called it "listening to the people." Well, okay, but don't ask me to do any more committees. I got my fill of that and so did a lot of the other committee members.

The plan was only a temporary fix. Within months, it was clear that the only real solution would be to build additional schools. About three years ago, the board asked district voters to approve funding to build three more elementary schools and a new high school. After a hard-sell campaign, school supporters were jubilant over a 56 percent passage rate. After all, only about 25 percent of the residents have children in the schools. Construction has been going on at a furious pace to meet the promise to open the new schools in time for the start of the next school year.

School Name	Student Capacity	Under (Over)	Attendance Area	Non-Caucasian		Free/Reduced Lunch %
				%	#	
Amelia Elementary	475	(70)	West	49	267	35
Beacon Elementary	475	(83)	Central	27	151	15
Central Elementary (math magnet)	150	0	East	23	35	15
Everett Elementary (arts magnet)	275	0	Central	26	72	12
Freedom Elementary	500	(108)	Northeast	9	55	9
Hanover Elementary	550	(200)	South	46	345	32
Henderson Elementary	550	(150)	South	44	308	42
Lipton Street Elementary (language magnet)	150	0	Central	22	33	13
McDonald Elementary	450	(59)	East	11	56	10
Nesbitt Elementary	450	(87)	Central	16	86	21
Norman Elementary	450	(130)	Northeast	16	93	10
Pritchard Elementary	650	76	Central	33	189	20
Sanders Elementary	600	(70)	South	27	181	10
Thomas Elementary	550	10	North	22	118	8
Valley Forge Elementary	550	24	Northeast	18	95	7
New elementary	450					
New elementary	450					
New elementary	450					
Current elementary population (grades K–5)	7,672					
Washington Middle	750	(65)	Central	37	301	28
Lincoln Middle	725	20	Central	48	338	32
Kennedy Middle	750	31	Northeast	28	201	14
Armstrong Middle	700	57	East	25	161	11
Anthony Middle	750	(73)	West	49	403	38
Current middle school population (grades 6–8)	3,705					
Henry High	1,600	(631)	Northeast	36	803	23
Clifton High	1,500	(512)	Central	42	845	20
New high school	1,500					
Current high school population (9–12)	4,243					

Completion of the building program will require the hiring of additional staff at all levels. Start-from-scratch staffs must be put in place at the new elementary schools and the new high school. In addition to new hires, a number of teachers must be transferred involuntarily to meet the staffing needs in the new buildings. At the administrative level, several district assistant principals and principals are vying for the new administrative positions, each seeking to convince the superintendent of his or her superior ability. No positions have been posted as yet, but inquiries from external sources are frequent.

In addition to staffing classrooms and hiring custodians, everything from school names and mascots to coaching assignments must be selected. Rumors are flying through the schools and the community: "The schools have been named for corporate donors," "No, the schools are going to be named by the students/senior citizens/a contest," "The high school mascot is a wild boar," "No, the high school mascot will be chosen by the new principal," "No, the high school mascot is a polar bear, which will be stuffed and placed in the lobby." Each week, new rumors surface. The district's public information officer is continually "putting out fires."

Attendance boundaries must be changed in order to balance populations at existing schools and fill the new schools with students. It is clear that attendance boundaries must be redrawn for all elementary, middle, and high schools. The prior redistricting efforts showed that this will not be an easy process. Most parents and students feel strong attachments to their "old" schools. Students, parents, and staff are demanding a say in the redistricting process. At this point, they are insisting on staying where they are. Hot gossip is circling around which students will be moved where. Letters to the editor are beginning to appear in the local paper.

> Excerpt from a citizen's letter: I moved here from New York City five years ago. I picked Clifton so that my children could go to a good school in a stable town. A year after we settled here, my children were forced to leave the school they had grown to love. They were uprooted and sent to another school to make room for somebody else in their previous school. I write to publicly beseech the Clifton Board of Education not to rip my children from their educational home again. Take your pound of flesh from someone else's neighborhood. . . .

Enrollment pressures are not the only reason for redistricting. The state requires that racially unbalanced schools must be brought into balance. Caucasian/non-Caucasian distributions should mirror the community's percentages. A school is considered "noncompliant" if it has a minority population equal to or greater than 15 percent higher than the community's minority population percentage. Six schools are above the "acceptable" level. If the district intends to comply with state regulations, students must be moved. Parent rumblings about forced busing abound. Dire predictions and reminders of failed busing programs in other cities are regularly recounted. The rumor mill is spinning rapidly. Clearly, tensions and suspicions are increasing steadily as the following comments illustrate:

■ Overheard at a local restaurant: Those kids shouldn't be shipped up north. It isn't fair to them. They moved to that area of town, they ought to be able to go to school there. I'm sure they'd be happier close to home, within their own culture. Now, I certainly don't intend to sound racist, and you know I'm not, but if I wanted to have a "multicultural environment" I wouldn't have moved to a subdivision like ours. I don't want my children going to school with poor children. I mean, really. I never thought we were building these new schools for a racial desegregation plan. . . .

■ A PTA president from the south end talks to her principal: Are we inferior in some way? Is that what they're saying? Are we to be shoved on buses and driven for miles to attend a different school because we need to be dispersed for some reason? Are we less of a threat if we're spread out somewhere? I resent the implications of all this and I will not sit quietly while my children and I are disparaged. I will say what needs to be said—loudly—when the time comes.

As Henry High School became more overcrowded, the high school English as a Second Language (ESL) programs were consolidated at Clifton High because there was more space available there. Other ESL units are housed at Lincoln Middle School, Hanover Elementary, Pritchard Elementary, and Lipton Street Elementary Magnet School. The ESL population has grown from 26 students across all grades six years ago to 280 students this school year. Sporadic incidents have occurred among ESL and non-ESL students at the high school and the middle school. Despite efforts by ESL teachers, tensions are on the increase. A recent incident illustrates the stress:

> A teacher discusses the incident: I don't know what started this latest fight. There'd been some talk that one of the boys was mad at the other, but I thought it was just typical adolescent stuff that blows over. You know how it is; sometimes all it takes is just a comment to set them off. But this time, it got out of hand. Apparently, they were on the bus this morning and the one boy said something about the other boy, laughed at his clothes and how he talked, said some things about his sister, that sort of thing. It escalated from there, and we ended up with a big fight in the schoolyard. Friends of both boys got into it, and there was plenty of punching and kicking. Now I hear that one of the boys is saying he is going to cut the other one tonight.

Just as space concerns led to the consolidation of the high school ESL program at Clifton High, space constrained the housing of a majority of the Multiple Handicapped (MH) and Severely Behaviorally Handicapped (SBH) units at Clifton High. And, because Clifton High was designed to accommodate vocational programming, the district's vocational programs (i.e., metal shop, auto repair technology, graphic design) are also housed there. The superintendent wants to divide the ESL, special education, and vocational programs among the three high schools.

Even though enrollment stress and racial imbalance present significant challenges to redistricting, the superintendent has also decided to use this opportunity to make other programmatic changes. His rationale is that a comprehensive change in one fell swoop now rather than piecemeal changes over the course of years will limit disruption to students and the community.

The superintendent has also decided that changes are in order for the district's well-established magnet school programs. The magnets were created in the late 1980s to serve as choice programs for parents, to be laboratory schools for district curricular delivery, and to provide effective educational use of the district's smallest, most historic school buildings. Over the years, the laboratory aspect of the schools has diminished extensively. It is now difficult to differentiate magnet curricula from the other elementary schools in the district. However, the magnets are consistently high achievers on state and national tests. They serve small populations and have long waiting lists to get in. In fact, their enrollment numbers have not increased since the inception of the program, even though the district has grown substantially. Student selection is done through a lottery each spring. Once selected for a magnet, students may stay through fifth grade. Parent involvement in the magnets is extensive and passionate. An aura of elitism surrounds the magnet populations even though no specific abilities are required for student admittance. Though hopeful of expanding the program and reenergizing the foci, the superintendent has not yet devised a plan or process for changing the magnets. However, magnet parents are decidedly uneasy and have begun to form "save our school" groups. Consider the following:

> A Central Elementary Magnet School parent recruits group members: We enrolled in this school because we believed in it. We believe in its size, we believe in its focus, we believe in its teachers. And we will *not* stand by and let all we have worked for, all we have achieved, all we believe be destroyed. This is a program that works. Our students are learning and they love what they're learning. If we want to stand up for our children, we have to stand up for Central. We will take our message to the papers, to the television stations, to this whole community. We will show the superintendent and the board that we are serious about our beliefs. We will be proactive about this. We will not wait until the decisions are made. We will fight for Central.

Shortly after arriving in the district, the superintendent proposed block scheduling at the high schools. After an immediate outcry from the teachers' union, the superintendent quickly suggested that a study of block scheduling would occur prior to any implementation. In addition to the educational information gathered on blocking, the study found a faculty schism over the teachers' willingness to move to blocking. Hence, the superintendent plans to implement blocking in only one of the high schools, which might be another choice program for parents and students.

"Choice" is an integral part of another change desired by the superintendent. Hoping to make high school course work more interesting and relevant to the post-high school lives of graduates, he suggests that career majors be formed within each high school. In addition to the major, students would be required to take core course offerings such as English, mathematics, sciences, and social studies. Costs prohibit operating all majors in each high school. Therefore, the superintendent and other central office staff are planning to recommend eight possible majors, to be divided across the district and open to all. The majors are: Communications; Fine and Performing Arts; Business and Business Management; Engineering; Information Management; Social Services; Health and Medicine; and Environmental Studies. If different majors are to be offered at different high schools, the redistricting plan must consider high school enrollments based on possible major enrollments as well as geographic populations. Though extensive discussion has occurred in the central office about this concept of majors, the parents, students, and community are currently unaware of this possibility. The teachers' union has been involved in the discussion to date. Though cautiously positive about the suggestion, the union is watchful and concerned about changes in workload and contract day.

School Name	Student Attendance Rate	State Average Attendance Rate	State Proficiency Test Passage Rate by Building	State Average Proficiency Passage Rate
Amelia Elementary	96.5%	75%	80.2%	63.3%
Beacon Elementary	95.2%	75%	75.3%	63.3%
Central Elementary (math magnet)	96.5%	75%	100.0%	63.3%
Everett Elementary (arts magnet)	96.8%	75%	93.8%	63.3%
Freedom Elementary	95.7%	75%	78.7%	63.3%
Hanover Elementary	95.1%	75%	66.0%	63.3%
Henderson Elementary	94.3%	75%	70.8%	63.3%
Lipton Street Elementary (language magnet)	96.5%	75%	92.3%	63.3%
McDonald Elementary	96.6%	75%	78.4%	63.3%
Nesbitt Elementary	94.7%	75%	67.4%	63.3%
Norman Elementary	95.8%	75%	85.4%	63.3%
Pritchard Elementary	96.1%	75%	64.9%	63.3%
Sanders Elementary	94.7%	75%	75.5%	63.3%
Thomas Elementary	97.1%	75%	81.5%	63.3%
Valley Forge Elementary	95.0%	75%	84.7%	63.3%
Washington Middle	95.7%	75%	86.0%	71.9%
Lincoln Middle	94.2%	75%	79.8%	71.9%
Kennedy Middle	95.5%	75%	83.5%	71.9%
Armstrong Middle	96.4%	75%	75.1%	71.9%
Anthony Middle	94.8%	75%	78.4%	71.9%
Henry High	94.3%	75%	90.4%	82.7%
Clifton High	92.9%	75%	89.6%	82.7%

To compound the stress inherent in this massive redistricting, the schools must ask the community's voters to pass a tax issue to operate the new schools. The district's current budget stands at approximately $100 million. If the new schools open without additional dollars, the district will face a deficit of about $4 million next year, even if no program changes are made. Adding the career majors, changing to block scheduling at one high school, and revamping the magnet schools could easily bring the deficit to $5 million next year, with growing deficits each year thereafter. Because of state-mandated election calendars, it looks as though the election will be held shortly after decisions are made on attendance boundaries and related programmatic changes. Decisions must be made quickly as to how much money the district will seek from taxpayers. Once that decision is made, a campaign strategy must be developed.

Staffing Needs	Number of Additional Full-Time Employees Needed	Approximate Annual Cost: Salary	Approximate Annual Cost: Benefits
Classroom Teachers, Bachelor's degree	15.0	$597,840.00	$179,352.00
Classroom, Master's degree and above	10.0	439,640.00	131,892.00
Administrators	5.0	425,600.00	127,680.00
Special Education	4.0	175,856.00	52,757.00
Art	4.0	159,424.00	47,827.00
Music	4.5	179,352.00	53 806.00
Physical Education	3.5	139,496.00	41,849.00
Guidance Counselors	4.8	211,027.00	63,308.00
Media	2.5	109,910.00	32,973.00
Nurse	2.0	87,928.00	26,378.00
School Psychologists	1.5	65,946.00	19,784.00
ESL	3.0	131,892.00	39,568.00
Speech Pathologist	1.5	65,946.00	19,784.00
Custodians	5.0	155,000.00	46,500.00
Office Staff	4.5	90,846.00	27,254.00
Duty Monitors (i.e., attendance, cafeteria, etc.)	1.8	27,846.00	8,354.00
Supplementals for Extracurriculars		86,980.00	26,094.00
IT Support Staff	2.0	77,936.00	23,219.00
Warehouse Worker	1.0	33,992.00	10,198.00
Total		$3,262,457.00	$978,667.00

Clifton's redistricting will not be an easy task. This is a project with multiple layers and multiple constituencies. Students, staff, and families will be directly affected. The community's beliefs about its schools and its residents may be challenged. Emotions are involved as much as rationality. The decisions made will have ramifications that endure for years to come. The challenge is to make sure the ramifications are positive. Although it is early in the process, several things seem clear. Determinations must be made about how to proceed. Time lines, committees, and charges must be developed. Decisions must be made.

Discussing the Case

- What are the necessary decisions?
- Who should be involved? When? What roles will be played?
- What information is needed? By whom?
- When, if ever, is process more important than product?

- How do the data inform your decision?
- What are the potential negative consequences of your actions?
- What is your plan to mute such consequences?
- How will you monitor the pace of change in the district?
- What is the most useful decision-making model for this case? Satisficing? Mixed Scanning? Others? Why?

Suggestions for a Group Project

We suggest a group approach with this case, perhaps extending it into a project over several class periods. We offer a few guidelines in this regard.

I. First, consider dividing the class into teams of about five or six students. Have each team identify the key actors and groups of the case. For example, consider the following roles and groups:
   A. Superintendent
   B. Board members
   C. Central Office staff (Human Resources, Curriculum Director, Planning, etc.)
   D. Principals of existing schools
   E. Teachers
   F. Teachers' Union reps
   G. Bus drivers
   H. Magnet school parents
   I. Elementary parents
      1. South
      2. West
      3. East
      4. North
   J. Immigrant parents
   K. Longtime resident parents
   L. Longtime residents
   M. Newspeople
   N. Student representatives

II. Each team may be assigned all the roles and groups or only a portion of the roles. List the key points and issues each of these participants will bring to the table. Assign liaisons between the group tasks for information gathering.

III. Identify the tasks that will have to be addressed. For example, determine:
   A. Demographics of the community
   B. Tax issues (including needed increases)
   C. Magnet changes
   D. Career changes
   E. Block scheduling
   F. Others

IV. Identify the problems that are likely to arise and prepare involvement strategies.

V. Develop a series of reports for public consumption in Clifton.

VI. Recombine the teams into two larger groups, and have each group develop and present a strategy for a successful redistricting. Focus on the superintendent's role in this process.

Other Suggested Activities

1. Have the class do the preliminary work presented above, but then have each student develop an action strategy as a term project or portfolio item.

2. Consider role-playing district meetings, specifically board meetings over multiple nights to reach district decisions.

3. Role-play a meeting with the superintendent and the board when the redistricting is first introduced.

4. Role-play an open board meeting to discuss redistricting with community members.

5. Role-play a meeting between the administration and the teachers.

ENDNOTE

1. This case was written by Professor Nancy Nestor-Baker of the University of Cincinnati for this book, and is used with her permission.

BIBLIOGRAPHY

Aditya, R. M., House, R. J., & Kerr, S. (2000). The theory and practice of leadership: Into new millennium. In G. Cooper & E. A. Locke (eds.), *Industrial and organizational psychology: Linking theory to practice*. Oxford, UK: Blackwell, 198–228.

Alinsky, S. (1971). *Rules for radicals*. New York: Vintage Books.

Allison, G. (1971). *Essence of decision: Explaining the Cuban missile crisis*. Boston: Little, Brown.

Alluto, J. A., & Belasco, J. A. (1972). A typology for participation in organizational decision making. *Administrative Science Quarterly, 17,* 117–125.

Alluto, J. A., & Belasco, J. A. (1973). Patterns of teacher participation in school system decision making. *Educational Administration Quarterly, 9,* 27–41.

Ashkanasy, N., Zerbe, W., & Hartel, C. (2002). *Managing emotions in the workplace*. New York: M. E. Sharpe.

Bachrach, S., Bamberger, P., Conley, S. C., & Bauer, S. (1990). The dimensionality of decision participation in educational organizations: The value of multi-domain evaluative approach. *Educational Administration Quarterly, 26,* 126–167.

Barnard, C. (1938). *The functions of the executive*. Cambridge, MA: Harvard University Press.

Bazerman, M. H., & Chugh, D. (2006). Decisions without blinders. *Harvard Business Review, 84,* 88–97.

Blau, P., & Scott, W. R. (1962). *Formal organizations: A comparative approach*. San Francisco: Chandler.

Bolman, L. G., & Deal, T. E. (1991). *Reframing organizations: Artistry choice, and leadership*. Jossey-Bass.

Boulding, K. (1964). Review of David Braybrooke & Charles E. Lindblom's A strategy of decision: Policy evaluation as a social process. *American Sociological Review, 29,* 930–931.

Brickley, A., Smith, C. W., & Zimmerman, L. (2001). *Managerial economics and organizational architecture* (2nd ed.). Chicago: Irwin.

Bridges, E. M. (1964). Teacher participation in decision making. *Administrator's Notebook, 12,* 1–4.

Bridges, E. M. (1967). A model for shared decision making in the school principalship. *Educational Administration Quarterly, 3,* 49–61.

Bridges, E. M., Doyle, W. J., & Mahan, D. J. (1968). Effects of hierarchical differentiation on group productivity, efficiency, and risk taking. *Administrative Science Quarterly, 13,* 305–319.

Brinton, C. (1990). *A history of western morals*. New York: Paragon House.

Buchanan, L., & O'Connell, A. (2006). A brief history of decision making. *Harvard Business Review, 84,* 33–41.

Charan, R. (2006). Conquering a culture of indecision. *Harvard Business Review, 84,* 108–116.

Chase, F. S. (1952). The teacher and policy making. *Administrator's Notebook, 1,* 1–4.

Cohen, D. K., & March, J. G. (1974). *Leadership and ambiguity: The American college president*. New York: McGraw-Hill.

Cohen, D. K., March, J. G., & Olsen, J. P. (1972). A garbage-can model of organizational choice. *Administrative Science Quarterly, 17,* 1–25.

Conley, S. (1990). A metaphor for teaching: Beyond the bureaucratic-professional dichotomy. In S. B. Bacharach (ed.), *Education reform: Making sense of it all*. Boston: Allyn and Bacon, 313–324.

Conway, J. A. (1984). The myth, mystery, and mastery of participative decision making in education. *Educational Administration Quarterly, 3,* 11–40.

Council of Chief State School Officers. (1996). *Interstate school leader licensure consortium: Standards for school leaders*. Washington, DC: Author.

Crozier, M., & Friedberg, E. (1977). *L'acteur et le systeme*. Paris: Editions du Seuil.

Culberston, J. A., Jacobson, P. B., & Reller, T. L. (1960). *Administrative relations: A case book*. Englewood Cliffs, NJ: Prentice-Hall.

Cusick, P. A. (1983). *The egalitarian ideal and the American high school*. New York: Longman.

Daft, R. L. (2001). *Organizational theory and design* (7th ed.). St. Paul: West.

Dewey, J. (1922). *Human nature and conduct*. New York: Henry Holt.

Dewey, J. (1938). *Logic: The theory of inquiry*. New York: Henry Holt.

Drucker, P. F. (1966). *The effective administrator.* New York: Harper & Row.

Duke, D. L., Showers, B. K., & Imber, M. (1980). Teachers and shared decision making: The costs and benefits of involvement. *Educational Administration Quarterly, 16,* 93–106.

Etzioni, A. (1967). Mixed scanning: A third approach to decision making. *Public Administration Review, 27,* 385–392.

Etzioni, A. (1986). Mixed scanning revisited. *Public Administration Review, 46,* 8–14.

Etzioni, A. (1988). *The moral dimension: Toward a new economics.* New York: Free Press.

Etzioni, A. (1989). Humble decision making. *Harvard Business Review, 67,* 122–126.

Etzioni, A. (1992). Normative-affective factors: Toward a new decision-making model. In Mary Zey (ed.), *Decision making: Alternatives to rational choice models.* Newbury Park, CA: Sage, 89–111.

Evers, C. W., & Lakomski, G. (1991). *Knowing educational administration.* Oxford: Pergamon.

Feldman, J., & Kanter, H. E. (1965). Organizational decision making. In J. G. March (ed.), *The handbook of organizations.* Chicago: Rand McNally.

Field, R. H. G. (1982). A test of the Vroom-Yetton model of leadership. *Journal of Applied Psychology, 67,* 523–532.

Georgiou, P. (1973). The goal paradigm and notes toward a counter paradigm. *Administrative Science Quarterly, 21,* 291–310.

Gigerenzer, G. (1996). On narrow norms and vague heuristics: A reply to Kahneman and Tversky. *Psychological Review, 103,* 556–559.

Gigerenzer, G. (2000). *Adaptive thinking: Rationality in the real world.* New York: Oxford University Press.

Gigerenzer, G., Todd, P. M., & ABC Research Group. (1999). *Simple heuristics that make us smart.* New York: Oxford University Press.

Gilovich, T. (1991). *How we know what isn't so: The fallibility of human reason in everyday life.* New York: Free Press.

Gladwell, M. (2005). *Blink: The power of thinking without thinking.* New York: Little, Brown and Company.

Hall, R. H. (1987). *Organizations: Structures, processes, and outcomes* (4th ed.). Englewood Cliffs, NJ: Prentice-Hall.

Haller, E. J., & Strike, K. A. (1986). *An introduction to educational administration.* New York: Longman.

Hammond, J. S., Keeney, R. L., & Raiffa, H. (1988). The hidden traps in decision making. *Harvard Business Review, 76,* 47–58.

Hammond, J. S., Keeney, R. L., & Raiffa, H. (2006). The hidden traps in decision making. *Harvard Business Review, 84,* 118–126.

Heller, F., Drenth, P., Koopman, P., & Rus, V. (1988). *Decisions in organizations.* Beverly Hills, CA: Sage.

Heller, F. A., Pusic, E., Strauss, G., & Bernhard, W. (1998). *Organizational participation: Myth and reality.* Oxford, UK: Oxford University Press.

Herrnstein, R. J. (1990). Rational choice theory: Necessary but not sufficient. *American Psychologist, 45,* 356–367.

Hickson, D., Butler, R., Cray, D., Mallory, G., & Wilson, D. (1986). *Top decisions: Strategic decision making in organizations.* Oxford, UK: Basil Blackwell.

Hoy, W. K. (2003). An analysis of enabling and mindful school structures: Some theoretical, research, and practical consideration. *Journal of Educational Administration, 41,* 87–108.

Hoy, W. K., Gage, Q. C., & Tarter, C. J. (2004). Theoretical and empirical foundations of mindful schools. In W. K. Hoy & C. Miskel (eds.), *Educational organizations, policy and reform: Research and measurement.* Greenwich, CN: Information Age, 305–335.

Hoy, W. K., Gage, Q., & Tarter, C. J. (2006). School mindfulness and faculty trust: Necessary conditions for each other? *Educational Administration Quarterly, 42,* 236–255.

Hoy, W. K., & Miskel, C. G. (2001). *Educational administration: Theory, research, and practice* (6th ed.). New York: McGraw-Hill.

Hoy, W. K., & Miskel, C. G. (2008). *Educational administration: Theory, research, and practice* (8th ed.). New York: McGraw-Hill.

Hoy, W. K., Newland, W., & Blazovsky, R. (1977). Subordinate loyalty to immediate superior, esprit, and aspects of bureaucratic structure. *Educational Administration Quarterly, 13,* 71–85.

Hoy, W. K., & Tarter, C. J. (1992). Collaborative decision making: Empowering teachers. *Canadian Administrator, 32,* 1–9.

Hoy, W. K., & Tarter, C. J. (1993a). A normative model of shared decision making. *Journal of Educational Administration, 31,* 4–19.

Hoy, W. K., & Tarter, C. J. (1993b). Crafting strategies, not contriving solutions: A response to Downey and Knight's observations on shared decision making. *Canadian Administrator, 32,* 1–6.

Hoy, W. K., Tarter, C. J., & Kottkamp, R. (1991). *Open schools/healthy schools: Measuring organizational climate.* Newbury Park, CA: Sage.

Imber, M., & Duke, D. L. (1984). Teacher participation in school decision making: A framework for research. *Journal of Educational Administration, 22,* 24–34.

Janis, I. L., & Mann, L. (1977). *Decision making: The psychological analysis of conflict, choice, and commitment.* New York: Free Press.

Kahneman, D. K., & Tversky, A. (1996). On the reality of cognitive illusions. *Psychological Review, 103,* 582–591.

Katona, G. (1975). *Psychological economics.* New York: Elsevier.

Klein, G. (1997). An overview of naturalistic decision making applications. In C. D. Zsambok & G. Klien (eds.), *Naturalistic decision making.* Mahwah, NJ: Erlbaum, 49–59.

Klein, G. (1998). *Sources of power: How people make decisions.* Cambridge, MA: MIT Press.

Klein, G. (2003). *The power of intuition.* New York: Doubleday.

Lafferty, J., & Eady, P. M. (1974). *The desert survival situation* (7th ed.). Plymouth, MI: Experimental Learning Methods.

Langer, E. J. (1989). *Mindfulness.* Cambridge, MA: Perseus Books.

Langley, A., Mintzberg, H., Pitcher, P., Posada, J., & Saint-Macary, J. (1995). Opening up decision making: The view from the black stool. *Organization Science, 6,* 260–279.

Likert, R. (1961). *New patterns of management.* New York: McGraw-Hill.

Lindblom, C. E. (1959). The science of muddling through. *Public Administrative Review, 19,* 79–99.

Lindblom, C. E. (1980). *The policy-making process* (2nd ed.). Englewood Cliffs, NJ: Prentice-Hall.

Litchfield, E. (1956). Notes on a general theory of administration. *Administrative Science Quarterly, 1,* 3–29.

Maitlis, S., & Ozcelik, H. (2004). Toxic decision processes: A study of emotion and organizational decision making. *Organization Science, 15,* 375–393.

March, J. G. (1994). *A primer on decision making.* New York: Free Press.

March, J. G., & Olsen, J. P. (1979). *Ambiguity and choice in organizations* (2nd ed.). Bergen, Norway: Universite-forlaget.

March, J. G., & Simon, H. A. (1968). *Organizations.* New York: John Wiley.

Masoner, M. (1988). *An audit of the case study method.* New York: Praeger.

Miner, J. B. (1984). The validity and usefulness of theories emerging in organizational science. *Academy of Management Review, 9,* 296–306.

Miner, J. B. (1988). *Organizational behavior: Performance and productivity.* New York: Random House.

Mintzberg, H. (1983). *The structuring of organizations.* Englewood Cliffs, NJ: Prentice-Hall.

Mintzberg, H. (1989). *Mintzberg on management.* New York: Free Press.

Mohrman, A. M., Cooke, R. A., & Mohrman, S. A. (1978). Participation in decision making: A multidimensional perspective. *Educational Administration Quarterly, 14,* 13–29.

Moon, N. J. (1983). The construction of a conceptual framework for teacher participation in school decision making. Ed.D. Dissertation, University of Kentucky.

Mulder, M. (1971). Power equalization through participation? *Administrative Science Quarterly, 16,* 31–38.

Nitzan, S., & Paroush, J. (1984). A general theorem and eight corollaries in search of correct decision. *Theory and Decision, 17,* 211–220.

Papandreou, A. G. (1952). Some basic problems in the theory of the firm. In B. F. Halley (ed.), *A survey of contemporary economics,* vol. 2. Homewood, IL: Irwin.

Pfeffer, J., & Sutton, R. I. (2006). Evidence-based management. *Harvard Business Review, 84,* 63–74.

Pinfield, L. T. (1986). A field evaluation of perspectives on organizational decision making. *Administrative Science Quarterly, 31,* 365–388.

Plous, S. (1993). *The psychology of judgment and decision making.* New York: McGraw-Hill.

Quade, E. S. (1982). *Analysis for public decisions* (2nd ed.). New York: North Holland.

Sargeant, C., & Belisle, E. (1955). *Educational administration: Cases and concepts.* Boston: Houghton Mifflin.

Salas, E., & Klein, G. (2001). *Linking expertise and naturalistic decision making.* Mahwah, NJ: Erlbaum.

Schneider, G. T. (1984) Teacher involvement in decision making, zones of acceptance, decision conditions, and job satisfaction. *Journal of Research and Development in Education, 18,* 25–32.

Simon, H. A. (1947). *Administrative behavior.* New York: Macmillan.

Simon, H. A. (1957). *Administrative behavior* (2nd ed.). New York: Macmillan.

Simon, H. A. (1964). On the concept of organizational goal. *Administrative Science Quarterly, 8,* 1–22.

Simon, H. A. (1976). From substantive to procedural rationality. In J. Latsis (ed.), *Methods and appraisal in economics.* Cambridge: Cambridge University Press, 129–148.

Simon, H. A. (1991). Keynote address. Baltimore, MD: UCEA Conference.

Simon, H. A. (1993). Decision making: Rational, nonrational, and irrational. *Educational Administration Quarterly, 29,* 392–411.

Slater, R. O., & Boyd, W. B. (1999). School as polities. In J. Murphy & K. S. Lewis (eds.), *Handbook on research in educational administration.* San Francisco: Jossey-Bass, 297–322.

Tarter, C. J., & Hoy, W. K. (1998). A contingency theory of decision making. *Journal of Educational Administration, 36,* 212–228.

Thomas, H. (1984). Mapping strategic management research. *Journal of General Management, 9,* 55–72.

Thompson, J. D. (1967). *Organizations in action.* New York: McGraw-Hill.

Torrance, E. P. (1955). Some consequences of power differences in decision making in permanent and temporary three-man groups. In A. P. Hare, E. F. Borgatta, & R. F. Bales (eds.), *Small groups.* New York: Alfred A. Knopf, 482–492.

Tschannen-Moran, M. (2001). Collaboration and the need for trust. *Journal of Educational Administration, 39,* 308–331.

Tversky, A., & Kahneman, D. K. (1982). *Judgments of and by representativeness.* In D. Kahneman, P. Slovic, & A. Tversky (eds.), *Judgment under uncertainty: Heuristics and biases.* New York: Cambridge University Press, 84–98.

Vazquez, X. H. (2004). Allocating decision rights on the shop floor: A perspective from transaction cost economics and organizational theory. *Organization Science, 15,* 463–480.

Vroom, V. H., & Jago, A. G. (1988). *The new leadership: Managing participation in organizations.* Englewood Cliffs, NJ: Prentice-Hall.

Vroom, V. H., & Yetton, P. W. (1973). *Leadership and decision making.* Pittsburgh, PA: University of Pittsburgh Press.

Weick, K. W., & Sutcliffe, K. M. (2001). *Managing the unexpected.* San Francisco: Jossey-Bass.

Wildavsky, A. (1991). *Searching for safety.* New Brunswick, NJ: Transaction Press.

Willower, D. (1991). Art and science in administration. *Education, 111,* 497–500.

Willower, D. (1992). *Educational administration: Philosophy, praxis and professing.* Madison, WI: National Council of Professors of Educational Administration.

Willower, D. (1993). Explaining and improving educational administration. *Educational Management and Administration, 21,* 153–160.

Willower, D. J. (1999). Values and valuation: A naturalistic inquiry. In P. J. Begley (ed.), *Values in educational leadership.* Albany: State University of New York Press.

Willower, D. (in press). Whither educational administration? The post post-positivist era. *Journal of Educational Administration and Foundations.*

Willower, D. J., & Licata, J. L. (1997). *Values and valuation in the practice of educational administration.* Thousand Oaks, CA: Corwin Press.

Wiseman, C. (1979a). Selection of major planning issues. *Policy Sciences, 12,* 103–113.

Wiseman, C. (1979b). Strategic planning in the Scottish health service—A mixed-scanning approach. *Long Range Planning, 12,* 71–86.

Zey, M. (ed.). (1992). *Decision making: Alternatives to rational choice models.* Newbury Park, CA: Sage.

INDEX

Case Name and Number	Vision	Student Learning Professional Development	In-School Environment	Community Collaboration	Ethics	General Context
Teachers Council (2.1)		X				
Controversial Speaker (2.2)		X				
Conflict at Christmas (3.1)	X					
Crisis in Marshall Cr. (3.2)						X
Critical Friends Group (4.1)		X				
Divided Loyalties (4.2)	X					
Politics at River Grove (4.3)				X		
Freak Dancing (5.1)			X	X		X
Sexual Harassment (5.2)					X	
Late Again (5.3)		X	X			
Excessive Force? (5.4)			X	X		
Discord and Disharmony (5.5)				X		
Superintendent's Hiring Dilemma (5.6)	X					
Electives (5.7)		X				
Sour Notes (5.8)		X				
Zero Tolerance (5.9)			X			
The Slap (5.10)		X	X		X	
Low Expectations (5.11)		X				
Kinky Hair (5.12)					X	
Reluctant Assistant (5.13)		X	X		X	
The Set Up (5.14)		X			X	
Dropped for a Loss (5.15)			X			
The Curriculum Dilemma (6.1)		X				
The Secretary's Office (6.2)			X			
Parking Lot (6.3)		X				
Computer Purchasing (7.3)			X			